MASCULINITIES IN THE COURT TALES OF DANIEL

> This volume is among the first to explore masculinity, or more precisely masculinities, in the Hebrew Bible. The analysis is methodologically sophisticated and clearly presented, and the author does not shy away from showing the contemporary implications of his findings. This book will be of interest to students and scholars of the Hebrew Bible/Old Testament, Gender Studies, and Masculinity Studies.
> —Marc Brettler, Duke University, USA

In this volume, Brian Charles DiPalma examines masculinities in the court tales of Daniel as a test case for issues facing the burgeoning area of gender studies in the Hebrew Bible. In doing so, it both analyzes how the court tales of Daniel portray the characters in terms of configurations of masculinity in their socio-historical context and also seeks to advance gender studies in the Hebrew Bible on theoretical, methodological, and political grounds.

Masculinities in the Court Tales of Daniel is therefore of interest not only to scholars working on Daniel, but also biblical scholars studying gender in the Hebrew Bible more broadly, including those engaged in feminist criticism, queer criticism, and studies of masculinity, as well as anyone studying gender within an ancient Near Eastern context.

Brian Charles DiPalma is an independent scholar, currently teaching in Fresno, California, USA.

ROUTLEDGE STUDIES IN THE BIBLICAL WORLD

Available titles

A COMMENTARY ON NUMBERS
Narrative, Ritual, and Colonialism
Pekka Pitkänen

MASCULINITIES IN THE COURT TALES OF DANIEL
Advancing Gender Studies in the Hebrew Bible
Brian Charles DiPalma

Forthcoming titles

RELIGION, ETHNICITY, AND XENOPHOBIA IN THE BIBLE
Foolish Nations
Brian Rainey

For more information about this series, please visit: www.routledge.com/classical studies/series/BIBWORLD

MASCULINITIES IN THE COURT TALES OF DANIEL

Advancing Gender Studies in the Hebrew Bible

Brian Charles DiPalma

LONDON AND NEW YORK

First published 2018
by Routledge
2 Park Square, Milton Park, Abingdon, Oxon OX14 4RN

and by Routledge
711 Third Avenue, New York, NY 10017

Routledge is an imprint of the Taylor & Francis Group, an informa business

© 2018 Brian Charles DiPalma

The right of Brian Charles DiPalma to be identified as author of this work has been asserted by him in accordance with sections 77 and 78 of the Copyright, Designs and Patents Act 1988.

All rights reserved. No part of this book may be reprinted or reproduced or utilised in any form or by any electronic, mechanical, or other means, now known or hereafter invented, including photocopying and recording, or in any information storage or retrieval system, without permission in writing from the publishers.

Trademark notice: Product or corporate names may be trademarks or registered trademarks, and are used only for identification and explanation without intent to infringe.

British Library Cataloguing-in-Publication Data
A catalogue record for this book is available from the British Library

Library of Congress Cataloging-in-Publication Data
A catalog record for this book has been requested

ISBN: 978-1-138-72473-0 (hbk)
ISBN: 978-1-315-19226-0 (ebk)

Typeset in Times New Roman
by Apex CoVantage, LLC

CONTENTS

List of figures   viii
Acknowledgements   ix

1 Introduction   1
   1.1 Introduction 1
   1.2 Contextualizing this study in biblical scholarship 2
   1.3 Goals, argument summary, and outline 4

2 Issues for gender studies in the Hebrew Bible   11
   2.1 Introduction 11
   2.2 The issues 11
      2.2.1 A question of method: how to study gender in biblical literature? 11
      2.2.2 Disciplinary fit of studies of masculinity 13
      2.2.3 Political implications of masculinity studies 14
      2.2.4 What happens when characters deviate from gendered norms? 15
   2.3 Summary 16

3 On gender and masculinity: framing the case study   21
   3.1 Introduction 21
   3.2 Studying gender in biblical literature informed by sociological perspectives 21
   3.3 Doing gender in sociological scholarship 22
   3.4 Masculinities 22
   3.5 Concluding comments 26

4 Masculinity and the court tales of Daniel: identifying the issues   33
   4.1 Introduction 33

4.2 Hypotheses about masculinity in the court tales of
      Daniel 33
    4.2.1 Daniel 1 – competing masculinities: brawn versus
          beauty and brains 33
    4.2.2 Daniel 2 – the power of knowledge 36
    4.2.3 Daniel 3 – the king's erect statue: a ritual of
          subordination gone awry 40
    4.2.4 Daniel 4 – is Nebuchadnezzar good at being a male
          ruler? 42
    4.2.5 Daniel 5 – Belshazzar and the problem (of) son(s) 44
    4.2.6 Daniel 6 – repetition and its significance 46
  4.3 Summary of hypotheses 48

5 **A predominant masculinity and the court tales of Daniel**　　58
  5.1 Introduction 58
  5.2 Sources for testing the hypotheses 59
  5.3 A culturally predominant masculinity 59
    5.3.1 Violence, power, and masculinity 59
    5.3.2 Producing sons, names, and masculinity 67
    5.3.3 Protection, provision, and masculinity 71
  5.4 Conclusions 74

6 **Scribal masculinity and the court tales of Daniel**　　83
  6.1 Introduction 83
  6.2 Scribal masculinity in the ancient near East and the
      Hebrew Bible 84
  6.3 Conclusions 96

7 **Beauty, masculinity, and the court tales of Daniel**　　101
  7.1 Introduction 101
  7.2 Approaching beauty and masculinity 101
  7.3 Beauty and the court tales of Daniel 108
  7.4 Conclusions 111

8 **Discourse, masculinity, and the court tales of Daniel**　　115
  8.1 Introduction 115
  8.2 Beyond persuasion: problems with "persuasive
      speech" 115
  8.3 Another approach: using discourse to do gender 118

8.4 Discourse and masculinity in the court tales of Daniel 120
8.5 Conclusions 125

9 Advancing gender studies in the Hebrew Bible   **130**
9.1 Introduction 130
9.2 Summary of arguments and areas for future research 130
9.3 Revisiting the issues 133
   9.3.1 A question of method: how to study gender in biblical literature? 133
   9.3.2 What happens when a narrative character deviates from culturally predominant norms of gender? 135
   9.3.3 Political implications of a study of masculinity in biblical literature 136
   9.3.4 Disciplinary fit of a study of masculinity in biblical literature 139

Bibliography   143
Index   157

FIGURES

5.1	Behistun relief of Darius	61
5.2	Tomb of Xerxes at Naqsi-Rustam	61
5.3	Seal of Darius	63
5.4a–d	Selection of Archer Series Coins	63
5.5	PFS 113*; cylinder seal impression from Persepolis	66
6.1	Wall relief; reign of Tiglath-Pileser III	87
6.2	Wall relief; northwest palace of Ashurbanipal	88
7.1	Behistun relief of Darius	107
7.2	Original central panel at Apadana	107
7.3	Relief of king and two attendants	108

ACKNOWLEDGEMENTS

I read acknowledgments with as much interest as the books themselves because I enjoy learning about a scholar's community of colleagues and friends, which helps humanize the name on the cover. Additionally, reading about the communities that support the work of others makes me think of my own community, which always brings me joy. It is with great pleasure that I can now acknowledge the caring and dedicated support of the people who have made this book possible, especially the editorial team at Routledge, including Amy Davis-Poynter and Elizabeth Risch.

This book is a revised version of my doctoral dissertation, which was written at Emory University. The Laney Graduate School provided generous funding throughout, making it possible to complete the dissertation in a timely fashion. I am especially grateful to the Hebrew Bible faculty, including William ("Bill") K. Gilders, Joel M. LeMon, Carol A. Newsom, Brent A. Strawn, and Jacob Wright. Bill proved untiringly helpful throughout my entire time at Emory, from coursework to guiding this project to completion through all its various stages. His insightful comments and engaging conversations always pushed me to develop this project to be the best it could. I can only hope that this completed form elicits no tearful denunciations from him and that his cat will be able to see more of him. Carol and Joel also provided critical feedback on multiple versions. Along with her first round of feedback, Carol provided a copy of her commentary on Daniel that became a trusted guide for exegetical difficulties in the court tales. Joel even provided additional feedback on my work as we subdued chaos in the Chattahoochee. At points when I thought I had written all I could as clearly as possible, their comments energized me to sharpen and clarify my arguments. I am grateful for the many ways each of them has supported and critiqued my work.

While my home at Emory was in the Graduate Division of Religion, faculty members in the Women's, Gender, and Sexuality department, including Lynne Huffer and Irene Brown, welcomed me into their classes. I am also grateful for occasions to teach at Candler School of Theology, including a special topics course on Feminist and Queer Approaches to Biblical Interpretation. Conversations with students in that course caused me to rethink several points in this project. I am also grateful for the Andrew Mellon Graduate Teaching Fellowship program at Emory, which entailed the honor of teaching at Morehouse College. The students at Morehouse who took a special topics course on Gender, Sexuality, and the Hebrew Bible with me helped me refine and clarify some of these ideas.

While this book is the culmination of my work at Emory, several other people significantly influenced me and my development prior to beginning at Emory. In particular, I am grateful to several of my undergraduate professors at Fresno Pacific University, including Richard Rawls, Pam and Marshall Johnston, Greg Camp, and Laura Schmidt Roberts, the latter of whom provided my first introduction to feminist scholarship. At Princeton Theological Seminary, Jacqueline Lapsley and Dennis T. Olson were especially influential in providing occasions to study feminist work on the Bible and to allow me space to begin exploring masculinity in biblical literature. Though I never studied with him, I am grateful to David J. A. Clines, who allowed me to incorporate some of his unpublished work into a paper I was researching on masculinity in Exodus 1–4. He also connected me with Ovidiu Creangă, who was editing a volume on masculinity in the Hebrew Bible. Ovidiu's insightful feedback on that piece significantly shaped it and me as I began my doctoral work at Emory.

The friendship of Ryan Bonfiglio, K. Parker Diggory, Josey Bridges Snyder, Johannes Kleiner, and Adam Strater sustained me through the rigors of doctoral studies. Seeing a look of terror in my eyes after my first seminar in course work, they invited me to coffee in what became a weekly gathering ritual.

I am also very grateful to my family for their love and support. I remember explaining to my parents, Dave and Kathryn, that learning Hebrew and Greek was important even though people had already translated the Bible. Even as I have struggled to convey just what it is that I do, they have proven unfailingly supportive. My wife's parents, Charlie and LuAnn Hindes, have welcomed me into their family even as their daughter has sojourned with me in New Jersey and Georgia. I rejoice with them that our latest move has brought us back home. Finally, I thank my wife, Audrey Hindes, who has been a wonderful partner. With substantial training in biblical studies herself, she has engaged my work in ways that pushed it and me to become even better, establishing herself as one of my finest teachers.

1

INTRODUCTION

1.1 Introduction

As the book of Daniel begins, King Nebuchadnezzar of Babylon defeats King Jehoiakim of Judah in war and takes four young men from the conquered people to serve his court: Daniel, Hananiah, Mishael, and Azariah (1:1–7). The latter three are better known by the names their Babylonian captors assign to them: Shadrach, Meshach, and Abednego. The narratives that follow in Dan 1–6, known as "the court tales of Daniel,"[1] contain memorable stories: the three youths in the fiery furnace (ch. 3), the writing on the wall (ch. 5), and Daniel and the lion's den (ch. 6). Except for the queen in 5:10–12, the stories feature an all-male cast. In studying these stories, which were compiled in the late Persian or early Hellenistic period,[2] biblical scholars have considered numerous issues, including how the narratives respond to imperial domination.[3] Accordingly, social identity is not a new topic to scholarship on the court tales of Daniel. Yet scholars typically confine social identity to ethnicity and exclude gender, failing to ask how the stories depict the characters with respect to configurations of masculinity even though warfare, the activity with which the stories begin, was integral to masculinity in the ancient Near East.[4]

This study will address this gap by showing how the court tales of Daniel portray the characters with respect to configurations of masculinity in the sociohistorical context. From the outset of this study, an obvious fact about the court tales of Daniel cannot be neglected: the stories never bring gender to the foreground. For instance, when the Babylonians defeat Judah in war (Dan 1:1–2), they do not ridicule the Judeans in the way that Nahum taunted the Assyrians: "Look at your army, they are women among you (הנה עמך נשים בקרבך)" (3:13). Nor do Daniel and his colleagues exhort one another to become men as David did in his final words to Solomon: "Display strength and (be)come a man (חזקת והיית לאיש)" (1 Kgs 2:2). Yet interpreting stories in light of gendered norms that are attested elsewhere in the cultural context is an integral approach to the growing area of gender studies in the Hebrew Bible.[5]

To introduce this study, this chapter has two goals. First, offering a concise assessment of developments in gender studies in the Hebrew Bible, I will show

how studying masculinity in the court tales of Daniel can advance this burgeoning area of scholarship. My second goal is to show what is at stake in this topic: failing to notice masculinity in these stories perpetuates the invisibility of masculinity, cloaking it as natural or normal rather than a product of cultural conventions and processes that change over time and across cultures. I conclude the chapter with a brief overview of the goals and argument in this project.

1.2 Contextualizing this study in biblical scholarship

While the emergence of modern feminist biblical criticism is often associated with the work of Elizabeth Cady Stanton in the late nineteenth century, feminist biblical scholarship has become an established part of biblical studies since the mid 1970s.[6] While the diversity of feminist perspectives, at least in some respects,[7] challenges characterizations of this scholarship, many scholars identify a shared interest in critiquing androcentric biases in biblical literature and its interpretations to dismantle gendered inequality in the world.[8]

Focusing on texts with female characters has been a central strategy in efforts to critique androcentrism in biblical texts and their interpreters.[9] Contributors to Stanton's project, for instance, adopted this process: "Each person purchased two Bibles, ran through them from Genesis to Revelation, marking all the texts that concerned women. The passages were cut out, and pasted in a blank book, and the commentaries then written underneath."[10] Producing a different kind of Jefferson's Bible, the impact of this methodological decision upon the texts discussed in *The Woman's Bible* cannot be underestimated. While it is difficult to assess whether this aspect of Stanton's work influenced subsequent feminist biblical scholarship in any traceable ways, the inclination of feminist biblical scholars to focus on texts with female characters persists.[11] Significant choices motivate this pattern, including resisting interpretations of biblical stories featuring female characters that oppress or marginalize women.[12] But this tendency can hide texts, like the court tales of Daniel, that feature male characters from thorough feminist analysis. Indeed, feminist biblical scholars have only devoted brief attention to the court tales of Daniel and this work has focused on the unnamed queen, who makes a brief appearance in 5:10–12, or the Greek addition Susanna.[13] At once acknowledging and seeking to move beyond this tendency in feminist work on Daniel, Carol A. Newsom argues that "the lack of female characters in the Hebrew and Aramaic version of Daniel should not mean that the book is of no interest to feminist reflection."[14] While Newsom presents a cogent case in showing how the book of Daniel holds multiple voices together, other feminist biblical scholars have not explored Newsom's vision of what feminist biblical scholarship on Daniel could become.[15]

Feminist biblical scholars often distinguish between "sex" – described as natural and pertaining to anatomy – and "gender" – understood as cultural ideas mapped onto or that express that sex.[16] This distinction combined with a tendency to focus on female characters in texts often results in conflating the term "gender" with women or "gender" becomes a shorthand for studies of female characters.[17] This equation explains the comments of Amy Merrill Willis about "gender" in Daniel: "Daniel is not concerned with gender in so much as the book is almost exclusively focused on male characters."[18] While not unique to Merrill Willis or feminist biblical scholarship,[19] this equation enables masculinity to masquerade as natural or inevitable, which hinders feminist efforts to expose and critique androcentrism in biblical texts and their interpretations. Devoting focused attention to masculinity in biblical literature presents an important avenue for growth in feminist biblical studies, and the predominantly male cast in the court tales of Daniel is an important test case for this possibility.[20]

A focus on masculinity in biblical texts often emerges in queer approaches, which critique and extend feminist approaches.[21] This diverse body of scholarship shares a goal of challenging uses of the Bible that "support heteronormative and normalizing configurations of sexual practices and sexual identities."[22] With this agenda, queer approaches can critique heterosexual biases in some feminist biblical scholarship.[23] Yet in drawing from Judith Butler's work, in which gender is not mapped onto a predetermined sex but rather the production of the illusion of a stable sex, queer biblical scholarship often focuses on gender because troubling ideas about gender simultaneously disrupts the framework heteronormativity requires: a binary production of sexed bodies.[24] In this way, queer approaches can align with and extend some feminist work.

Common understandings of gender in queer approaches invite rather than preclude analyzing the nearly all-male cast of the court tales of Daniel in terms of gender, though this has not yet occurred apart from a discussion of male beauty in the stories and a general discussion of "queer" elements in the book.[25] Various factors explain this gap, including the recent emergence of queer approaches to biblical interpretation and their marginal(ized) status.[26] The marginal status of queer biblical studies may be changing as the Society of Biblical Literature has recently published a volume of queer essays, though even this collection positions itself at the "margins" of biblical studies.[27] While understandings of gender in queer approaches clearly enable an analysis of masculinity in the court tales of Daniel, questions emerge about where to locate such inquiry.

A growing body of scholarship explores masculinity in the Hebrew Bible without always articulating its relationship to feminist or queer approaches.[28] Failing to describe how a study of masculinity relates to feminist or queer scholarship can clearly create tension. For instance, a major theme in the work of David J. A. Clines – that the Hebrew Bible is written in an androcentric language of "maschlish"[29] – has elicited critiques:

> Feminists . . . may well respond to Clines that they have been noticing for a very long time that the Hebrew Bible is written, almost entirely, in Maschlish. This has been one of the founding rationales of feminism. . . . But it is gratifying to see the recognition dawning across the discipline.[30]

INTRODUCTION

Indeed, critiquing the androcentrism of the Hebrew Bible and its interpretation has been a mainstay of feminist biblical scholarship.[31] While Guest offers a generous response, Esther Fuchs accuses Clines of appropriating feminist thought, including her own, without acknowledging his debt in ways that elide feminist contributions to scholarship.[32]

The growing work on masculinity in the Hebrew Bible has not generated sustained interest in the court tales of Daniel, leaving many questions unanswered and even unasked.[33] T. M. Lemos devotes approximately three pages to Daniel in a discussion of gender in a Judean post-exilic context, asking bluntly: "Is Daniel masculine?"[34] Her answer is less straightforward than her question, positing about Daniel himself that "the traditional Israelite conception of masculine honor that is found in exaggerated form in Ezekiel is absent here."[35] Lemos at least implies that Daniel himself is not masculine in relation to some constructions of masculinity from ancient Israel (e.g., martial prowess) as the title for her discussion of Daniel suggests: "Daniel and Diasporic *Emasculation*" (emphasis mine). Still, Lemos's work offers only tentative reflections and suggests that further work is needed. Indeed, simply because Daniel deviates from some gendered norms need not require the conclusion that he is non-masculine, a possibility I will test in this book. Likewise, what about Daniel's colleagues? And in what ways does the relationship between God and the foreign kings engage cultural norms about masculinity?

1.3 Goals, argument summary, and outline

This study will show how the court tales of Daniel portray the characters with respect to configurations of masculinity in the historical context of the stories. As this goal engages issues facing gender studies in the Hebrew Bible, my second goal is to advance such work on theoretical, methodological, and political grounds. For instance, through focusing on masculinity in these stories, I will show how a study of masculinity can relate to central emphases and goals of feminist biblical scholarship. Similarly, as the topic of gender never rises to the foreground in the court tales of Daniel, the stories present a difficult case study for a methodological question of how to analyze gender in ancient texts.

I begin by contextualizing four issues for which I use this project to advance gender studies in the Hebrew Bible (Chapter 2): (1) How can scholars study gender in ancient literature? (2) How does a study of masculinity in biblical literature fit in relation to existing approaches? (3) What are the political implications of studying masculinity in biblical literature? (4) What happens when characters deviate from predominant constructions of gender? While biblical scholarship has become increasingly indebted to Butler for understanding "gender," I also include sociological studies of gender, which are generally described as social constructionist and overlap in a significant way with Butler's work (Chapter 3).[36] But sociological work introduces dynamics, especially the possibility that multiple masculinities can be produced in hierarchical relationships with each other in a given setting, that I argue are crucial for understanding the court tales of Daniel.[37]

INTRODUCTION

My analysis of the court tales of Daniel begins with a reading of the stories in terms of the activities scholars have linked to masculinity in other portions of the Hebrew Bible and its ancient Near Eastern context (Chapter 4). This chapter proposes hypotheses about gender in the court tales of Daniel that subsequent chapters test in light of the socio-historical context. Chapter 5 argues that a predominant masculinity in this cultural setting entailed three interwoven activities: (1) physical violence, especially in war; (2) producing sons to perpetuate the father's name; and (3) protecting and providing for subordinates. After sketching this predominant masculinity, I discuss scribal masculinity, a recurring dynamic in the Hebrew Bible and its ancient Near Eastern context that illumines the representation of Daniel and his colleagues (Chapter 6). Chapter 7 assesses the court tales of Daniel in terms of ideas about male beauty in the Hebrew Bible and its ancient Near Eastern context. Next, I show how characters use discourse to do gender in the stories (Chapter 8). I conclude by revisiting the issues I articulate in Chapter 2 in order to advance gender studies in the Hebrew Bible (Chapter 9).

Throughout this book, I will argue that the court tales of Daniel are androcentric beyond the obvious predominantly male cast: the stories (re)produce configurations of masculinity attested in the cultural context. For instance, even though Daniel and his colleagues depart from a culturally predominant masculinity, I show that they are differently masculine in light of an ancient Near Eastern scribal masculinity. Similarly, the narrative question of whether God or a foreign king protects and provides for Daniel and his colleagues (re)produces threads of a culturally predominant masculinity. Likewise, descriptions of physical appearances in the stories (re)produce an equation of a better-looking male with a higher position of power. With these claims, I raise consciousness about the androcentricism in the court tales of Daniel and a subtle dynamic that (re)produces gendered inequality, which aligns with feminist biblical scholarship. Likewise, showing a plurality of masculinities that disrupts a strictly binary configuration of gender aligns with emphases in queer biblical criticism. In these ways, this study participates in gender studies, which draws from feminism and queer theory. Locating the study in this place renders it accountable, intellectually and politically, to the critical perspectives upon which it relies and to which I hope to contribute.[38]

Notes

1 The designation "court tales" for Dan 1–6 is based on the genre of these stories in contrast with the apocalyptic literature in chs. 7–12. Court tales are found elsewhere in the Hebrew Bible (Gen 37–50; Esth) in two basic variations: (1) a court conflict, where an official is endangered and subsequently triumphs; and (2) a court contest in which a courtier completes a difficult task. See Carol A. Newsom, *Daniel: A Commentary*, OTL (Louisville: Westminster John Knox, 2014), 12–18. For a proposal that the genre of the stories is an "ancient story collection," see Tawny L. Holm, *Of Courtiers and Kings: The Biblical Daniel Narratives and Ancient Story-Collections*, EANEC 1 (Winona Lake, IN: Eisenbrauns, 2013).

2 The entire book of Daniel (i.e., chs. 1–12) came together prior to the death of Antiochus IV (164 BCE). But scholars argue that the court tales were compiled independently

before being joined with chs. 7–12. The court tales were likely compiled in the late Persian or early Hellenistic period. See Newsom, *Daniel*, 6–12; Louis F. Hartman, *The Book of Daniel*, AB (Garden City, NY: Doubleday, 1978), 11–13; John J. Collins, *Daniel: A Commentary on the Book of Daniel*, Hermeneia (Minneapolis: Fortress, 1993), 24–38; Choon Leong Seow, *Daniel*, WC (Louisville: Westminster John Knox, 2003), 4–9.

3 See David M. Valeta, "The Book of Daniel in Recent Research (Part One)," *CurBR* 6 (2008): 333–40. For the suggestion that the court tales of Daniel are "accommodationist" literature, see W. Lee Humphreys, "Life-Style for Diaspora: A Study of the Tales of Esther and Daniel," *JBL* 92 (1973): 211–23. More recently, biblical scholars have found elements of "resistance" in these stories. See David M. Valeta, *Lions and Ovens and Visions: A Satirical Reading of Daniel 1–6*, Hebrew Bible Monographs 12 (Sheffield: Sheffield Phoenix, 2008); Anathea Portier-Young, *Apocalypse Against Empire: Theologies of Resistance in Early Judaism* (Grand Rapids: Eerdmans, 2011), esp. 223–280. For a cogent argument that the stories are "negotiating" claims of imperial rule, simultaneously accommodating and resisting, see Newsom, *Daniel*, 15–18.

4 Harry A. Hoffner, "Symbols for Masculinity and Femininity: Their Use in Ancient Near Eastern Sympathetic Magic Rituals," *JBL* 85 (1966): 327. More recently, see Cynthia R. Chapman, *The Gendered Language of Warfare in the Israelite-Assyrian Encounter*, HSM 62 (Winona Lake, IN: Eisenbrauns, 2004).

5 For examples and discussion, see Beatrice Lawrence, "Gender Analysis: Gender and Method in Biblical Studies," in *Method Matters: Essays on the Interpretation of the Hebrew Bible in Honor of David L. Petersen*, eds. Joel M. LeMon and Kent Harold Richards, RBS 56 (Atlanta: Society of Biblical Literature, 2009), 333–48; Ken Stone, "Gender Criticism: The Un-Manning of Abimelech," in *Judges & Method: New Approaches in Biblical Studies*, ed. Gale A. Yee, 2nd ed. (Minneapolis: Fortress, 2007), 183–201; Deryn Guest, *Beyond Feminist Biblical Studies*, The Bible in the Modern World 47 (Sheffield: Sheffield Phoenix, 2012). For an introduction to similar work among sociologists, who analyze whether gendered norms in the modern world are (re)produced in various types of media in a practice known as "content-analysis," see Frank Taylor, "Content Analysis and Gender Stereotypes in Children's Books," *Teaching Sociology* 31 (2003): 300–311. For surveys of this approach, see Rena M. Rudy, Lucy Popova, and Daniel G. Linz, "The Context of Current Content Analysis of Gender Roles: An Introduction to a Special Issue," *Sex Roles* 62 (2010): 705–20; Rebecca L. Collins, "Content Analysis of Gender Roles in Media: Where Are We Now and Where Should We Go?" *Sex Roles* 64 (2011): 290–98.

6 For Stanton's work, see Elizabeth Cady Stanton, *The Woman's Bible* (Mineola, NY: Dover, 2002). Some suggest a "two wave" model of feminist biblical scholarship in which Stanton represents a "first wave" in the late 19th century and Phyllis Trible's work marks a "second wave" in the mid-1970s. For this periodization, see Susan Brayford, "Feminist Criticism: Sarah Laughs Last," in LeMon and Richards, *Method Matters*, 314; Naomi Steinberg, "Feminist Criticism," in *Methods for Exodus*, ed. Thomas B. Dozeman (New York: Cambridge University Press, 2010), 163–4. But others point out that feminist or proto-feminist readings of biblical texts clearly exist. For discussion of examples, see Kathleen M. O'Connor, "The Feminist Movement Meets the Old Testament: One Woman's Perspective," in *Engaging the Bible in a Gendered World: An Introduction to Feminist Biblical Interpretation in Honor of Katharine Doob Sakenfeld*, eds. Linda Day and Carolyn Pressler (Louisville: Westminster John Knox, 2006), 9–10; Susanne Scholz, *Introducing the Women's Hebrew Bible* (New York: T&T Clark, 2007); Carol A. Newsom, "Women as Biblical Interpreters Before the Twentieth Century," in *Women's Bible Commentary, Revised and Updated*, eds. Carol A. Newsom, Sharon H. Ringe, and Jacqueline E Lapsley, 3rd ed. (Louisville: Westminster John

Knox, 2012), 11–23. A resurgence of work in the mid-1970s is associated with Phyllis Trible, *God and the Rhetoric of Sexuality*, OBT (Minneapolis: Fortress, 1978); idem., "Depatriarchalizing in Biblical Interpretation," *JAAR* 41 (1973): 30–48; idem., *Texts of Terror: Literary-Feminist Readings of Biblical Narratives* (Philadelphia: Fortress, 1984). Evidence of the impact of feminist approaches can be seen, for instance, in that the *Women's Bible Commentary*, an edited collection of essays on each biblical book, is now in its third edition. See Carol A. Newsom, Sharon H. Ringe, and Jacqueline E. Lapsley, eds., *Women's Bible Commentary, Revised and Updated*, 3rd ed. (Louisville: Westminster John Knox, 2012). Likewise, the Feminist Companion to the Bible exists in two series, and each series contains multiple volumes of essays on individual books or sections of biblical literature. Two books are devoted to surveying feminist scholarship by biblical book. See Alice Ogden Bellis, *Helpmates, Harlots, and Heroes*, 2nd ed. (Louisville: Westminster John Knox, 2007); Susanne Scholz, ed., *Feminist Interpretation of the Hebrew Bible in Retrospect*, Recent Research in Biblical Studies 5 (Sheffield: Sheffield Phoenix, 2013). Moreover, collections of essays on methods of biblical interpretation typically include feminist criticism. See, for instance, Danna Nolan Fewell, "Reading the Bible Ideologically: Feminist Criticism," in *To Each Its Own Meaning: An Introduction to Biblical Criticisms and Their Application*, eds. Steven L. McKenzie and Stephen R. Haynes (Louisville: Westminster John Knox, 1999), 268–82; J. Cheryl Exum, "Feminist Criticism: Whose Interests Are Being Served?" in *Judges & Method: New Approaches in Biblical Studies*, ed. Gale A. Yee, 2nd ed. (Minneapolis: Fortress, 2007), 65–89; Brayford, "Feminist Criticism"; Steinberg, "Feminist Criticism."

7 On the reliance of feminist biblical studies on liberal feminism, see Esther Fuchs, "Biblical Feminisms: Knowledge, Theory and Politics in the Study of Women in the Hebrew Bible," *BibInt* 16 (2008): 205–26.

8 Scholz, *Introducing the Women's Hebrew Bible*, 25; O'Connor, "The Feminist Movement," 12–14; Brayford, "Feminist Criticism," 313–14.

9 For a discussion of this general tendency, see Guest, *Beyond Feminist Biblical Studies*, 25–26.

10 Stanton, *The Woman's Bible*, 6.

11 See, for instance, Tikva Simone Frymer-Kensky, *Reading the Women of the Bible*, 1st ed. (New York: Schocken, 2002); Bellis, *Helpmates, Harlots, and Heroes*. For the suggestion that Stanton's work influences later feminist biblical scholarship in a direct way, though without discussion, see Scholz, *Introducing the Women's Hebrew Bible*, 19.

12 For the suggestion that in Stanton's work it is not even possible to distinguish between feminism as a political movement and feminism as a mode of biblical interpretation, see Deborah F. Sawyer, "Gender Criticism: A New Discipline in Biblical Studies or Feminism in Disguise?" in *A Question of Sex? Gender and Difference in the Hebrew Bible and Beyond*, eds. Deborah W. Rooke and Hebrew Bible Monographs 14 (Sheffield: Sheffield Phoenix, 2007), 2. See also Sarah Schectman, *Women in the Pentateuch: A Feminist and Source-Critical Analysis*, Hebrew Bible Monographs 23 (Sheffield: Sheffield Phoenix, 2009), 11.

13 A notable exception is Carol A. Newsom, "Daniel," in Newsom, Ringe, and Lapsley, *Women's Bible Commentary*, 293–98. Focusing on female characters in Daniel can be seen in Athalya Brenner, "Who's Afraid of Feminist Criticism? Who's Afraid of Biblical Humour? The Case of the Obtuse Foreign Ruler in the Hebrew Bible," in *A Feminist Companion to Prophets and Daniel*, ed. Athalya Brenner (Sheffield: Sheffield Academic, 2001), 228–45; idem., "Self-Response to 'Who's Afraid of Feminist Criticism?'" in Brenner, *A Feminist Companion to Prophets and Daniel*, 245–46; Emily Sampson, "Daniel, Belshazzar, and Julia: The Rediscovery of the Translation of

Julia E. Smith (1792–1886)," in Brenner, *A Feminist Companion to Prophets and Daniel*, 262–82; H. J. M. van Deventer, "Another Wise Queen (Mother) – Women's Wisdom in Daniel 5.10–12?," in Brenner, *A Feminist Companion to Prophets and Daniel*, 247–61. For feminist work on Susanna, see Toni Craven, "Daniel and Its Additions," in *The Women's Bible Commentary*, ed. Carol A. Newsom and Sharon H. Ringe (Louisville: Westminster John Knox, 1992), 191–94; Jennifer A. Glancy, "The Accused: Susanna and Her Readers," in *A Feminist Companion to Esther, Judith, and Susanna*, ed. Athalya Brenner (Sheffield: Sheffield Academic, 1995), 288–302; Amy-Jill Levine, "'Hemmed in on Every Side': Jews and Women in the Book of Susanna," in Brenner, *A Feminist Companion to Esther, Judith, and Susanna*, 303–23.
14 Newsom, "Daniel," 293.
15 Ibid., 298.
16 See Fewell, "Reading the Bible Ideologically," 273; Susan E. Haddox, "(E)Masculinity in Hosea's Political Rhetoric," in *Israel's Prophets and Israel's Past: Essays on the Relationship of Prophetic Texts and Israelite History in Honor of John H. Hayes*, eds. Brad E. Kelle and Megan Bishop Moore, LHBOTS 446 (New York: T&T Clark, 2006), 178, fn. 18; Exum, "Feminist Criticism," 68, fn. 5.
17 On the equation of "gender" with women or studies of female characters, see Guest, *Beyond Feminist Biblical Studies*, 12–13.
18 Amy C. Merill Willis, "Heavenly Bodies: God and the Body in the Visions of Daniel," in *Bodies, Embodiment, and Theology of the Hebrew Bible*, eds. S. Tamar Kamionkowski and Wonil Kim, LHBOTS 465 (New York: T&T Clark, 2010), 13, fn. 2.
19 Guest, *Beyond Feminist Biblical Studies*, 13.
20 For this argument, see Sawyer, "Gender Criticism," 5.
21 For examples of queer biblical scholarship that focus primarily on masculinity, see Ken Stone, "Lovers and Raisin Cakes: Food, Sex and Divine Insecurity in Hosea," in *Queer Commentary and the Hebrew Bible*, ed. Ken Stone, JSOTSSup 334 (Sheffield: Sheffield Academic, 2001), 116–39; Stuart Macwilliam, "Ideologies of Male Beauty and the Hebrew Bible," *BibInt* 17 (2009): 265–87.
22 Ken Stone, "Queer Commentary and Biblical Interpretation: An Introduction," in Stone, *Queer Commentary and the Hebrew Bible*, 33.
23 See Deryn Guest, "Looking Lesbian at the Bathing Bathsheba," *BibInt* 16 (2008): 227–62; idem., "From Gender Reversal to Genderfuck: Reading Jael Through a Lesbian Lens," in *Bible Trouble: Queer Reading at the Boundaries of Biblical Scholarship*, eds. Teresa J. Hornsby and Ken Stone, SemeiaSt 67 (Atlanta: Society of Biblical Literature, 2011), 9–44.
24 Judith Butler, *Gender Trouble: Feminism and the Subversion of Identity*, 2nd ed. (New York: Routledge, 2010). Butler clearly was not the first to suggest the point about a normative heterosexual framework requiring a strictly binary construction of gender. See also, for example, Gayle Rubin, "The Traffic in Women: Notes on the 'Political Economy' of Sex," in *Toward an Anthropology of Women*, ed. Rayna R. Reiter (New York: Monthly Review Press, 1975), 157–210.
25 See, respectively, Macwilliam, "Ideologies of Male Beauty and the Hebrew Bible,"; Mona West, "Daniel," in *The Queer Bible Commentary*, ed. Deryn Guest et al. (London: SCM, 2006), 427–31.
26 Notice, for instance, that the editor to a milestone in queer biblical scholarship offered this introductory comment: "while soliciting contributions to this volume I spoke with several scholars who were interested in the project but felt that, given the focus of the volume, institutional or ecclesial politics prevented their participation." See Stone, *Queer Commentary and the Hebrew Bible*, 7. This comment does not detract from the important work that has been done in queer biblical studies, including Robert E. Goss and Mona West, eds., *Take Back the Word: A Queer Reading of the Bible* (Cleveland,

INTRODUCTION

OH: Pilgrim Press, 2000); Stone, *Queer Commentary and the Hebrew Bible*; Guest et al., *The Queer Bible Commentary*; J. Teresa, and Ken Stone, eds. *Bible Trouble: Queer Reading at the Boundaries of Biblical Scholarship*. Semeia St 67 (Atlanta: Society of Biblical Literature, 2011); Stuart Macwilliam, *Queer Theory and the Prophetic Marriage Metaphor in the Hebrew Bible* (Sheffield: Equinox, 2011). For monographs on related topics, see Martti Nissinen, *Homoeroticism in the Biblical World: A Historical Perspective*, trans. Kirsi Stjerna (Minneapolis: Augsburg Fortress, 1998); Neal H. Walls, *Desire, Discord, and Death: Approaches to Ancient Near Eastern Myth* (Boston: American Schools of Oriental Research, 2001); S. Parpola and R. M. Whiting, eds., *Sex and Gender in the Ancient Near East: Proceedings of the 47th Rencontre Assyriologique Internationale, Helsinki, July 2–6, 2001* (Helsinki: Neo-Assyrian Text Corpus Project, 2002).

27 Hornsby and Stone, *Bible Trouble*. The subtitle to the volume is "Queer Readings at the Boundaries of Biblical Scholarship."

28 Three contributions emerged in the mid 1990s: Howard Eilberg-Schwartz, *God's Phallus and Other Problems for Men and Monotheism* (Boston: Beacon, 1994); John Goldingay, "Hosea 1–3, Genesis 1–4, and Masculist Interpretation," *HBT* 17 (1995): 37–44; David J. A. Clines, "David the Man: The Construction of Masculinity in the Hebrew Bible," in *Interested Parties: The Ideology of Writers and Readers of the Hebrew Bible*, 2nd ed. (Sheffield: Sheffield Academic, 2009), 212–43. Clines's essay has exercised the most influence on recent studies of masculinity in the Hebrew Bible. For examples, see Ovidiu Creangă, ed., *Men and Masculinity in the Hebrew Bible and Beyond*, The Bible in the Modern World 33 (Sheffield: Sheffield Phoenix, 2010); Ovidiu Creangă, and Peter-Ben Smit, eds., *Biblical Masculinities Foregrounded*, Hebrew Bible Monographs 62 (Sheffield: Sheffield Phoenix, 2014). The latter contains essays on the New Testament. For essays on masculinity in the New Testament, see Stephen D. Moore and Janice Capel Anderson, eds., *New Testament Masculinities*, SemeiaSt 45 (Atlanta: Society of Biblical Literature, 2003). For some monographs on masculinity in the Hebrew Bible, see Chapman, *The Gendered Language of Warfare*; Susan E. Haddox, *Metaphor and Masculinity in Hosea*, StBibLit 141 (New York: Peter Lang, 2011); Roland Boer, *The Earthy Nature of the Bible: Fleshly Readings of Sex, Masculinity, and Carnality* (New York: Palgrave Macmillan, 2012).

29 David J. A. Clines, "He-Prophets: Masculinity as a Problem for the Hebrew Prophets and Their Interpreters," in *Sense and Sensitivity: Essays on Reading the Bible in Memory of Robert Carrol*, eds. Alastair G. Hunter and Philip R. Davies, JSOTSup 348 (Sheffield: Sheffield Academic, 2002), 311–28; idem., "Being a Man in the Book of the Covenant," in *Reading the Law: Studies in Honour of Gordon J. Wenham*, eds. J. G. McConville and Karl Möller, LHBOTS 461 (London: T&T Clark, 2007), 3–9; idem., "Dancing and Shining at Sinai: Playing the Man in Exodus 32–34," in Creangă, *Men and Masculinity in the Hebrew Bible and Beyond*, 54–63. Clines continues to suggest similar themes in his presentation for the 2015 Ethel M. Wood Lecture at King's College London "The Scandal of a Male Bible." A video is available online: www.youtube.com/watch?v=sfXfeaC7WTE. A copy of the manuscript, which closely corresponds to the actual words, is also available: David J. A. Clines, "The Scandal of a Male Bible," www.academia.edu/10977758/The_Scandal_of_a_Male_Bible.

30 Guest, *Beyond Feminist Biblical Studies*, 128.

31 See, for instance, Trible, "Depatriarchalizing in Biblical Interpretation," 30–31.

32 Esther Fuchs, "Men in Biblical Feminist Scholarship," *JFSR* 19 (2003): 107–8.

33 T. M. Lemos, "'They Have Become Women': Judean Diaspora and Postcolonial Theories of Gender and Migration," in *Social Theory and the Study of Israelite Religion: Essays in Retrospect and Prospect*, ed. Saul M. Olyan (Atlanta: Society of Biblical Literature, 2012), 81–109.

34 Ibid., 103.
35 Ibid.
36 On the influence of Butler's *Gender Trouble*, see, for instance, Honsby and Stone, *Bible Trouble*. I do not intend to suggest that sociological perspectives are the only way to approach gender. For discussion of sociological ideas in relation to others, see Mary Holmes, *What Is Gender? Sociological Approaches* (Los Angeles: Sage, 2007). For a critique and responses to that critique, see J. Richard Udry, "Biological Limits of Gender Construction," *American Sociological Review* 65 (2000): 443–57; Ivy Kennelly, Sabine N. Merz, and Judith Lorber, "What Is Gender," *American Sociological Review* 66 (2001): 598–605; Cecilia L. Ridgeway, *Framed by Gender: How Gender Inequality Persists in the Modern World* (New York: Oxford University Press, 2011), 18–23.
37 R. W. Connell, *Masculinities*, 2nd ed. (Berkeley: University of California Press, 2005).
38 See also Guest, *Beyond Feminist Biblical Studies*, 119; Martti Nissinen, "Biblical Masculinities: Musings on Theory and Agenda," in *Biblical Masculinities Foregrounded*, eds. Ovidiu Creangă and Peter-Ben Smit, Hebrew Bible Monographs 62 (Sheffield: Sheffield Phoenix, 2014), 272.

2

ISSUES FOR GENDER STUDIES IN THE HEBREW BIBLE

2.1 Introduction

This chapter contextualizes four issues facing gender studies in the Hebrew Bible and demonstrates their significance: (1) a methodological issue of how to study gender in biblical literature, (2) the fit of the topic of masculinity in biblical studies, (3) the socio-political interests served through studying masculinity in biblical texts, and (4) the implications of depicting a character transgressing predominant gendered norms. Rather than being comprehensive, these four issues are ones that intersect with this study of the court tales of Daniel.[1]

2.2 The issues

2.2.1 *A question of method: how to study gender in biblical literature?*

A central concern for gender studies in the Hebrew Bible is analyzing how texts portray characters with respect to gendered norms.[2] Texts that directly equate an action or characteristic with being (like) or becoming male or female make this task easier than others as they provide evidence of culturally particular gendered norms. For example, when the Philistines prepare for battle in 1 Sam 4:9, they say to one another: "Strengthen yourselves and be(come) men (התחזקו והיו לאנשים) . . . be(come) men and engage in war (והייתם לאנשים ונלחמתם)." Statements like this one provide compelling evidence about the gendered norms the text engages, but they are very rare.[3] When texts like the court tales of Daniel lack these explicit cues, researchers must determine which activities or characteristics are gendered and which ones are not. While this methodological issue has surfaced in scholarship,[4] this section will offer some parameters for making claims about gender in narrative texts from the Hebrew Bible and evaluating the cogency of such arguments. Many of these are implicit in previous studies, and I intend to bring them to the foreground to facilitate discussion.

Using a single text to determine the gendered norms assumed in that text and subsequently comparing characters in that text to those norms can lead to a problematically circular argument.⁵ To avoid this circular argumentation, some have turned to anthropological studies of more recent socio-cultural groups in the circum-Mediterranean world to provide data with which to read biblical texts.⁶ But the possibility of changes in configurations of gender across cultures and times suggests that this approach may not be fully adequate for analyzing texts from ancient societies.⁷ Instead, evidence from geographically and chronologically proximate socio-cultural groups should be consulted, and the most promising research has adopted this sort of approach.⁸

Building on the points above, some parameters begin to emerge: the text should be located in a historical context. Noticing gender in that text requires assessing other sources, both the cultural group that produced the text as well as any neighboring cultural groups, which are proximate to the text. The genre of these sources must also be considered. Legal texts, for example, that prescribe or prohibit particular actions in terms of socially defined positions as male or female provide valuable information about cultural values.⁹ For non-legal genres, I propose two heuristic categories for organizing and assessing the evidence. First, *a relatively explicit statement about gender* is one in which a text directly equates some activity or characteristic with being like or becoming male or female. In biblical Hebrew, these statements typically use a form of the verb היה with the preposition ל (to be or become) or the preposition כ (to be like).¹⁰ The rallying cry of the Philistines in 1 Sam 4:9 exemplifies this type of evidence. These statements provide the best evidence for culturally specific ideas about gender.

The second category of evidence is *implicit descriptions*: a text simply attributes features or actions to a character without connecting either to a gendered identity. A regular finding of a sociological method known as "content analysis" enables some criteria to emerge for working with this type of evidence, which constitutes the overwhelming majority of biblical literature.¹¹ Content analyses of media in the modern world consistently find that characters typically conform to the gendered norms that the researchers knew at the beginning of the study.¹² Thus, if the sociologists had not known the gendered norms in advance, but instead asked what sorts of behaviors or characteristics are repeatedly, consistently, and positively linked with particular bodies, they would have been able to determine the gendered norms in modern contexts with a high degree of accuracy. This finding suggests some criteria that biblical scholars can use in working with this type of evidence: repetition, consistency, and ideology. The first criterion of repetition asks what behaviors or characteristics are repeatedly associated with particular bodies. "Relatively consistent" association with particular bodies is preferable to "exclusive" association because gendered norms are culturally constructed without a natural or essential link between them and the bodies with which they are typically associated.¹³ The third criterion – ideology – is the most ambiguous. It asks questions such as: Are such actions or characteristics that are repeatedly and relatively consistently associated with particular bodies represented *positively* or *negatively*? Are those actions or characteristics *celebrated* or *criticized*? Are the outcomes *advantageous* or *harmful*? While such binary categories are simplistic, they provide starting points for assessing how texts portray such activities or characteristics. These criteria assume that biblical texts are not typically subversive in their cultural contexts with respect to how they represent characters vis-à-vis configurations of gender, which may appear at odds with desires to find subversive deviations from gendered norms in biblical texts. But noticing deviations requires knowing the gendered norm. The framework above presents a way of working with this type of evidence and renders some assumptions, which are needed to produce knowledge about the topic, available for debate.

2.2.2 Disciplinary fit of studies of masculinity

As was clear in the introduction to this study, masculinity has been a topic of study in feminist approaches, and others contend that feminist approaches can grow by including studies of masculinity more directly.[14] Yet it is also possible to study masculinity without any commitments to and even in opposition to feminism. As Stephen Moore cautions, some studies of masculinity "have tended to amount . . . to an uncritical celebration of traditional masculinities conducted . . . in reaction to the erosive effects on them of feminism and women's studies."[15] While Moore notes that most studies of masculinity in biblical literature avoid this critique, it remains an important concern because a study of masculinity need not be feminist. Indeed, queer approaches, which can critique feminist approaches, also study masculinity in the Hebrew Bible.[16] Clearly, masculinity has been studied from each of the approaches to gender in the Hebrew Bible.[17] Where should a study of masculinity fit?[18]

When masculinity in biblical texts came into explicit scholarly focus with renewed attention, two options emerged for relating the work to existing scholarship. Many recent studies of masculinity in the Hebrew Bible do not articulate how they relate or contribute to feminist or queer biblical scholarship, which has followed David Clines's lead in construing an analysis of masculinity as a topic of study that is independent from feminist criticism.[19] The dangers of this path became clear in the introduction to this study: failing to articulate how a study of masculinity relates to feminist or queer scholarship can lead to uncertainty about locating the work or critiques of appropriation, leaving lingering questions about whose interests are served through the work.[20]

Writing about the same time as Clines, John Goldingay pursued another route, positioning his article as a new approach. In defining "masculist interpretation," he acknowledged that the approach could avoid or subvert feminism, but proposes instead to provide male insights about God that need "to be complemented by female ones."[21] Yet the "complementarity" of his arguments is not always clear. For instance, his critique of violence and masculinity in an intimate partner relationship is muted, and the supposed "naturalness" or "normality" of male power remains unquestioned. Even the proposal to provide "complementary" male insights with its implied essentialism, which becomes more explicit in places,[22] will leave current feminist and queer biblical scholars suspicious. Still, it may not be clear whether the problem lies with the proposal itself to construe masculinity studies as an approach or simply with Goldingay's efforts. The latter seems more likely because Dennis T. Olson follows Goldingay's lead in pursuing masculist interpretation, which he describes as one that is "generally pro-feminist in its orientation" but that shifts "from a focus on the feminine to a focus on the masculine."[23] Unlike Goldingay, Olson argues that a link between violence and masculinity in the Hebrew Bible is not inevitable. Yet it is not evident that Olson's study of masculinity amounts to a new approach because it could just as easily be "feminist" rather than "pro-feminist."[24]

From the outset, I situate this project's focus on masculinity in the court tales of Daniel as a topic of study in gender studies rather than a new or unique "approach." Locating it in this place renders it accountable to feminist and queer approaches, upon which I rely and to which I seek to make contributions. In light of Guest's contention that a study be deemed "feminist" or "queer" based on the work it does rather than on the identity of the interpreter,[25] this issue can only be adequately assessed after presenting my analysis of masculinity in the court tales of Daniel.

2.2.3 *Political implications of masculinity studies*

The general lack of reflection about how a study of masculinity in biblical literature relates to existing approaches leads to another important issue, especially when a study of masculinity need not necessarily be aligned with feminist or queer politics: the social or political implications of studying masculinity in the Hebrew Bible.[26]

Social and political goals have been a persistent part of feminist biblical criticism. For instance, Deborah Sawyer argues that with respect Elizabeth Cady Stanton's work in the context of the late nineteenth century women's suffrage movement, "there is no observable division between the secular feminist agenda and the aims of feminist biblical scholarship."[27] A concern with political engagement and social transformation in feminist biblical scholarship persists in varying degrees. For instance, Kathleen O'Connor describes her experience with feminist biblical scholarship as a constant "call to conversion."[28] Framed in this way, feminist biblical scholarship involves more than curiosity about issues such as when texts were written or how they were compiled. While these questions have and serve social interests, feminist biblical criticism embraces the political interestedness of the scholarship as an integral component of the work. Even in work with less-explicit political goals in view, political concerns surface. For instance, Carol Meyers introduces her study of the social status of non-elite women in ancient Israel by arguing that "although effecting current social change is not a central goal here, the search for the life experiences of Israelite women has an indirect role to play in understanding biblical based inequities in the contemporary world."[29] In short, while social or political involvement occupies various roles in feminist biblical scholarship,[30] it remains integral to this body of scholarship.

Queer biblical criticism also embraces an explicit political agenda. While Ken Stone identifies two primary emphases in queer biblical criticism,[31] they share a political goal of resisting uses of the Bible that support a heteronormative framework.[32] In this respect, queer biblical criticism moves beyond merely seeking to understand representations of gender and sexuality in the Bible. It embraces a goal of contesting and disrupting interpretations that oppress people in the modern world based on categories of gender and sexuality. While Stone frames the interestedness of queer biblical scholarship as an anti-normative project, the agenda clearly involves the transformation of those oppressive ideologies as well. Like feminist biblical criticism, queer biblical criticism involves commitments to and engagement with social movements.

In contrast to the embrace of social agendas in feminist and queer biblical scholarship, many recent studies of masculinity in biblical texts lack this component. Arguing that recent studies of masculinity in biblical literature lack the "passion" of earlier feminist biblical scholarship, Clines argues for "a masculinity movement, not, as with feminism's project to assert the rights of women and to redress inequality, but to assess, critique and row back from the kinds of unthinking masculinity that are spread all over the Hebrew Bible."[33] A lack of "passion" should not be equated with the absence of politics, and it is misleading to suggest that generating knowledge about masculinity in the Hebrew Bible does not serve various social and political interests.[34] Nissinen offers an alternative explanation of what Clines observes: "scholars (especially young ones who have to worry about their tenures) may be hesitant about expressing too much passion in their scholarly writings, but there is certainly an engagement involved in every contribution to the present volume."[35] Even as aspects of Clines's passionate plea might be formulated more carefully, he forces a key question that others have echoed: what are the political implications of studying masculinity in the Hebrew Bible?[36] Or to put the issue in the way that J. Cheryl Exum articulates a central concern of feminist biblical criticism: Whose interests are served in the production of knowledge about masculinity in the Hebrew Bible?[37] Engaging Clines and others who have pressed this issue, I will directly address the social implications of this project in the conclusion.[38]

2.2.4 *What happens when characters deviate from gendered norms?*

Scholars who work from the perspective that gendered norms are cultural conventions that do not naturally flow from or adhere to particular bodies should expect that characters in texts will deviate from gendered expectations.[39] But what happens in such cases? Are these deviations subversive? Or do they reinforce the norm even as it may be exposed as a product of cultural processes? To press this issue, I will briefly describe the arguments of two scholars, Clines and Guest, who arrive at rather different conclusions regarding what happens when particular biblical characters deviate from gendered norms.

While Clines's conclusion about the representation of David is problematically circular,[40] he models an example of describing what can happen when a character deviates from gendered norms. Clines notes some instances where David appears to depart from ideas about masculinity found in Samuel, such as David's fearful flight from Jerusalem after hearing that Absalom has been proclaimed king (2 Sam 15:13–23).[41] But rather than view this deviation as "subversive," Clines asks rhetorically: "Is it not, from the point of view of the narrator, a weakness in David as a man . . . that he has caved in at the first rumour of opposition to him by Absalom?"[42] In this respect, he suggests that the text utilizes David's transgression of a gendered norm as a rhetorical strategy for negatively characterizing David.[43] For Clines, even though a character deviating from gendered norms may expose those norms as cultural conventions, it need not subvert those norms.[44]

Another way of engaging this issue emerges in Guest's argument about Jael (Judg 4–5). Guest argues that Jael's violent penetration of Sisera's head with a tent peg (4:21) provokes questions about "whether *geber* [man, warrior] can ever be fixed so unthinkingly to 'men' ever again and, simultaneously, whether our certainties about 'women' can ever be the same."[45] Guest critiques feminist scholars who describe Jael in terms of "gender reversal" because this terminology reinforces a rigidly binary construction of gender. Instead, Guest describes Jael as performing "genderfuck": a confusion, destabilizing, or subverting of "the normalcy of sex/gender regimes."[46] For Guest, Jael "breaks the borders between male and female and reveals that all gendered acts are performative."[47] In contrast with Clines, Guest offers a different answer to what occurs when a character transgresses gendered norms: a subversive moment of gender confusion occurs in the exposure of the norms as culturally contingent.

As these examples demonstrate, different options exist for assessing what happens when a character deviates from gendered norms. The issue can be further defined as follows: When is a deviation from a gendered norm subversive, and when is it not subversive? Moreover, if a deviation is subversive, in what way is it subversive? The court tales of Daniel provide a few examples for considering what happens when characters deviate from predominant gendered norms.

2.3 Summary

The study of masculinity in the court tales of Daniel will provide important data for engaging these four issues facing gender studies in the Hebrew Bible: (1) a methodological issue of how to study of gender in biblical literature, (2) the disciplinary fit of the topic of masculinity in biblical studies, (3) the political implications of a study of masculinity in biblical literature, and (4) what occurs when characters deviate from predominant gendered norms. As the methodological issue required attention to enable the study of masculinity in the court tales of Daniel, I sketched some parameters for making and assessing claims about gender in biblical literature. The remaining three issues will occasionally surface in the study itself, but I will defer engaging them until the conclusion to develop my argument.

Notes

1. As will become clear, other scholars raise many of these issues.
2. Beatrice Lawrence, "Gender Analysis: Gender and Method in Biblical Studies," in *Method Matters: Essays on the Interpretation of the Hebrew Bible in Honor of David L. Petersen*, eds. Joel M. LeMon and Kent Harold Richards, RBS 56 (Atlanta: Society of Biblical Literature, 2009), 335; Ken Stone, "Gender Criticism: The Un-Manning of Abimelech," in *Judges & Method: New Approaches in Biblical Studies*, ed. Gale A. Yee, 2nd ed. (Minneapolis: Fortress, 2007), 192; Deryn Guest, *Beyond Feminist Biblical Studies*, The Bible in the Modern World 47 (Sheffield: Sheffield Phoenix, 2012), 20.
3. On the idea that such texts are rare, see also Stone, "Gender Criticism," 188. The only examples I have found include Judg 8:20–1; 1 Sam 4:9; 17:33; 1 Kgs 2:2; 3:7–8; Job 38:3; 40:7; Jer 1:6, 31:22; 50:37; 51:30; Nah. 3:13.
4. In addition to Stone, Guest, for example, writes "exactly how one goes about letting ancient masculinities speak for themselves is a thorny issue." Guest, *Beyond Feminist Biblical Studies*, 129.
5. This sort of approach weakens the weight of the conclusions about David in David J. A. Clines, "David the Man: The Construction of Masculinity in the Hebrew Bible," in *Interested Parties: The Ideology of Writers and Readers of the Hebrew Bible*, 2nd ed. (Sheffield: Sheffield Academic, 2009), 212–43. He begins with the defensible assumption that: "I am quite sure that the construction of masculinity in the David story ... reflects the cultural norms of men of the author's time" (216). Beginning with the servant's description of David in 1 Sam 16:18, Clines studies the characterization of David to determine those norms and concludes that David is "a fully-fledged traditional male" (231). Any one of these steps and the conclusion Clines reaches may be defensible, but the approach leads to a problematically circular argument.
6. Stone, "Gender Criticism," 188.
7. Guest, *Beyond Feminist Biblical Studies*, 130.
8. See, for instance, Cynthia R. Chapman, *The Gendered Language of Warfare in the Israelite-Assyrian Encounter*, HSM 62 (Winona Lake, IN: Eisenbrauns, 2004). Chapman devotes more attention to working with the problem of evidence in working with Neo-Assyrian evidence than with her point of comparison: prophetic literature in the Hebrew Bible.
9. See, for instance, Cheryl B. Anderson, *Women, Ideology, and Violence: Critical Theory and the Construction of Gender in the Book of the Covenant and the Deuteronomic Law* (New York: T&T Clark, 2004); Mark K. George, "Masculinity and Its Regimentation in Deuteronomy," in *Men and Masculinity in the Hebrew Bible and Beyond*, ed. Ovidiu Creangă, The Bible in the Modern World 33 (Sheffield: Sheffield Phoenix, 2010), 64–82.
10. See also Chapman's work on Neo-Assyrian sources when she offers similar ideas pertaining to the activities accompanying two Neo-Assyrian royal epithets, "man" (*zikaru*) and "young man" (*eṭlu*), which she argues "do not have grammatically feminine forms and are explicitly and essentially masculine titles." Chapman, *The Gendered Language of Warfare*, 21.
11. For an introduction to the practice of content analysis, see Frank Taylor, "Content Analysis and Gender Stereotypes in Children's Books," *Teaching Sociology* 31 (2003): 300–311.
12. Jennifer L. Krafchick et al., "Best-Selling Books Advising Parents About Gender: A Feminist Analysis," *Family Relations* 54 (2005): 84–100; Kathleen E. Denny, "Gender in Context, Content, and Approach: Comparing Gender Messages in Girl Scout and Boy Scout Handbooks," *Gender & Society* 25 (2011): 27–47; Jo Ann M. Buysse, and

Melissa Sheridan Embser-Herbert, "Constructions of Gender in Sport: An Analysis of Intercollegitate Media Guide Cover Photographs," *Gender & Society* 18 (2004): 66–81; Rebecca L. Collins, "Content Analysis of Gender Roles in Media: Where Are We Now and Where Should We Go?" *Sex Roles* 64 (2011): 290–98.

13 This idea will be described in detail in Chapter 3. This basic concept was articulated in Candace West and Don H. Zimmerman, "Doing Gender," *Gender & Society* 1 (1987): 125–51.

14 On the inclusion of masculinity within feminist approaches, see Guest, *Beyond Feminist Biblical Studies*, 25–26. For the argument that feminist approaches can grow by including this topic, see Deborah F. Sawyer, "Gender Criticism: A New Discipline in Biblical Studies or Feminism in Disguise?" in *A Question of Sex? Gender and Difference in the Hebrew Bible and Beyond*, ed. Deborah W. Rooke, Hebrew Bible Monographs 14 (Sheffield: Sheffield Phoenix, 2007), 2–17.

15 Stephen D. Moore, "'O Man, Who Art Thou...?' Masculinity Studies and New Testament Studies," in *New Testament Masculinities*, eds. Stephen D. Moore and Janice Capel Anderson, SemeiaSt 45 (Atlanta: Society of Biblical Literature, 2003), 4. For an example, see Robert Bly, *Iron John: A Book About Men* (Reading, MA: Addison-Wesley, 1990). A similar approach in relation to biblical literature is Richard Rohr, *Soul Brothers: Men of the Bible Speak to Men Today* (New York: Orbis Books, 2004).

16 Stuart Macwilliam, "Ideologies of Male Beauty and the Hebrew Bible," *BibInt* 17 (2009): 265–87. See also Ken Stone, "Lovers and Raisin Cakes: Food, Sex and Divine Insecurity in Hosea," in *Queer Commentary and the Hebrew Bible*, ed. Ken Stone, JSOTSSup 334 (Sheffield: Sheffield Academic, 2001), 116–39; idem., "Queer Reading Between Bible and Film: Paris Is Burning and the 'Legendary Houses' of David and Saul," in *Bible Trouble: Queer Reading at the Boundaries of Biblical Scholarship*, eds. Teresa J. Hornsby and Ken Stone, SemeiaSt 67 (Atlanta: Society of Biblical Literature, 2011), 75–98. Similarly, masculinity has been studied under the framework of "gender criticism." See Stone, "Gender Criticism."

17 For an example of masculinity being the primary topic of a scholar focusing on "gender criticism," see Stone, "Gender Criticism."

18 See also Guest, *Beyond Feminist Biblical Studies*, 125.

19 For discussion, see ibid., 122–25.

20 Esther Fuchs, for instance, has criticized Clines on the point of appropriation in relation to his article on the Song of Songs. See David J. A. Clines, "Why Is There a Song of Songs, and What Does It Do to You If You Read It?" in *Interested Parties: The Ideology of Writers and Readers of the Hebrew Bible*, 2nd ed. (Sheffield: Sheffield Academic, 2009), 94–121; Esther Fuchs, "Men in Biblical Feminist Scholarship," *JFSR* 19 (2003): 107–8. On the lingering questions some feminists have about the social interests served through masculinity studies, see Stephen D. Moore, "Final Reflections on Biblical Masculinity," in Creangă, *Men and Masculinity in the Hebrew Bible and Beyond*, 242.

21 John Goldingay, "Hosea 1–3, Genesis 1–4, and Masculist Interpretation," *HBT* 17 (1995): 44.

22 For instance, in seeking to account for the violence in Hosea 1–3, Goldingay suggests that "Perhaps male ambiguity about violence finds expression here: we are both attracted to it and afraid of it within ourselves. We need to feel it is under control. Perhaps male awareness of responsibility for the world also finds further expression here: it is important to men that someone is in control, that things are not out of hand" (43). With this "we," Goldingay creates a universal and transhistorical masculinity in significant tension with many feminist and queer perspectives understanding gender as something produced in particular socio-historical settings.

23 Dennis T. Olson, "Untying the Knot? Masculinity, Violence, and the Creation-Fall Story of Genesis 2–4," in *Engaging the Bible in a Gendered World: An Introduction to Feminist Biblical Interpretation in Honor of Katharine Doob Sakenfeld*, eds. Linda Day and Carolyn Pressler (Louisville: Westminster John Knox, 2006), 77.
24 Though Olson does not explain why he describes his work as "pro-feminist" rather than "feminist," he is likely responding to questions about whether a male scholar can do feminist scholarship. For a discussion of men in feminist biblical scholarship, see Fuchs, "Men in Biblical Feminist Scholarship."
25 Guest, *Beyond Feminist Biblical Studies*, 152–62. Guest suggests that "the genderqueer hermeneut is identified not by who one *is*, but what one *does* with biblical texts" (162). Guest suggests this idea moves beyond defining approaches exclusively in terms of the social location of the scholar to make room for straight feminists to do genderqueer work. While not explicit, Guest's argument shares significant affinity with Butler's thoughts on performativity wherein an identity does not preexist a deed but is rather constituted through its doing. See Judith Butler, *Gender Trouble: Feminism and the Subversion of Identity*, 2nd ed. (New York: Routledge, 2010), 34. To extend Guest's argument, there is potential to exploit the convention of referring to a piece of scholarship as a "work." Framing the issue in this way requires asking what work the work does.
26 On feminist suspicions of masculinity studies, see Moore, "O Man," 3.
27 Sawyer, "Gender Criticism," 2.
28 Kathleen M. O'Connor, "The Feminist Movement Meets the Old Testament: One Woman's Perspective," in Day and Pressler, *Engaging the Bible in a Gendered World*, 3.
29 Carol L. Meyers, *Rediscovering Eve: Ancient Israelite Women in Context* (Oxford: Oxford University Press, 2012), 10.
30 Compare the different perspectives in Phyllis A. Bird, "What Makes a Feminist Reading Feminist? A Qualified Answer," in *Escaping Eden: New Feminist Perspectives on the Bible*, eds. Harold C. Washington, Susan Lochrie Graham, and Pamela Thimmes (New York: New York University Press, 1999), 124–31; Pamela Thimmes, "What Makes a Feminist Reading Feminist? Another Perspective," in Washington, Graham, and Thimmes, *Escaping Eden*, 132–40.
31 As a heuristic, I suggest that these emphases may be described as identity-based and deconstructive. The first tends to use "queer" as an umbrella term for readings by LGBT people with the idea that reading from those social locations impacts the questions one asks of texts and the answers that may arise. See Ken Stone, "Queer Commentary and Biblical Interpretation: An Introduction," in Stone, *Queer Commentary and the Hebrew Bible*, 19. For this basic position, see Mona West, "Reading the Bible as Queer Americans: Social Location and the Hebrew Scriptures," *Theology and Sexuality* 10 (1999): 28–42. For examples of this type of queer biblical criticism, see Robert E. Goss, and Mona West, eds., *Take Back the Word: A Queer Reading of the Bible* (Cleveland, OH: Pilgrim Press, 2000). The second approach to queer biblical interpretation, a "deconstructive one," highlights the ambiguities and fluidity in categories of identity, such as gender or sexuality, in the Hebrew Bible. See Stone, "Queer Commentary and Biblical Interpretation," 22. For examples, see Hornsby and Stone, *Bible Trouble*.
32 Stone, "Queer Commentary and Biblical Interpretation," 33.
33 David J. A. Clines, "Final Reflections of Biblical Masculinity," in *Men and Masculinity in the Hebrew Bible and Beyond*, ed. Ovidiu Creangă, The Bible in the Modern World 33 (Sheffield: Sheffield Phoenix, 2010), 239.
34 Martti Nissinen, "Biblical Masculinities: Musings on Theory and Agenda," in *Biblical Masculinities Foregrounded*, eds. Ovidiu Creangă and Peter-Ben Smit, Hebrew Bible Monographs 62 (Sheffield: Sheffield Phoenix, 2014), 281; Guest, *Beyond Feminist Biblical Studies*, 135–42.

35 Nissinen, "Biblical Masculinities," 281.
36 In addition to Nissinen and Guest, see Ovidiu Creangă, "Introduction," in Creangă and Smit, *Biblical Masculinities Foregrounded*, 3–14; Björn Krondorfer, "Biblical Masculinity Matters," in Creangă and Smit, *Biblical Masculinities Foregrounded*, 286–96.
37 J. Cheryl Exum, "Feminist Criticism: Whose Interests Are Being Served?" in Yee, *Judges & Method*, 65–89. See also Danna Nolan Fewell, "Reading the Bible Ideologically: Feminist Criticism," in *To Each Its Own Meaning: An Introduction to Biblical Criticisms and Their Application*, eds. Steven L. McKenzie and Stephen R. Haynes (Louisville: Westminster John Knox, 1999), 268–82.
38 I see this issue as an extension of Guest's argument about the need for "mobile theorists." See Guest, *Beyond Feminist Biblical Studies*, 162 emphasis original.
39 This idea is developed in Chapter 3.
40 For discussion, see note 5 above.
41 Clines, "David the Man," 230–31.
42 Ibid., 231.
43 Ibid.
44 In my work on masculinity in Exod 1–4, I make a similar suggestion about the characterization of Pharaoh in relation to cultural assumptions about masculinity. See Brian Charles DiPalma, "De/Constructing Masculinity in Exodus 1–4," in Creangă, *Men and Masculinity in the Hebrew Bible and Beyond*, 36–53.
45 Deryn Guest, "From Gender Reversal to Genderfuck: Reading Jael Through a Lesbian Lens," in Hornsby and Stone, *Bible Trouble*, 30.
46 Ibid., 9.
47 Ibid., 31.

3
ON GENDER AND MASCULINITY
Framing the case study

3.1 Introduction

For scholars of masculinity in biblical texts to align their work more closely with masculinity studies outside biblical studies, they must be conversant with key concepts in masculinity studies.[1] This chapter participates in that work as a foundation for analyzing masculinity in the court tales of Daniel. While Judith Butler's ideas about gender have become prominent in biblical studies,[2] I also incorporate sociological approaches to gender, which introduce key concepts, especially about masculinity, that are not part of Butler's work.[3] After briefly discussing the contributions of sociological research on gender to biblical scholars, I show the similarities between a sociological idea of "doing gender" and Butler's concept of gender. Finally, I will discuss developments in the concept of "hegemonic masculinity" that are critical for understanding my arguments about masculinity in the court tales of Daniel.

3.2 Studying gender in biblical literature informed by sociological perspectives

Sociologists R. W. Connell and James Messerschmidt remind that scholarly concepts like gender or hegemonic masculinity have been developed through various sociological methods to account for social dynamics and systems in the modern world.[4] Given the possibility of changes in configurations of gender, biblical scholars cannot use this scholarship to fill in gaps of knowledge about gendered norms in the ancient world. Connell and Messerschmidt even caution that due to changes in gender through time and across cultures: "It is desirable to eliminate any usage of hegemonic masculinity as a fixed, transhistorical model."[5] In other words, an idea like "hegemonic masculinity" may not explain gender in every social context, and biblical scholars must avoid making the evidence fit a mold developed elsewhere.[6] Modern sociological research on gender can only provide clarity on key concepts and distinctions that biblical scholars may *or may not* find relevant for the unique evidence each case presents.

3.3 Doing gender in sociological scholarship

The phrase "doing gender" encapsulates a highly influential sociological understanding of gender.[7] Critiquing those who describe gender as a "role" or a "display,"[8] Candace West and Don Zimmerman suggest that people "do gender" in interactions with others: "gender is the activity of managing situated conduct in light of normative conceptions of attitudes and activities appropriate for one's sex category."[9] They distinguish between "sex," typically assigned at birth on the basis of socially agreed upon criteria, and "sex-category," which is "established and sustained by the socially required identificatory displays that proclaim one's membership in one or the other category."[10] In other words, doing gender involves activities that constitute or produce an individual into particular sex-categories in accordance with cultural norms. To make these distinctions concrete with an example from the Hebrew Bible, consider the rallying cry of the Philistines before battle in 1 Sam 4:9: "Strengthen yourselves and be(come) men (התחזקו והיו לאנשים)... be(come) men and engage in war (והייתם לאנשים ונלחמתם)." In this example, acts of strength and war are ways the Philistine soldiers do gender and seek to produce themselves into a sex-category of "men." In the modern world, people do gender in numerous ways (e.g., gestures, dress, patterns or topics of speech, sports, or using gender segregated public restrooms).[11] While this influential paradigm has attracted critiques,[12] it remains a predominant concept in sociological research.[13]

A clear similarity exists between Butler's performative conception of gender and West and Zimmerman's idea of doing gender. For Butler, gender is "the repeated stylization of the body, a set of repeated acts within a highly rigid regulatory frame that congeal over time to produce the appearance of substance, of a natural sort of being."[14] In other words, gender is not inscribed on preexisting biological identities. Nor does gender "express" an identity that preexists an action. For Butler, gender is a performative action that produces those identities: "there is no gender identity behind the expressions of gender; that identity is performatively constituted by the very 'expressions' that are said to be its results."[15] As gender identities are constituted by actions, they are never fully achieved, but rather "tenuously constituted in time."[16] While a full comparison of Butler's work with the sociological idea of "doing gender" cannot be addressed in this context,[17] a clear similarity exists: gender entails things done that constitute individuals into social categories. Indeed, one sociologist describes Butler as "a humanities-based cousin to 'doing gender.'"[18] In this study, I work primarily with the framework West and Zimmerman articulate, especially with respect to the concepts of masculinity and masculinities that emerge in conversation with it in sociological scholarship.

3.4 Masculinities

While early work on masculinity in the Hebrew Bible construed masculinity as a singular concept,[19] many biblical scholars have been influenced by sociologist Raewyn Connell and now write about masculin*ities*.[20] Why did this shift occur?

In her early work, Connell defined masculinity as "simultaneously *a place* in gender relations, the *practices* through which men and women engage that place in gender, and the *effects* of these practices in bodily experience, personality, and culture."[21] This tripartite definition of masculinity (a place, practices, and effects) aligns with West and Zimmerman's idea of "doing gender." For Connell, things done in interactions with others (i.e., practices) produce an individual into a sex-category (i.e., a place) and have implications at various levels of social life (i.e., the effects). Influenced by the idea of intersectionality, which attends to the interaction of multiple social categories (e.g., race or class) in individuals and groups,[22] Connell asserts that multiple masculinities are discernible, but not all masculinities are equal as they are produced with intricate relationships of power between them.[23] Still, Connell proposes that one masculinity, "hegemonic masculinity," emerges "as the currently accepted answer to the problem of the legitimacy of patriarchy, which guarantees (or is taken to guarantee) the dominant position of men and the subordination of women."[24] The key feature of hegemonic masculinity is its capacity to legitimate a gendered social order, and the mechanism for structuring these relationships is not necessarily a result of violence.[25] Other masculinities negotiate relationships (e.g., subordinate or complicit) with hegemonic masculinity because most men do not meet this idealized configuration, and Connell suggests that non-hegemonic masculinities can reap a "patriarchal dividend, the advantage men in general gain from the overall subordination of women."[26] Connell describes these masculinities as "complicit," allowing researchers to describe how individuals may simultaneously deviate and benefit from hegemonic masculinity.

It is the framework of masculinity, masculinities, and hegemonic masculinity that biblical scholars have incorporated, though not without some difficulties. For instance, while Dennis T. Olson substantially advanced studies of masculinity in the Hebrew Bible by introducing Connell's framework, his concluding sketch of "alternative masculinities" becomes reductionist: each male character has his own type of masculinity, which unintentionally reduces masculinity to any act a male character does.[27] A notable omission from Connell's framework in biblical studies is its political investments, which may partially contribute to the ongoing absence of explicit social engagement in work on masculinities in the Hebrew Bible.[28] Finally, biblical scholars have relied upon an early framework for understanding masculinities that has been critiqued and reformulated.[29] Biblical scholars must attend to these important developments, discussed below, to respond to Nissinen's call for biblical scholars of masculinity to "differ from their colleagues in masculinity studies only with respect to their knowledge of their source materials."[30]

Responding to critiques of Connell's initial concept, Connell and Messerschmidt abandon certain ideas but retain three key points: a *plurality* of masculinities are produced in *hierarchical relationships* to each other and the mechanism for the reproduction of this hierarchy is *hegemonic*.[31] They also propose an expanded model to account for different geographic locations of masculinities.[32] The local level focuses on "face-to face interaction," while the regional level considers a "culture or the nation-state," and the global level entails "transnational arenas such as world politics and transnational business."[33] The authors caution that although there are links between these, "it is tempting to assume a hierarchy of power or authority, running from global to regional to local, but this could be misleading."[34] While Connell's basic framework for masculinities remained, it has developed in significant ways.

Even as this reformulated concept has proven very productive in studies of masculinity, it has experienced refinement in light of further work.[35] In particular, Christine Beasley demonstrates that while the term "hegemonic masculinity" was intended to describe a cultural mechanism (re)producing male dominance, scholars often conflate it with or use it as a synonym for a dominant masculinity or dominant men.[36] Biblical scholars are not immune to this conflation. Ovidiu Creangă, for instance, writes that "'hegemonic masculinity' connotes the most dominant representation of what it means to be a man in a given gender order."[37] Similarly, Susan Haddox, argues that "while all cultures in actuality display multiple masculinities, in most societies, one ideal is dominant, the standard against which all other masculinities are judged. This is known as hegemonic masculinity."[38] To be clear: Creangă and Haddox do *not* misread Connell as the ambiguity exists in her work. But this conflation becomes an issue because the practices of dominant men may not necessarily legitimate male dominance: "Dominant forms of masculinity . . . may not always, at all times, legitimate men's power, and those that do legitimate it may not always be socially celebrated or common."[39] Accordingly, Beasley proposes that scholars narrowly use the term "hegemonic masculinity" for the practices of any masculinity that legitimate male dominance.[40] While Beasley may overstate the position of Connell and Messerschmidt on the question of multiple hegemonic masculinities,[41] all clearly agree that aspects of a culturally dominant masculinity may or may not be hegemonic, and this point narrows the use of term "hegemonic" to practices that legitimate male dominance.[42]

With a narrowing of the definition of "hegemonic masculinity," alternative terminology is needed for other ways scholars had used the term.[43] I will use the term "predominant" for a culturally idealized or influential masculinity. Using the modifier "predominant" with reference to a masculinity (e.g., a predominant masculinity) only describes its relationship with other masculinities without commenting upon what sort of positions of power those producing that configuration of practices are in. For a masculinity associated with a particularly high position of power, I use "dominant masculinity."

Recent discussions of masculinity also emphasize the need for attentiveness to the multifaceted relationships between masculinities. The way that Connell describes masculinities as complicit, subordinated, or marginalized easily leads scholars to describe a masculinity with one of these relational terms (e.g., a complicit masculinity) without specifying the masculinity with which it is complicit. This reification of a relational term becomes a problem when a masculinity is simultaneously subordinate to one masculinity and dominant in relation to another, a point that receives exceptional clarity of expression by Tony Coles:

"there are subfields within the field of masculinity that have their own dynamics of dominant and subordinate masculinities. Therefore, one may be subordinated as a gay man within the field of masculinity yet be dominant within the field of gay masculinity."[44] An example of the problematic implications of using a relational term for a masculinity by itself can be drawn from recent biblical scholarship. Haddox argues that "Genesis favors those patriarchs expressing subordinate masculinities as the best choice for the emerging nation of Israel, both as a political entity and as a people in relationship to God."[45] While Haddox works with a singular idea of hegemonic masculinity and a slippage between hegemonic and predominant masculinity,[46] it may be the case that patriarchs are subordinate vis-à-vis a "hegemonic masculinity." But an additional question emerges: are they dominant in relation to others? If so, referring to the masculinity of the patriarchs as "subordinate" in isolation from other masculinities neglects the complex web of relationships in which their masculinity is constructed in Genesis. A relational term should be reserved for describing relationships between masculinities rather than a masculinity by itself to avoid reifying it into a single type and neglecting other relationships with which the masculinity in question exists.

The research of C. J. Pascoe on masculinity in an American High School provides a helpful case study to illustrate how these distinctions can work. Pascoe argues that among the students she studied "by symbolically or physically mastering girls' bodies and sexuality, boys at River High [a fictional name for the high school] claim masculine identities."[47] Demonstrating physical mastery over the bodies of girls could come through various practices done in routine interactions, such as rituals of flirtatious touching that "escalated, becoming increasingly violent, until a girl squealed, cried, or just gave up."[48] Another common practice was discourse about sex in which boys sought to demonstrate knowledge about and desire for sex as well as acts of physical domination over girls' bodies.[49] Through a variety of practices, both discursive and non-discursive, a predominant masculinity entailed mastery and power while "girls' bodies . . . became the conduit through which boys established themselves as masculine."[50] While this masculinity was well attested, Pascoe found ways that individuals negotiated with this predominant configuration of masculinity.

Some adolescent males found aspects of a situationally predominant masculinity incompatible with their religious commitments about sexuality. Initially, it seemed that their refusal to participate in typical ways of doing masculinity would have presented a challenge to their efforts to constitute themselves as masculine. But rather than rejecting the basic equations of a predominant masculinity, these boys accepted them and did masculinity differently. One of these boys described the others "as out of control" and suggested that the others "engaged in practices of 'getting girls' because they were ruled by their emotions."[51] This boy reframed the issue to portray the others as possessing less control than he demonstrated by refraining. While the individual acted in a way that differed from a contextually predominant masculinity, he accepted and (re)produced an equation of masculinity with power and control while reframing it to allow him to meet its expectations. Similarly, when Pascoe asked one of these boys whether he felt any less masculine because of his religious convictions, he responded: "No. If anything, more. Because you can resist. You don't have to give into it."[52] Rather than reject a configuration of masculinity as control, mastery, and domination, these boys were instead "drawing on masculinizing discourses of self-control and maturity."[53] Accordingly, Pascoe concludes that "the Christian boys . . . may have been less interactionally sexist, but their investment in gender difference and gender inequality was little different from that of the other boys."[54] These boys negotiated with a predominant masculinity by appealing to religious convictions and reframing the issue in a way that permitted them to constitute themselves as masculine even as their practices differed.

Pascoe's work demonstrates dynamics and distinctions that are crucial for this study. Multiple masculinities can be produced in a particular setting even as not all are equal. Moreover, Pascoe describes a dynamic wherein a non-predominant masculinity accepts aspects of a predominant masculinity even while the practices of each differ. While this non-predominant masculinity initially appears less interested in (re)producing gendered inequality, the conclusion cannot hold. These deviations from a predominant configuration of masculinity did not subvert gendered inequality.[55] Quite to the contrary—the non-predominant masculinity Pascoe describes was differently invested in (re)producing gendered inequality. In this way, aspects of multiple masculinities were hegemonic in the way that they (re)produce male dominance. This dynamic occurred by equating masculinity with control and domination.

3.5 Concluding comments

A sociological perspective on gender, which understands the concept to involve things done in interactions that constitute individuals into particular sex categories, presents some challenges in working with texts from an ancient culture. For this study in particular, the court tales of Daniel are textualized descriptions of actions. They are not sociological field notes based upon observation or interviews, especially given the fictional nature of the stories.[56] Moreover, the stories are highly selective in what is represented. They attest to the (re)production of gender at a cultural or symbolic level of social life and the interactional lives of those that produced the texts may be impossible to explore.[57] Moreover, unlike sociologists, who are able to interview and conduct participant observation studies, I am not able to ask one of the authors of the court tales of Daniel what they think doing masculinity involves. At this point, a primary issue this study engages comes to the foreground again: how to study and make claims about gender in ancient texts. The sociological perspective of "doing gender" provides clarity on the concept itself and important dynamics or distinctions involved in studying it. But sociological scholarship cannot provide the gendered norms with which to read the court tales of Daniel because of the idea that gendered norms are products of particular socio-historical situations that change over time and across cultures.

While I draw several important points from critical studies of masculinities, I do not consider them a mold for the court tales of Daniel. These studies raise the possibility that there may be multiple masculinities in any given socio-historical context. Only those aspects of a masculinity that (re)produce male dominance should described as hegemonic. The key issue for this project is whether sufficient evidence attests to the presence of multiple masculinities in the socio-historical context in which the court tales of Daniel emerged. I do not consider it a foregone conclusion that the stories portray Daniel and his colleagues in accordance with a culturally intelligible masculinity. This problematic assumption would perpetuate another one that must be surpassed, namely understanding whatever any male character does as yet another doing of masculinity.[58] Quite to the contrary, whether the court tales of Daniel depict any of the characters as masculine is an idea that I will test in this study.

Notes

1 For a recent argument in favor of this closer integration, see Martti Nissinen, "Biblical Masculinities: Musings on Theory and Agenda," in *Biblical Masculinities Foregrounded*, eds. Ovidiu Creangă and Peter-Ben Smit, Hebrew Bible Monographs 62 (Sheffield: Sheffield Phoenix, 2014), 273. For similar calls in feminist biblical scholarship, see Pamela J. Milne, "Toward Feminist Companionship: The Future of Feminist Biblical Studies and Feminism," in *A Feminist Companion to Reading the Bible: Approaches, Methods and Strategies*, eds. Athalya Brenner and Carole Fontaine (Sheffield: Sheffield Academic, 1997), 39–60; Esther Fuchs, "Biblical Feminisms: Knowledge, Theory and Politics in the Study of Women in the Hebrew Bible," *BibInt* 16 (2008): 205–26.
2 Judith Butler, *Gender Trouble: Feminism and the Subversion of Identity*, 2nd ed. (New York: Routledge, 2010). Note the similarity in Teresa J. Hornsby, and Ken Stone, eds., *Bible Trouble: Queer Reading at the Boundaries of Biblical Scholarship*, SemeiaSt 67 (Atlanta: Society of Biblical Literature, 2011).
3 As noted in the introduction, this approach is generally known as "social constructionist." On the need to draw from various approaches, see Peter Hennen, *Faeries, Bears, and Leathermen: Men in Community Queering the Masculine* (Chicago: University of Chicago Press, 2008), 13–14.
4 R. W. Connell and James W. Messerschmidt, "Hegemonic Masculinity: Rethinking the Concept," *Gender & Society* 19 (2005): 853.
5 Ibid., 838.
6 Even the concept of "hegemonic masculinity," which clearly predominates studies of masculinity in the modern world, is not always found to be the most explanatory for some contexts. See, for instance, Jeff Hearn, "A Multi-Faceted Power Analysis of Men's Violence to Known Women: From Hegemonic Masculinity to the Hegemony of Men," *The Sociological Review* 60 (2012): 589–610; Jeff Hearn et al., "Hegemonic Masculinity and Beyond: 40 Years of Research in Sweden," *Men and Masculinities* 15 (2012): 1–25; Clare Bartholomaeus, "'I'm Not Allowed Wrestling Stuff': Hegemonic Masculinity and Primary School Boys," *Journal of Sociology* 48 (2012): 227–47.
7 Candace West, and Don H. Zimmerman, "Doing Gender," *Gender & Society* 1 (1987): 125–51. For discussion, see Adam Isaiah Green, "Queer Theory and Sociology: Locating the Subject and Self in Sexuality Studies," *Sociological Theory* 25 (2007): 30–32; Kristen Schilt, *Just One of the Guys? Transgender Men and the Persistence of Gender Inequality* (Chicago: University of Chicago Press, 2010), 8.

8 They argue that describing gender as a "role" illumines dynamic aspects of interactions but neglects the idea that some roles are already gendered (130). Although their approach overlaps with Erving Goffman's idea that gender is a "display" through which individuals align themselves in social groups, they argue that describing gender as a "display" makes gender seem optional or peripheral to interactions (130). On this point, West and Zimmerman agree with Goffman's ideas. He writes: "feminine expression is an indication of the alignment a person of the female sex class proposes to take (or accept) in the activity immediately to follow – *an alignment which does not merely express subordination but in part constitutes it.*" See Goffman, *Gendered Advertisements*, 8. Granting important critiques of the phrase "expression," Goffman clearly does not think of a gendered act as expressing something that preexists the action. Instead, it is the action itself that produces what might have been claimed as its effect.

9 Ibid., 127.

10 Ibid.

11 West and Zimmerman, "Doing Gender," 137–138.

12 For some critiques, primarily in terms of calls for new directions in future research, see Francine M. Deutsch, "Undoing Gender," *Gender & Society* 21 (2007): 106–27; Barbara J. Risman, "From Doing to Undoing: Gender as We Know It," *Gender & Society* 23 (2009): 81–84. For a response, see Candace West and Don H. Zimmerman, "Accounting for Doing Gender," *Gender & Society* 23 (2009): 112–22. On the central role of "accountability" to gender and the difficulty it creates for those that might wish to avoid doing gender, see especially Betsy Lucal, "What It Means to Be Gendered Me: Life on the Boundaries of a Dichotomous Gender System," *Gender & Society* 13 (1999): 791. For discussions of the multiple levels of social level at which gender can be produced that extend beyond West and Zimmerman's primary focus on interactions, see Janet Saltzman Chafetz, "The Varieties of Gender Theory in Sociology," in *Handbook of the Sociology of Gender*, ed. Janet Saltzman Chafetz (New York: Kluwer Academic/Plenum Publishers, 1999), 3–24; Judith Lorber, *Paradoxes of Gender* (New Haven: Yale University Press, 1994); Michael A. Messner, "Barbie Girls Versus Sea Monsters: Children Constructing Gender," *Gender & Society* 14 (2000): 765–84; Barbara J. Risman, "Gender as a Social Structure: Theory Wrestling with Activism," *Gender & Society* 18 (2004): 429–50; Pei-Chia Lan, *Global Cinderellas: Migrant Domestics and Newly Rich Employers in Taiwan* (Durham: Duke University Press, 2006); Carla Shows, and Naomi Gerstel, "Fathering, Class, and Gender: A Comparison of Physicians and Emergency Medical Technicians," *Gender & Society* 23 (2009): 161–87; Miliann Kang, *The Managed Hand: Race, Gender, and the Body in Beauty and Service Work* (Berkeley: University of California Press, 2010); Cecilia L. Ridgeway, *Framed by Gender: How Gender Inequality Persists in the Modern World* (New York: Oxford University Press, 2011).

13 For some examples where the concept of "doing gender" is central, see Ridgeway, *Framed by Gender*; C. J. Pascoe, *Dude, You're a Fag: Masculinity and Sexuality in High School* (Berkeley: University of California Press, 2007); Kang, *The Managed Hand*.

14 Butler, *Gender Trouble*, 45.

15 Ibid., 34.

16 Ibid., 191.

17 For a discussion of issues related to this topic, see Green, "Queer Theory and Sociology."

18 Schilt, *Just One of the Guys?*, 8.

19 Harry A. Hoffner, "Symbols for Masculinity and Femininity: Their Use in Ancient Near Eastern Sympathetic Magic Rituals," *JBL* 85 (1966): 326–34; David J. A. Clines, "David the Man: The Construction of Masculinity in the Hebrew Bible," in *Interested*

Parties: The Ideology of Writers and Readers of the Hebrew Bible, 2nd ed. (Sheffield: Sheffield Academic, 2009), 212–43; John Goldingay, "Hosea 1–3, Genesis 1–4, and Masculist Interpretation," *HBT* 17 (1995): 37–44. Clines makes room for multiple masculinities, but argues against this idea (228–231).

20 Raewyn Connell began publishing as "Robert W." or "Bob" and later as "R. W." See R. W. Connell, *Masculinities*, 2nd ed. (Berkeley: University of California Press, 2005). This book was first published in 1995. But the concept of "hegemonic masculinity" had its earliest articulation in Tim Carrigan, Bob Connell, and John Lee, "Toward a New Sociology of Masculinity," *Theory and Society* 14 (1985): 551–604. According to Connell and Messerschmidt, another of Connell's books is "the most cited source for the concept of hegemonic masculinity" ("Hegemonic Masculinity," 831). They refer to R. W. Connell, *Gender and Power* (Sydney: Allen and Unwin, 1987). For biblical scholarship incorporating these ideas, see the essays in Ovidiu Creangă, ed., *Men and Masculinity in the Hebrew Bible and Beyond*, The Bible in the Modern World 33 (Sheffield: Sheffield Phoenix, 2010); Creangă and Smit, *Biblical Masculinities Foregrounded*.

21 Connell, *Masculinities*, 71. Emphasis mine.

22 For discussion of intersectionality, see Patricia Hill Collins, *Black Feminist Thought: Knowledge, Consciousness, and the Politics of Empowerment*, 2nd ed. (New York: Routledge, 2009); Irene Browne and Joya Misra, "The Intersection of Gender and Race in the Labor Market," *Annual Review of Sociology* 29 (2003): 487–513; Leslie McCall, "The Complexity of Intersectionality," *Signs* 30 (2005): 1771–1800; Candace West, and Sarah Fenstermaker, "Doing Difference," *Gender & Society* 9 (1995): 8–37. For a case study in the difference an intersectional perspective makes, see Christine L. Williams, "The Glass Escalator: Hidden Advantages for Men in the 'Female' Professions," *Social Problems* 39 (1992): 253–67; Adia Wingfield, "Racializing the Glass Escalator: Reconsidering Men's Experiences with Women's Work," *Gender & Society* 23 (2009): 5–26. For additional work on this concept, see Lan, *Global Cinderellas*; Kang, *The Managed Hand*; Kristen Barber, "The Well-Coiffed Man: Class, Race, and Heterosexual Masculinity in the Hair Salon," *Gender & Society* 22 (2008): 455–76.

23 Connell, *Masculinities*, 37.

24 Ibid., 77.

25 Ibid.

26 Ibid., 79.

27 Dennis T. Olson, "Untying the Knot? Masculinity, Violence, and the Creation-Fall Story of Genesis 2–4," in *Engaging the Bible in a Gendered World: An Introduction to Feminist Biblical Interpretation in Honor of Katharine Doob Sakenfeld*, ed. Linda Day and Carolyn Pressler (Louisville: Westminster John Knox, 2006), 84–85.

28 Connell, *Masculinities*, 7. The influence of Michel Foucault on Connell about the social interests served through the production of knowledge is clear and acknowledged. See Michel Foucault, *The History of Sexuality: An Introduction*, trans. Robert Hurley (New York: Vintage Books, 1990); idem., *Discipline and Punish: The Birth of the Prison*, trans. Alan Sheridan (New York: Vintage Books, 1995); idem., *History of Madness*, ed. Jean Khalfa, trans. Jonathan Paul Murphy and Jean Khalfa (New York: Routledge, 2006).

29 See, for example, Ovidiu Creangă, "Variations on the Theme of Masculinity: Joshua's Gender In/stability in the Conquest Narrative," in Creangă, *Men and Masculinity in the Hebrew Bible and Beyond*, 83–109; Brian Charles DiPalma, "De/Constructing Masculinity in Exodus 1–4," in Creangă, *Men and Masculinity in the Hebrew Bible and Beyond*, 36–53; Susan E. Haddox, "Favoured Sons and Subordinate Masculinities," in Creangă, *Men and Masculinity in the Hebrew Bible and Beyond*, 2–19. Each relies on Connell's second edition of *Masculinities* published in 2005 with the basic

text unchanged from 1995. The most recent collection of essays on masculinities in biblical literature may be subject to a similar critique. Some contributors incorporate a reformulated version of Connell's initial idea: Connell and Messerschmidt, "Hegemonic Masculinity." For examples of contributors working with this version, see Hilary Lipka, "Masculinities in Proverbs: An Alternative to the Hegemonic Ideal," in Creangă and Smit, *Biblical Masculinities Foregrounded*, 86–103; Nissinen, "Biblical Masculinities." As will become clear below, even this reformulated idea has developed.

30 Nissinen, "Biblical Masculinities," 273.
31 Connell and Messerschmidt, "Hegemonic Masculinity," 846. An aspect rejected is any description of hegemonic masculinity "as a fixed character type" so as to better account for its fluid aspects (847). For a study of how hegemonic masculinity can change over an individual's life, see Beth A. Eck, "Compromising Positions: Unmarried Men, Heterosexuality, and Two-Phase Masculinity," *Men and Masculinities* 17 (2014): 147–72. For an account of how social context, specifically social/work versus romantic/familial, can alter perceptions of desirable masculinity, see Kirsten Talbot, and Michael Qualye, "The Perils of Being a Nice Guy: Contextual Variation in Five Young Women's Constructions of Acceptable Hegemonic and Alternative Masculinities," *Men and Masculinities* 13 (2010): 255–78. Connell and Messerschmidt also suggest that a better understanding of the relationship of masculinity to men's bodies is needed than only viewing bodies "as objects of a process of social construction" (851). Aspects of this point have clearly been part of their work from much earlier stages. See, for example, Connell's discussion of the concept of body-reflexive practices where the body is both subject and object of a variety of social practices and intricately involved in the production of a social world within which those practices are possible. Connell, *Masculinities*, 52–66. See also Michael A. Messner, "When Bodies Are Weapons: Masculinity and Violence in Sport," *International Review for the Sociology of Sport* 25 (1990): 203–20.
32 Connell and Messerschmidt, "Hegemonic Masculinity," 849.
33 Ibid.
34 Ibid., 850.
35 For an account of the use of the reformulated concept, see James W. Messerschmidt, "Engendering Gendered Knowledge: Assessing the Academic Appropriation of Hegemonic Masculinity," *Men and Masculinities* 15 (2012): 56–76.
36 Christine Beasley, "Rethinking Hegemonic Masculinity in a Globalizing World," *Men and Masculinities* 11 (2008): 88. Emphasis original.
37 Creangă, "Variations on the Theme of Masculinity," 85.
38 Haddox, "Favoured Sons and Subordinate Masculinities," 3.
39 Beasley, "Rethinking Hegemonic Masculinity," 88–89.
40 Ibid., 94–95.
41 Connell and Messerschmidt's most definitive statement is cautious: "Whatever the empirical diversity of masculinities, the contestation for hegemony *implies* that gender hierarchy does not have multiple niches at the top." Connell and Messerschmidt, "Hegemonic Masculinity," 845. Emphasis mine. Their choice of "implies" rather than "requires" suggests that they hold open the possibility depending on the evidence in particular situations. Indeed, when expanding the geographies at which masculinities may be studied (local, regional, and global), Connell and Messerschmidt use the phrase "hegemonic masculinities" (849) and even state that "although local models of hegemonic masculinity may differ from each other, they generally overlap" (850). Messerschmidt clearly embraces the idea in subsequent work. See James W. Messerschmidt, "And Now, The Rest of the Story: A Commentary on Christine Beasley's 'Rethinking Hegemonic Masculinity in a Globalizing World,'" *Men and Masculinities* 11 (2008): 104–8. Messerschmidt's later work reiterates this point and the key criteria

for describing a masculinity as "hegemonic" is whether it legitimates male dominance. See James W. Messerschmidt, *Hegemonic Masculinities and Camouflaged Politics: Unmasking the Bush Dynasty and Its War Against Iraq* (Boulder, CO: Paradigm Publishers, 2010), 161ff. The title of his book signals his embrace of the concept of multiple hegemonic masculinities

42 See Messerschmidt, "Engendering Gendered Knowledge," 72. Messerschmidt is influenced by Mimi Schippers, who suggests defining hegemonic masculinity as "the *qualities defined as manly that establish and legitimate a hierarchical and complementary relationship to femininity* and that, by doing so, guarantee the dominant position of men and the subordination of women" (emphasis original). See Mimi Schippers, "Recovering the Feminine Other: Masculinity, Femininity, and Gender Hegemony," *Theory and Society* 36 (2007): 94.

43 Beasley suggests the term "dominant masculinity" for a masculinity that is either widespread or associated with a high position of power. But this ambiguity creates a problem in light of a dynamic Connell identified: a high position of power may not be associated with the most idealized masculinity. "Most widespread" and "high position of power" are not synonymous, nor will the two always overlap. Messerschmidt offers these clarifications: " 'Dominant' forms of masculinity refer to the most powerful or the most widespread types in the sense of being the most celebrated. . . . 'Dominate' forms of masculinity involve commanding and controlling particular interactions. . . . However, neither a dominant nor a dominating masculinity functions in such a way as to necessarily legitimate a hierarchical relationship between men and women, masculinity and femininity." See *Hegemonic Masculinities and Camouflaged Politics*, 38. With these proposals, Messerschmitt adopts a similar perspective as Beasley on how to use the term "dominant masculinity" and perpetuates the same ambiguities (either widespread or powerful). A problem also emerges with his second proposal: "dominate" is a verb, making the initial phrase "dominate forms of masculinity" grammatically awkward and necessitates alternate formulations (e.g., a dominating masculinity).

44 Tony Coles, "Negotiating the Field of Masculinity: The Production and Reproduction of Multiple Dominant Masculinities," *Men and Masculinities* 12 (2009): 42.

45 Haddox, "Favoured Sons and Subordinate Masculinities," 16.

46 See above for discussion.

47 Pascoe, *Dude, You're a Fag*, 87.

48 Ibid., 98.

49 Ibid., esp 101–104.

50 Ibid., 104.

51 Ibid., 111.

52 Ibid., 112.

53 Ibid.

54 Ibid., 113.

55 For studies of what happens when individuals deviate from predominant configurations of gender, see Hennen, *Faeries, Bears, and Leathermen*; Marci D. Cottingham, "Recruiting Men, Constructing Manhood: How Health Care Organizations Mobilize Masculinities as Nursing Recruitment Strategy," *Gender & Society* 28 (2014): 133–56; Jesse Wozniak, and Christopher Uggen, "Real Men Use Nonlethals: Appeals to Masculinity in Marketing Police Weaponry," *Feminist Criminology* 4 (2009): 275–93; Claire Duncanson, "Forces for Good? Narratives of Military Masculinity in Peacekeeping Operations," *International Feminist Journal of Politics* 11 (2009): 63–80; Matthew B. Ezzell, " 'I'm in Control': Compensatory Manhood in a Therapeutic Community," *Gender & Society* 26 (2012): 190–215; J. Edward Sumerau, " 'That's What a Man Is Supposed to Do': Compensatory Manhood Acts in an LGBT Christian Church," *Gender & Society* 26 (2012): 461–87. On the ways that masculinities can be hybrid

configurations of hegemonic and non-hegemonic aspects, see Akihiko Hirose and Kay Kei-ho Pih, "Men Who Strike and Men Who Submit: Hegemonic and Marginalized Masculinites in Mixed Martial Arts," *Men and Masculinities* 13 (2010): 190–209; Tristan Bridges and C. J. Pascoe, "Hybrid Masculinities: New Directions in the Sociology of Men and Masculinities," *Sociology Compass* 8 (2014): 246–58.

56 My thinking on this point is influenced by William K. Gilders, who addresses similar issues in his studies of biblical representations of rituals. For an introduction, see William K. Gilders, "Anthropological Approaches: Ritual in Leviticus 8, Real or Rhetorical?" in *Method Matters: Essays on the Interpretation of the Hebrew Bible in Honor of David L. Petersen*, eds. Joel M. LeMon and Kent Harold Richards, RBS 56 (Atlanta: Society of Biblical Literature, 2009), 233–50.

57 For an especially insightful discussion of this dynamic, see Gale A. Yee, *Poor Banished Children of Eve: Woman as Evil in the Hebrew Bible* (Minneapolis: Fortress, 2003).

58 For further discussion of this point, see Chapter 2.

4

MASCULINITY AND THE COURT TALES OF DANIEL

Identifying the issues

4.1 Introduction

The nearly all-male cast of the court tales of Daniel invites rather than precludes an analysis of gender in the stories when construing gender as things done in interactions with others that constitute individuals in particular sex categories.[1] While I begin with the texts to delimit the relevant issues rather than fully discussing masculinity in the late Persian and early Hellenistic periods, previous research on masculinity in the Hebrew Bible and its ancient Near Eastern context inevitably informs my reading of the court tales of Daniel. To highlight the point that my claims in this chapter about the court tales of Daniel depend on a discussion of the historical context, which subsequent chapters undertake, I present them using hypothetical language.

I will advance two main hypotheses about masculinity in the court tales of Daniel. First, while Daniel and his colleagues depart from some configurations of masculinity, the stories may present them as negotiating with those practices to produce a different masculinity through knowledge and loyalty.[2] Second, by asking who provides for and protects Daniel and his colleagues, the stories appear to construct the struggles between God and the foreign kings as a rivalry for masculine dominance. Other issues related to masculinity will also emerge in my reading, such as physical beauty and persuasive speech. Considering these issues provides a foundation for assessing whether the court tales of Daniel (re)produce cultural configurations of masculinity.

4.2 Hypotheses about masculinity in the court tales of Daniel

4.2.1 Daniel 1 – competing masculinities: brawn versus beauty and brains

Numerous activities that scholars have associated with masculinity in the Hebrew Bible and its ancient Near Eastern context occur in Dan 1, including (1) warfare and violence, (2) knowledge, (3) protection and provision, (4) beauty,

(5) persuasive speech, and (6) producing sons.[3] While I discuss each issue below, this section introduces two competing masculinities in Dan 1 that are central to this study: (1) the power of physical violence versus the power of knowledge and (2) a competition between Nebuchadnezzar and God regarding who protects and provides for Daniel and his colleagues.

The court tales of Daniel begin with two kings at war, perhaps the most frequently discussed activity configured as masculine in the Hebrew Bible and its ancient Near Eastern context (Dan 1:1).[4] After setting the martial arena, the narrator introduces Yahweh, who allows Judah to fall (v. 2). Attentiveness to a cultural equation of masculinity with martial prowess suggests that Jehoiakim suffers an emasculating defeat while Nebuchadnezzar triumphs. Yahweh is more powerful than Nebuchadnezzar, who succeeds because of what Yahweh does for him. This move may exculpate Yahweh from one gendered charge (i.e., he *lacked strength*) while allowing another to emerge (i.e., he *failed to protect* his people). The text makes no mention of wrongdoing on Judah's part, a strategy earlier Israelite writers adopted to produce Yahweh's masculinity in such situations.[5] While the court tales of Daniel do not rationalize Judah's fall in this way, Yahweh appears to fall short of gendered expectations that he protect his people from the military advances of a foreign king.[6]

Emerging victorious on the martial arena, Nebuchadnezzar extracts goods from Judah: vessels from the temple and young men from the upper classes (vv. 2–4). Daniel and his colleagues are among the conquered, which suggests that they are presented with difficulties in negotiating cultural norms of masculinity, especially in light of the interactions of multiple social categories (gender, ethnicity, and socio-political status). Moreover, a structural parallel between the vessels and Daniel and his colleagues puts the latter into a similar position as the former. Nebuchadnezzar has both objects "brought" (*hiph.* of בוא) to Babylon: the vessels to display the king's power over foreign lands and Daniel and his colleagues to demonstrate the king's martial prowess over foreign people and their own lack of it. This point helps explain the specification that the personnel extracted from Judah are to be "without any blemish (מאום) and good looking (וטובי מראה)" (v. 4): as displays of his power, the king wants his jewels to look their best.[7] But what is the significance of their beauty with respect to cultural norms of masculinity? While scholars have not extensively discussed beauty and masculinity in the Hebrew Bible, it clearly needs attention to understand gender in these stories.[8]

In addition to their beauty, Daniel and his colleagues have "insight in each matter of wisdom, knowing knowledge, and skilled in knowledge (ומשכילים בכל־חכמה וידעי דעת ומביני מדע)" (v. 4). They are well-functioning adornments for the king's court, a combination of beauty and brains. Is there a connection between their knowledge and masculinity? Among their attributes is "strength" (כח), specifically strength "to stand in the palace of the king" (v. 4). Perhaps knowledge will enable them to negotiate a cultural equation of masculinity with strength.[9] A way of assessing this idea emerges in relation to the king's purpose in bringing them to Babylon: "to teach them the literature and language of the Chaldeans (ללמדם ספר ולשון כשדים)" (v. 4). This training is a scribal education to prepare them to serve the court.[10] Scribal masculinity clearly needs attention to understand the court tales of Daniel.[11]

Nebuchadnezzar intends to improve Daniel and his colleagues with respect to their beauty and their brains. Nebuchadnezzar's intention to improve their knowledge is clear when the narrator reports the purpose of bringing them to Babylon. That Nebuchadnezzar desires to improve, or at least to maintain, their physical appearance is implied when Daniel requests another diet. Daniel's attempt to procure another diet appears to be gendered activity in light of suggestions that persuasive speech is configured as masculine in the Hebrew Bible.[12] The guard's response to Daniel is crucial: "He [the king] will *see your appearance* (יראה את פניכם) looking worse than the boys and you will endanger my head with the king" (v. 10). The guard insists that he must maintain their physical appearance, a concern understandable in light of the idea that they must look their best as displays of the king's power. As Nebuchadnezzar provides the rations, he could be credited with providing the sustenance to maintain or improve their brains and their beauty. He even seems successful on both counts because after their training, Daniel and his colleagues are superior to the others (vv. 15, 19–20).

Yet the narrator suggests that Yahweh provides for Daniel and his colleagues, making the point explicit for their knowledge: "God *gave* (נתן) these four boys knowledge and insight in each matter related to literature and wisdom. He [God] made Daniel insightful [*hiph.* of בין] in each vision and dreams" (v. 17). Whatever Nebuchadnezzar provided, the narrator asserts that their knowledge comes from God. In this way, the text creates a difference between what readers know (i.e., God has provided) and what Nebuchadnezzar thinks (i.e., he has provided).[13] In this struggle for correct knowledge, the narrative asks who provides for Daniel and his colleagues.[14] God's role in their physical appearance is at best implied. After Daniel decides to refrain from the royal rations, the narrator reports that "God bestowed kindness and mercy on Daniel before the chief of the eunuchs" (v. 9). This opening suggests that God is at work. Likewise, the surprising result of their diet implies that God should receive the credit for their appearance.[15] In light of suggestions that acting as a protector or provider were configured as masculine in the ancient Near East,[16] this rivalry appears as a wrestling match between God and Nebuchadnezzar for status as the culturally dominant male.

Amidst this rivalry, food consumption could have significance for how Daniel and his colleagues are represented with respect to masculinity. Their diet is a vegetal one, and Newsom argues that while the foods are not specified, "the symbolic contrast between the two diets is one between 'strong' foods and 'weak' foods."[17] More recently, Newsom does not revisit this suggestion, a possibility needing attention given the frequent configuring of strength as masculine and weakness as feminine.[18]

Daniel 1 concludes with a comparison of Daniel and his colleagues with the others in their class. The narrator first reports that the king could not find any other like Daniel and his colleagues (v. 19). The second statement clarifies: "in every matter of wisdom and discernment concerning which the king inquired of them, he found them ten times better" (v. 20). The court tales imagine a situation in which an individual can publicly display knowledge and be evaluated by others in a way that hierarchically differentiates some males from other males. Presenting knowledge in this way suggests that the court tales of Daniel configure knowledge as masculine in some way.

While the preceding discussion raises several issues, an additional issue needs introduction: fathers and sons. Whose sons are Daniel and his colleagues? The text claims that they are from royal or noble descent (v. 3).[19] More importantly for cultural configurations of masculinity, are they married, and have they produced male children? When introducing them, the narrator omits mention of wives or children and describes them as "boys (ילדים)" (v. 4), a term other characters use for them in Dan 1 (vv. 10, 13, 15, 17). Their status as "boys" may explain the narrator's omission of including wives or children: they are too young. Status as a "boy" may be subordinately masculine vis-à-vis an adult male status, but one that might not be unmasculine. Another possibility emerges in interpretive traditions asserting that Daniel and his colleagues are eunuchs.[20] Indeed, the "chief of eunuchs (שר הסריסים)" supervises them (vv. 7, 9–10), which leads some scholars to speculate that Daniel and his colleagues are eunuchs if they are under him.[21] Still, the text never describes them with terms for "eunuchs." Instead, the text refers to them as "boys" in Dan 1 and as "men" in the rest of the court tales.[22] While later traditions understand them as eunuchs, the text does not address the question. At this point in the court tales, a question emerges that could have significance to gender in light of the suggestion that producing male children to perpetuate a male's name was important for masculinity in earlier literature from ancient Israel.[23]

In terms of the categories scholars have developed for masculinity in other texts from the Hebrew Bible and its ancient Near Eastern context, numerous issues appear important in Dan 1. Nebuchadnezzar achieves a martial victory while Jehoiakim loses. Yet the narrator makes Nebuchadnezzar's success contingent on what Yahweh permits, which positions Yahweh as dominant. Further tension between Yahweh and Nebuchadnezzar emerges regarding who protects and provides for Daniel and his colleagues. For Daniel and his colleagues, belonging to a people who have been defeated in war and exiled appears to create difficulty with respect to their masculinity. They also seem to lack wives or male children, but their knowledge differentiates them hierarchically from other males and may be linked with displays of strength.

4.2.2 Daniel 2 – the power of knowledge

Daniel 2 depicts a public display of knowledge as powerful enough to produce subordinating gestures from a king (2:46) while minimizing the utility of physical violence. When reading this clash in terms of the possible configurations of masculinity in the cultural context, a less-common masculinity involving knowledge appears to triumph over a masculinity produced through physical violence.

The narrative conflict occurs early: Nebuchadnezzar has a dream and summons his officials to him "to declare (להגיד) to the king his dreams" (v. 2). Nebuchadnezzar reiterates his lack of knowledge when he tells them that he wants "to *know* (לדעת) the dream" (v. 3). While the king's lack of knowledge makes him dependent on his officials, this situation need not be entirely problematic: he has experts, who should be able to interpret the dream.[24] The courtiers request that the king "tell" (אמר) them the dream so that they can "make known" (*pa'el* of חוה) the interpretation. But the king clarifies: they are to cause the king *to know* (*haph'el* of ידע) the dream and its interpretation. The repetition of words involving knowledge emphasizes the king's lack of knowledge. Responding to this situation, Nebuchadnezzar threatens physical violence. Those who do not comply will be dismembered (lit. "made into limbs") and their houses turned into a dunghill (v. 5). This threat appears to engage cultural norms of masculinity in two respects: (1) the end of their line and the ability to preserve their names and (2) failing to protect their houses. This dynamic creates conflict between two activities concerned with power: physical violence and knowledge. In light of suggestions about masculinity elsewhere in the Hebrew Bible and its ancient Near Eastern context, this conflict appears as a clash of two masculinities.

Those summoned reiterate their position. Previously, they commanded the king: "tell (אמר) the dream to your servants" (v. 4). Now, they use a jussive: "may (יאמר) the king tell the dream to his servants" (v. 7). They also refer to themselves in the third person (i.e., *his* servants) as opposed to the second person they used earlier (i.e., *your* servants). They are trying to persuade the king through a careful use of language to tell them the dream. If there is a link between persuasive speech and masculinity, they are trying to conform to gendered expectations.[25]

The conflict caused by Nebuchadnezzar's lack of knowledge comes to an initial climax when the courtiers say to the king: "every great and masterful king has not asked for something like this" (v. 10). By suggesting that Nebuchadnezzar departs from royal expectations, the courtiers may be rebuking the king for behavior they consider unbecoming. They may also be seeking to persuade the king to tell them the dream. Or perhaps they indicate their submissiveness to the king, suggesting that their inability to comply will not reflect poorly on him. However one construes their intent, their words suggest that Nebuchadnezzar has set himself apart from other kings. But this exceptionality could be taken in various ways: are they suggesting that he has asked for much or rather that he has asked for *too* much?

Understandings of dreams in Mesopotamian culture partly explain Nebuchadnezzar's anger: the negative portends of dreams could be averted through rituals, and he seeks to compel his officials to give the dream.[26] Moreover, his response appears as an attempt to (re)constitute his position of power through physical violence, possibly a culturally predominant way of doing masculinity. Yet killing the wise men of Babylon would eliminate any chance of resolving the conflict of this story: his lack of knowledge. Moreover, lacking knowledge would perpetuate his powerlessness, especially as he would be unable to ward off any negative implications of the dream. With these dynamics, the story binds Nebuchadnezzar in a complex knot: the action through which he could constitute himself as a dominant male (physical violence) would leave him powerless with respect to his dream and less than a wise ruler. Violence would be an inadequate means to power, incapable of addressing the king's predicament. In this way, Dan 2 suggests that knowledge can be more powerful than physical violence. This tension appears as a duel of two masculinities, both of which equate masculinity with power even as they differ in how to display it.

Although absent to this point, the eponymous hero of the court tales enters as Nebuchadnezzar's decree is about to be executed and Daniel is wise from the outset.[27] The narrator reports: באדין דניאל התיב עטא וטעם לאריוך (v. 14). Scholars typically understand this statement in the way reflected in the NRSV: "Daniel responded with prudence and discretion to Arioch."[28] But because the verb is in the *haph'el* stem (i.e., causative nuance), it can be translated as: "Daniel caused counsel and sense to return to Arioch."[29] Regardless of how the translation issues are resolved, the point is that Daniel is wise: he obtains more time and prevents the decree from being executed.

After having the dream and its interpretation revealed to him, Daniel blesses Yahweh and describes two of Yahweh's attributes: "wisdom and power (חכמתא וגבורתא)" (v. 20). Daniel subsequently describes examples of these attributes: Yahweh's *power* is evident because he "changes times and seasons, removes kings and causes kings to arise" (v. 21). Yahweh's *wisdom* receives greater elaboration: "he gives wisdom to those who are wise, knowledge to those knowing discernment. He reveals deep and hidden things. He knows what is in the dark" (vv. 21–22). Daniel also praises Yahweh for giving him "wisdom and power (חכמתא וגבורתא)," the same things he attributed to Yahweh (v. 23). But only knowledge receives attention as Daniel continues: "You have caused me to know (הודעתני) what we sought from you; for the matter of the king you have caused us to know (הודעתנא)" (v. 23). Perhaps for Daniel knowledge is power and a comment upon the former simultaneously makes a claim about the latter.[30] While most scholars do not understand Daniel's claim to have received "wisdom and power" as a hendiadys (powerful wisdom or wise power),[31] it could explain why Daniel only describes the wisdom he received from God. Moreover, the court tales of Daniel consistently construe knowledge as powerful. As Anathea Portier-Young puts it: "Wisdom and knowledge, not weapons, are the strength of the faithful in the book of Daniel."[32] While the configuring of power as knowledge has not been lost in scholarship on Daniel, its significance for gender has not been addressed.[33]

Before Daniel delivers his interpretation to the king, Arioch introduces him as "a man from the exiles of Judah (גבר מן־בני גלותא די יהוד)" (v. 25). This opening uses various social categories to describe Daniel, one related to socio-political status (i.e., "exiles") and another related to ethnicity (i.e., "of Judah"). The social categories are interconnected for Daniel and his colleagues: they are exiles and Judahites, both of which mark them as subordinate to their Babylonian conquerors.[34] Arioch also introduces Daniel as a גבר, a term derived from the same root as one of the things Daniel claimed to have received from God, "power" (גבורתא).

There are two options for understanding גבר: (1) גבר functions as an impersonal pronoun that is not gender specific (someone) or (2) גבר conveys a particular social location (a man). The latter possibility is more likely because the other terms denote *specific* social locations. Moreover, if Arioch were using גבר to refer to a single indefinite person without defining Daniel in terms of a gendered identity, it would depart from the convention in the court tales.[35] Indeed, the term seems to occur only with reference to groups of men elsewhere in the court tales.[36] Having been positioned as a "man" (גבר), how does Daniel manage the perception of his actions in light of cultural norms of masculinity? From the perspective on gender adopted in this project, where actions produce social identities, appeals to biology or physical features cannot provide a sufficient answer. Perhaps Daniel's powerful knowledge produces an image of Daniel as masculine in the court tales. If so, configuring knowledge as strength enables him to negotiate cultural assumptions about masculinity more typically defined in terms of physical violence.

Daniel's words to Nebuchadnezzar constitute most of the remainder of Dan 2 and consist of three parts: (1) introductory comments (vv. 27–30), (2) recounting Nebuchadnezzar's dream (vv. 31–36), and (3) interpreting the dream (vv. 37–45). Daniel's speech amounts to just under 40 percent of the chapter (nineteen verses), and he was not introduced at the beginning. Utilizing categories from scholarship on masculinity in the Hebrew Bible, his speech should be analyzed in terms of "persuasion."[37] Does Daniel persuade the king? Posing the question in this way exposes a problem with the category of "persuasive speech" for all discourse: it is not clear that Daniel is trying to persuade the king. Perhaps Daniel seeks to persuade the king that he has the dream and its interpretation correct. But this idea forces Daniel's words into a category other than what is most obvious about them: they are an interpretation of a dream. Clearly, a category of persuasive speech appears limiting for assessing the use of discourse to do gender.

After Daniel's interpretation, the chapter concludes quickly: "King Nebuchadnezzar fell upon his face and prostrated before Daniel" (v. 46). Both actions, "falling" (נפל) and "prostrating" (סגד), involve lowering the body, which are subordinating physical gestures.[38] Even as the text does not seem troubled by the idea of Nebuchadnezzar worshiping Daniel, commentators offer other explanations.[39] While there are different implications depending upon to whom Nebuchadnezzar directs his actions, the plot is clear: Daniel's powerful knowledge produces subordinating gestures from the one who should be the dominant human male. Even if the gestures are directed to Daniel's God, Nebuchadnezzar submits himself to Daniel as God's representative and reverses expectations for a "normal" order of things: a king should be the recipient rather than the doer of these gestures. A masculinity involving knowledge appears strong enough to bring a masculinity involving violence, or at least the threat of it, to its knees.

While Nebuchadnezzar begins with subordinating gestures, his subsequent actions attempt to (re)establish a position as the supremely powerful male in the stories. He makes Daniel great (*pa'el* of רבה), "gives" (יהב) him numerous gifts, and makes him "rule" (*haph'el* of שלט) over the province of Babylon (v. 48).

Doing these things at once empowers Daniel and the king for claiming the authority to do them.

In addition to the power of knowledge, Dan 2 raises the issue of wives and children. After Daniel obtains time to determine the interpretation of the dream, he returns "to his house (לביתה)" and encounters his colleagues (v. 17). But the text does not mention a wife or children. Issues of narrative chronology because of redactional activity complicate assessing this point. While the narrative sequence suggests that Dan 2 occurs after the conclusion of Dan 1, the time reference in Dan 2 indicates otherwise. The time allotted for the training of Daniel and his colleagues is three years (1:5), but the narratorial time stamp places Dan 2 amidst their training.[40] Still, the image of Daniel and his colleagues remains consistent: wives and children are not mentioned. At home, they have each other. As producing male children to perpetuate a father's name may have been important to some ancient constructions of masculinity, Daniel and his colleagues appear presented with a challenge in negotiating those ideas.[41]

A few points appear important to understanding the role of gender in Dan 2. Daniel and his colleagues do not clearly have wives or children, and they are Judean exiles. Yet at least Daniel is described as a "man," and his knowledge is so powerful that it causes the king to respond with subordinating physical gestures. Moreover, physical violence appears inferior to knowledge to display strength.

4.2.3 Daniel 3 – the king's erect statue: a ritual of subordination gone awry

Several issues with masculinity appear important to Dan 3, especially the king's erect statue and a ritual of subordination centered around it, which are ways that Nebuchadnezzar seeks to (re)produce his dominance. But the ritual does not go as planned. The God of Shadrach, Meshach, and Abednego protects them against the king. Moreover, despite uncertainty about whether Shadrach, Meshach, and Abednego produce children, they manage to have their names memorialized in a royal decree.

The image that Nebuchadnezzar erects is a public display of power. At sixty cubits high and six cubits wide, the proportions are clearly hyperbolic (Dan 3:1).[42] Erecting a large image of gold displays the king's power because it shows that he has the resources (the raw material and the personnel) to erect it. While I share Clines's reticence to describe all tall structures as "phallic,"[43] it seems hard to avoid given the repetitious use of קום in the *hap'el* (i.e., to cause to arise or to "erect") to describe the statue (vv. 2–3, 5, 7, 12, 14, 18). Although no clear lexical links between the words used for the image or the action done to it suggest a double-entendre would be recognizable in the historical context,[44] I refer to this image as the "king's erect statue" to convey the text's repetition of this phrase and that the king's masculinity appears at stake through his erected statue.

An additional display of power accompanies the king's erect statue: a ritual of subordination.[45] The herald instructs imperial personnel to come and all come dutifully, "standing" (קום) before it and mirroring its own posture (v. 3). The ritual is simple. Upon hearing the music, all are to "fall" (נפל) and "lay prostrate" (סגד) before the image (vv. 5–6), the same actions that Nebuchadnezzar performed before Daniel (2:46) and that would (re)produce the subordination of his subjects as well his own dominance.[46] But almost as soon as the narrator reports that all appears to go according to script (3:7), the possibility that something has gone awry is raised (vv. 8–12). As rituals can produce particular social relationships,[47] when Shadrach, Meshach, and Abednego refuse to participate, they threaten a mechanism that (re)produces their relationship of inequality. This threat partly explains Nebuchadnezzar's rage.

When Nebuchadnezzar confronts Shadrach, Meshach, and Abednego, he raises a crucial issue for this study: "Who is the god who *will save you* (ישיזבנכון) from my hand?" (v. 15). Indeed, the court tales of Daniel repeatedly raise this question: Who protects Daniel and his colleagues? At the opening to the court tales, the narrator left God open to the charge that he failed to protect his people. Especially with the question raised explicitly at this point, God has an opportunity to establish himself as one who can protect his own and to (re)establish a masculine position.

The response of Shadrach, Meshach, and Abednego conveys that this ritual has not gone according to plan and Nebuchadnezzar responds accordingly. He attempts to show that he has the power to fulfill his word by carrying out his decree: binding them and throwing them into the fiery furnace.[48] In this way, he responds with actions scholars suggest are configured as masculine elsewhere in the Hebrew Bible: violence. Yet even this attempt goes awry. Those who obey the king are killed in their obedience (vv. 20–22) while those who disobeyed are saved (vv. 23–27)! In the process, God intervenes to protect Shadrach, Meshach, and Abed-nego. That others witness the entire scene makes the king's failure more significant. Moreover, even if Nebuchadnezzar had killed them, they would have been unable to produce the "proper" order of things through complying with the ritual of subordination that (re)establishes his dominance. The court tales again imagine a situation where acts of physical violence are an inadequate approach to power.

Working from the perspective that social positions are never uncontestably "achieved" and are produced through repeated actions,[49] Nebuchadnezzar's failures are highly significant. His concluding decree, which seeks to protect the God of Shadrach, Meshach, and Abednego from being spoken against (v. 29), continues his effort to display power. But this story has asserted that the God of Shadrach, Meshach, and Abednego can protect himself and his own, rendering the decree unnecessary. Moreover, while a decree would ordinarily (re)produce unequal relations between king and subject people, this decree memorializes and celebrates as its *raison d'être* an occasion on which others refused to comply with a decree and prospered. The contradictory logic of the decree undermines its powerful potential: obey this decree because others prospered when they disobeyed another decree. Through subtle twists, the very thing that should enable him to produce himself as masculine further exposes his failures.

The decree also preserves the names of Shadrach, Meshach, and Abednego. It repeats all three of their names twice: once in the preamble (v. 28) and again in the decree itself (v. 29). Indeed, Dan 3 repeats their names thirteen times, and they are not introduced at the beginning of the chapter (vv. 12–14, 16, 19–20, 22–23, 26 (x2), 28–30). This repetition contrasts with the typically economical prose in the Hebrew Bible.[50] Sending their names through the empire in the decree becomes a literary climax of this repetition. The concern to preserve a name appears to intersect with cultural configurations of masculinity. But rather than produce male children, Shadrach, Meshach, and Abednego preserve a name through devotion to God.[51]

Aspects of masculinity that scholars identify elsewhere in the Hebrew Bible appear in Dan 3. The clear critique of Nebuchadnezzar can be formulated in gendered terms: despite his efforts to display his power through a ritual of subordination centered around his erect statue, he appears rather flaccid. God demonstrates his ability to protect his own, even against the king. Finally, the king memorializes the names of Shadrach, Meshach, and Abednego as a result of their fidelity to their God.

4.2.4 Daniel 4 – is Nebuchadnezzar good at being a male ruler?

Daniel 4 presents another occasion for Daniel to demonstrate his knowledge, which raises similar issues to those I discussed about Dan 2. To avoid repeating those issues, I focus on Nebuchadnezzar's dream. I suggest this dream appears to engage gendered anxieties by asking whether he is good at being a male ruler.[52] While the phrase "male ruler" may seem redundant, it conveys how royal rule in the ancient Near East could intersect with predominant configurations of masculinity. I also suggest that the animalic imagery used to describe Nebuchadnezzar in his banishment shows God's power over him. Finally, Daniel memorializes his name through knowledge and loyalty to the king.

Upon having the dream, Nebuchadnezzar claims that he was frightened (דחל) and terrified (4:2) (בהל). Earlier, Nebuchadnezzar is disturbed (פעם) by his dream (2:1–3). In the final collection of the court tales of Daniel, Nebuchadnezzar's fear appears surprising as he should know that he has a skilled dream interpreter who was able to determine the dream earlier. Part of his fear arises from the disturbing imagery of a tree being cut down. The extent to which the dream may rely upon and engage cultural concerns of masculinity provides additional explanation for his fear.

Newsom suggests that the tree imagery in Nebuchadnezzar's dream has associations with femininity because of a connection between trees and goddesses in the ancient Near East.[53] Even if this point is granted,[54] the issues in the dream appear rooted in concerns about masculinity. The tree has a great height: it "stretches to the heavens" (v. 8). The tree "grows great (רבה) and strong (תקף)" such that it is "visible to the ends of the entire earth" (v. 8). As Daniel interprets the thinly veiled symbolism, the tree represents an empire of vast size and strength.⁵⁵ The tree also has abundant fruit that *provides* food (v. 9). Likewise, the tree provides a place to rest (v. 9). In other words, there is *protection* in the shadow of this tree. In these ways, the dream engages issues that scholars suggest were integral to the masculinity of rulers in the ancient Near East: protection, provision, and strength.⁵⁶ The tree is being good at being a male ruler.

The watcher's announcement would provoke the king's anxiety about whether he will maintain a performance consistent with cultural configurations of masculinity. The watcher commands that the tree be "cut down" and that its branches be "chopped" (v. 11). If engaging in physical violence was part of a culturally predominant masculinity, being the recipient of these violent actions entails trouble for the masculinity of Nebuchadnezzar. Cultural ideas about masculinity may also make the content even more upsetting: its fruit will be scattered, preventing it from providing food for the animals that relied upon it (v. 11). Moreover, the watcher declares that animals will be forced to "flee" from it. The tree will no longer protect those in its shadow. The judgment appears to narrate the failure of the tree to sustain a performance in accordance with cultural expectations of being good at being a male ruler, provoking a gendered anxiety, especially a fear of being overpowered by another.⁵⁷

The animalic imagery describing Nebuchadnezzar may heighten the gendered concerns of the dream concerning power (v. 30). Christopher Hays argues that the animalic imagery evokes creatures of the underworld, conveying the "extreme affliction" of the sufferer who takes on features of the dead.⁵⁸ Though more compelling than other explanations Hays critiques, his explanation overlooks the political symbolism of animals in the dream where animals are not creatures of the underworld. They are subordinate political entities in the world that finds "refuge" in the empire (v. 12).⁵⁹ For Nebuchadnezzar to become like an animal is to become like those that previously depended on him. The animalic imagery reverses social relationships and displays God's power over the king as Nebuchadnezzar's final words convey: "Those who walk with pride, he [God] is able to bring low (להשפלה)" (v. 34). In Nebuchadnezzar's view, being like an animal shows God's power to bring him low.⁶⁰

Like Dan 2, knowledge is a major issue in Dan 4. The crux of Dan 4 is that the king does not *know* the interpretation of a dream and requires others to "cause him to know" (*haph'el* of ידע) it (v. 3). The stated purpose of the watcher's decree against the king is that "all who live may *know* (ידע) the most high is sovereign" (v. 14). In this way, the decree serves a pedagogic function. Daniel's interpretation slightly alters the role of knowledge: Nebuchadnezzar will remain in an animalic state until *he knows* (ידע) that the most high rules (v. 22). In this respect, a lack of knowledge partly explains the decree against Nebuchadnezzar. Moreover, Nebuchadnezzar will be reestablished once he *knows* (ידע) that the most high rules (v. 23). Knowledge is powerful enough to remove and reestablish a king from his throne.⁶¹

Daniel's powerful knowledge does not lead to a promotion as it did previously (Dan 2:48). But Dan 4 imagines a scenario in which a king sends a letter to the entire kingdom memorializing Daniel's ability to interpret the dream and Daniel's name, which contrasts strongly with the nameless courtiers who failed.[62] Like his colleagues, Daniel makes a name for himself apart from producing male children. While his colleagues accomplished this task through their fidelity to their God, Daniel makes a name for himself through his intellectual potency and fidelity to the king.

Configurations of masculinity scholars identify elsewhere in the Hebrew Bible or its ancient Near Eastern context occur in Dan 4. The tree in Nebuchadnezzar's dream appears to evoke gendered anxieties about whether he is good at being a male ruler, and the animalic image of him underscores his subordination to Yahweh. In this respect, the court tales again appear to assert that Yahweh is the most powerful male. Moreover, knowledge appears potent enough to memorialize Daniel's name throughout the empire.

4.2.5 Daniel 5 – Belshazzar and the problem (of) son(s)

Daniel 5 presents Daniel with another occasion to demonstrate his knowledge. While I will briefly discuss the relationship between knowledge and power in this story, I will return to the significance of this repeated theme in the following section. This section will explore the idea that Dan 5 presents Belshazzar as a problem son of Nebuchadnezzar and a representative of the problem of sons for some ancient constructions of masculinity: they may preserve a father's name, but they can also tarnish that name.[63]

The queen in Dan 5 receives some of the only feminist analysis of the court tales of Daniel.[64] Athalya Brenner analyzes various foreign rulers characterized as "obtuse" in the Hebrew Bible (e.g., Pharaoh and Eglon) and argues that by depicting the queen as a better statesperson than the king, the narrative "achieves a serious critical aim: the subversion of (proverbial) foreign powers who act against Jews and Judaism."[65] In a self-response to this article, Brenner clarifies that this "positive" image of a wise woman intends to make the male ruler appear more stupid, which is not a positive representation of women.[66] This argument clearly has implications for the masculinity of Belshazzar.

The repetition of familial terms emphasizes the importance of father-son dynamics in Dan 5. When the narrator describes the vessels used in the drinking party, they are those "which Nebuchadnezzar, *his father*, had taken" (v. 2). Describing Daniel to Belshazzar, the queen makes specific reference to "your father" (v. 11). Likewise, Belshazzar describes Daniel as one "whom *my father*, the king, brought from Yehud" (v. 13). Daniel's response to Belshazzar begins with a lengthy description of Nebuchadnezzar's actions (vv. 18–21). Daniel even introduces Nebuchadnezzar to Belshazzar explicitly as "your father" (v. 18). Similarly, after Daniel recounts the lessons learned from Nebuchadnezzar, his transition describes Belshazzar as "his son" (v. 22). Disregarding historical realities, the narrative emphatically represents Belshazzar as the son of Nebuchadnezzar his father.[67]

The succession of this son is especially bad.[68] Belshazzar improperly uses the vessels his father had taken in a martial victory for a drinking party (vv. 2–3), constituting a *misuse* of what his father handed down to him. This act makes a clear contrast between Nebuchadnezzar the accomplished warrior (1:1–2) and his son the excessive reveler. Newsom even reads Belshazzar's commandeering of the vessels as an attempt to lay claim to the status his father obtained through a military victory, though she does not specify what she intends by "status."[69] If that is his intent, the plan backfires, perhaps describable as a son playing with his father's sword and getting cut in the process. Additionally, according to the queen, Belshazzar's father promoted Daniel over the wise (vv. 11–12). While the text does not indicate why Daniel was not present among them, Belshazzar *fails to utilize* a valuable resource that his father established: Daniel. Finally, Belshazzar loses the kingdom itself, which he had received intact. The text clearly portrays Belshazzar as a problem son. His actions reflect negatively on his father and on himself for falling short of the expectations that he be a good son. With this story of a problem son, the narrative contains a rationale for seeking to preserve a name apart from male children: the beginning of the son's story is the end of the father's[70] and a son can ruin what the father hands down to him, including his own name.[71]

Though Dan 5 shifts from dream interpretation to interpreting mysterious writing, knowledge remains powerful. As Donald Polaski suggests, there may be a word play involving Belshazzar and the root קרא: he can "call" (קרא) for his wise men, but he cannot "read" (קרא) the writing.[72] His inability to read the writing puts him into a relatively powerless position in relation to his courtiers. In this way, the text equates writing and the (in)ability to read and interpret it with power. Polaski summarizes these dynamics cogently: "God, via scribal mediation addresses a recalcitrant king and his bureaucracy, again showing the extent to which notions of power are 'textualized' in . . . the book of Daniel."[73] Even as Daniel displays power differently, Dan 5 similarly configures knowledge as powerful. After describing the experience of Nebuchadnezzar (vv. 18–21), Daniel says to Belshazzar: "You did not humble your heart even though *you knew* (ידעת) all this" (v. 22). In this case, the issue is a failure to understand the significance of what he knows. Acting inappropriately despite that knowledge costs him his life and his kingdom. Moreover, just as Dan 4 confirms the truth of Daniel's words after the interpretation of the dream, Belshazzar loses the kingdom and dies after Daniel interprets the writing. This situation contrasts somewhat with what transpired in Dan 2, where the narrator did not immediately demonstrate the accuracy of Daniel's interpretation about the successive kingdoms. But at this point, Daniel's interpretation of Nebuchadnezzar's dream in Dan 2:39 appears to be occurring: another kingdom has arisen, that of Darius the Mede. Regardless of the historical inaccuracy, Daniel's powerful knowledge can do what it claims in these stories.[74] In both instances, it leads to his promotion (2:48; 5:29). Clothing and adornments even accompany Daniel's new position in this case. Daniel 5 clearly portrays writing and the ability to interpret it properly as exceptionally powerful, powerful enough to bring a king and his kingdom to an end. This (re)configuring of power in terms of writing, interpretation, and knowledge may be a way Daniel negotiates a culturally predominant construction of masculinity.

Daniel 5 develops numerous issues related to masculinity that have surfaced previously. Again depicting Daniel as knowledgeable, this story shows the power of his knowledge in a new manner. Though Belshazzar should perpetuate his father's name in a positive way, he ruins his father's name and his own name. This first father-to-son transition in the court tales of Daniel contrasts strongly with Daniel and his colleagues, who continue to appear to lack wives or children. Yet each of the Judean courtiers has managed to make his own name apart from producing children.

4.2.6 Daniel 6 – repetition and its significance

While Dan 6 presents some new issues in the court tales, it reiterates themes encountered earlier.[75] The composition history of the court tales provides a partial explanation of this repetitiveness: the stories originally existed independently and were compiled later.[76] But what is the rhetorical significance of this repetition? The repetitiveness in the court tales may be an ideological strategy of seeking to "naturalize" and "normalize" its constructions of masculinity. Though not wanting to be repetitive in this context, I will note the repetitive elements in Dan 6 but focus on the new aspects and subsequently discuss the significance of repetition in the court tales of Daniel.

Whereas Dan 3 focuses on Shadrach, Meshach, and Abednego, with no mention of Daniel, Dan 6 reverses the situation: Daniel is the focus, and his colleagues are absent. The king in Dan 3 is the Babylonian Nebuchadnezzar, whereas it is Darius the Mede in Dan 6. Darius is more benevolent than Nebuchadnezzar, even desiring to save Daniel. In Dan 6, the imperial officials conspire against Daniel to entrap him in contrast to the decree in Dan 3 that does not target Shadrach, Meshach, and Abednego. The source of the life-threatening danger changes from a fiery furnace to a pit of lions. But both chapters depict God protecting an endangered court official who disobeyed a decree.[77]

Daniel 6 goes beyond reiteration to emphasize God's protection of Daniel through the repeated use of verbs related to "saving." Upon hearing the charge against Daniel, the king was determined "to *save* him (לשיזבותה)" and "was exerting effort to *deliver* him (להצלותה)" (v. 15). In his concluding confession of God's power, Darius acknowledges that Daniel's God "saves and delivers (משיזב ומצל)" (v. 28). As evidence for his assertion about Daniel's God, Darius explains: "for he [God] has saved (שיזב) Daniel" (v. 28). Darius acknowledges that Daniel's God succeeds where he failed to protect Daniel. Between these bookends to the endangering and rescuing of Daniel, Darius expresses his wish that Daniel's God will "save" (שיזב) him (v. 17). Upon visiting the pit in the morning, the king asks Daniel if his God has "saved" (שיזב) him (v. 21). Daniel states that God sent an angel to protect him not because the king asked, but because he was innocent (v. 23). The narrator echoes Daniel's claim when he states that Daniel is protected "because he trusted his God" (v. 24). The text clearly conveys that God, not the king, is Daniel's protector.

One reason for the emphasis on this point may be related to the change of heroes: it permits Daniel to show loyalty to God. Because Dan 3 does not mention Daniel, readers may be left wondering if he participated in the ritual of subordination.[78] Even if Daniel has delivered critical messages to kings, he has been an obedient official, and his loyalty to the king is even emphasized at the outset of Dan 6 (vv. 2–5). This story presents Daniel an opportunity to display loyalty to his God. Darius even notes Daniel's fidelity to his God, when he twice describes Daniel's God as the one "whom you constantly serve" (vv. 17 and 21). Likewise, when Darius checks on Daniel in the morning, he describes him as a "servant of the living God" (v. 21). Previously Daniel's loyalty to his king led to his name to being proclaimed throughout the empire (ch. 4). Now, Daniel's loyalty to his God enables his name to be proclaimed throughout the kingdom (6:26–27). Indeed, though Daniel appears to lack a wife or children, especially given the glimpse into his house that reveals Daniel alone (vv. 10–11), devotion to his God enables his name to be memorialized.

The emphasis on God's ability to protect his own is especially important because God failed to protect his people at the opening of the court tales. While Dan 3 shows God protecting his own, socially constructed identities are contingent on repeated performances, and this story provides another occasion for God to establish that he can protect his own, even against foreign kings. In the process, the stories create and sustain a rivalry between God and foreign kings along what appears to be gendered lines: protecting subordinates. By the conclusion of the court tales, God has repeatedly demonstrated success where he earlier fell short. This repetition may seek to give the appearance of "normalcy" or "naturalness" to God's masculinity even as the repetition may betray some anxiety in seeking to (over?)compensate for the initial failure.

Extending my suggestions about repetition, Darius's concluding words fit the pattern in the court tales of concluding a story with a confession of God's sovereignty.[79] He praises Daniel's God as the living God whose kingdom and dominion last forever, which contrasts with his own kingdom, which will soon be succeeded by the Persian Cyrus (6:27–29). Nebuchadnezzar begins the pattern of concluding a story with a king's praise of God's reign (Dan 2:48). Likewise, at the conclusion of Dan 3, Nebuchadnezzar affirms that no other God can save as the God of Daniel's colleagues has done (vv. 28–29). At the outset and ending of the fourth story in the court tales, Nebuchadnezzar makes similar affirmations (3:32–33; 4:31–34). The only deviation from this pattern is Dan 5, in which the problem son Belshazzar fails to confess God's sovereignty, a departure underscoring the characterization of Belshazzar. This repetition appears as a narrative and rhetorical strategy by which the text "naturalizes" and "normalizes" a particular relationship between God and the kings: God, not a foreign king, is the dominant male.

Whereas earlier chapters presented (the threat of) physical violence as an inferior or inadequate way of establishing power, Dan 6 presents others attempting to force the king to kill Daniel. But the king's sword has the opposite effect: they, along with "their sons (בניהון)" and "their wives (נשיהון)," are thrown into a pit of lions where they are torn apart (6:25; v. 24 Eng.). In terms of configurations of masculinity introduced above, their failure to protect their houses appears quite significant. Moreover, the killing of their (male) children and their wives precludes any possibility of memorializing their names, which the text does not include. In contrast to their memorialized namelessness, Daniel prospers and his name is memorialized because of his loyalty to his God. In this case, loyalty to God and king is a more effective way of preserving one's name than wrongly used physical violence. The repetition of this dynamic may seek to "normalize" or "naturalize" a masculinity that departed from a culturally predominant one.

Another significant repeated element in the court tales of Daniel involves knowledge, though there are slight differences in this topic. In Dan 1, the narrator does not describe the knowledge that Daniel and his colleagues display. But the public display itself leads to their differentiation from and empowerment over their classmates (vv. 19–20). Dan 2 depicts Daniel's knowledge at its highest: he determines not only the interpretation of the dream but the dream itself as well. This powerful knowledge leads to his promotion and subordinating physical gestures from the king (vv. 48–49). By contrast, Daniel's interpretation of Nebuchadnezzar's second dream is anti-climactic when he receives the dream in advance, but it leads to Daniel's name being proclaimed throughout the empire. Moreover, his interpretation of the dream is powerfully true as Nebuchadnezzar experiences exactly what Daniel says. Daniel's final public display of knowledge involves writing rather than a dream. But the social effect of that knowledge is very powerful, leading to his own promotion (5:29) and the end of a king's life and kingdom. While slight differences exist between each episode, they reiterate a basic equation: knowledge is powerful.[80] This repetitiveness is partly explainable from the perspective that socially constructed positions are contingent upon repeated displays. The repetition is also explainable as an attempt to "naturalize" and "normalize" this equation in producing a masculinity that was less common in the cultural context.

While Dan 6 repeats themes pertaining to masculinity, this repetition presents God with another opportunity to show that he can protect his own from a foreign king, serving to normalize a hierarchical relationship between God and foreign kings. Likewise, it allows Daniel to show his devotion to God and enables his name to be proclaimed throughout the entire kingdom. This repetition appears to function as a rhetorical strategy to normalize or naturalize the texts' construction of gender. If the court tales are portraying Daniel and his colleagues as having a different masculinity through knowledge or faithful service, this task would have been especially necessarily.

4.3 Summary of hypotheses

I have suggested numerous things about masculinity in the court tales of Daniel that subsequent chapters in this study will evaluate through a discussion of the socio-historical context in which the stories emerged. In particular, Daniel and his colleagues appear to deviate from a culturally predominant masculinity involving physical violence in war. Moreover, they seem to lack sons or wives. In terms of these cultural norms of masculinity, Daniel and his colleagues may appear as non-masculine. But the court tales of Daniel show them perpetuating their names apart from sons, and their knowledge is exceptionally powerful in the stories. These points suggest a different conclusion about Daniel and his colleagues: they appear differently masculine. Moreover, the court tales would depict a gendered rivalry between the other court officials and Daniel and his colleagues in their struggles to interpret dreams or mysterious writing.

With respect to God and the various kings, the question about who protects and provides for Daniel and his colleagues appears intelligible in terms of predominant cultural norms of masculinity. If this point withstands further analysis, the rivalry between God and the foreign kings can be seen to entail a significantly gendered component as the narrative asks who is the dominant male. In this wrestling match, God emerges as the dominant male. As long as kings accept their subordination to God, they are not presented with problems. Moreover, the negative depictions of various kings, such as when Nebuchadnezzar's ritual of subordination goes awry or in the representation of Belshazzar as a paradigmatic problem son, may take on new significance in light of culturally specific configurations of masculinity.

Notes

1 See Chapter 3 and the discussion of Candace West and Don H. Zimmerman, "Doing Gender," *Gender & Society* 1 (1987): 125–51.
2 This proposal would challenge the idea that they are non-masculine as suggested in T. M. Lemos, "'They Have Become Women': Judean Diaspora and Postcolonial Theories of Gender and Migration," in *Social Theory and the Study of Israelite Religion: Essays in Retrospect and Prospect*, ed. Saul M. Olyan (Atlanta: Society of Biblical Literature, 2012), 81–109.
3 On the introductory nature of Dan 1 in relation to the court tales, see Carol A. Newsom, *Daniel: A Commentary*, OTL (Louisville: Westminster John Knox, 2014), 38–39.
4 Harry A. Hoffner, "Symbols for Masculinity and Femininity: Their Use in Ancient Near Eastern Sympathetic Magic Rituals," *JBL* 85 (1966): 326–34. More recently, see David J. A. Clines, "David the Man: The Construction of Masculinity in the Hebrew Bible," in *Interested Parties: The Ideology of Writers and Readers of the Hebrew Bible*, 2nd ed. (Sheffield: Sheffield Academic, 2009), 212–43; John Goldingay, "Hosea 1–3, Genesis 1–4, and Masculist Interpretation," *HBT* 17 (1995): 37–44; Harold C. Washington, "'Lest He Die in the Battle and Another Man Take Her': Violence and the Construction of Gender in the Laws of Deuteronomy 22," in *Gender and Law in the Hebrew Bible and the Ancient Near East*, eds. Victor H. Matthews, Bernard M. Levinson, and Tikva Frymer-Kensky (New York: T&T Clark, 2004), 185–213; Cynthia R. Chapman, *The Gendered Language of Warfare in the Israelite-Assyrian Encounter*, HSM 62 (Winona Lake, IN: Eisenbrauns, 2004); Susan E. Haddox, "(E)Masculinity in Hosea's Political Rhetoric," in *Israel's Prophets and Israel's Past: Essays on the Relationship of Prophetic Texts and Israelite History in Honor of John H. Hayes*, eds. Brad E. Kelle and Megan Bishop Moore, LHBOTS 446 (New York: T&T Clark,

2006), 174–200; Ovidiu Creangă, "Variations on the Theme of Masculinity: Joshua's Gender In/stability in the Conquest Narrative," in *Men and Masculinity in the Hebrew Bible and Beyond*, ed. Ovidiu Creangă, The Bible in the Modern World 33 (Sheffield: Sheffield Phoenix, 2010), 83–109.

5 Chapman, *The Gendered Language of Warfare*, 111.

6 On this idea for constructions of masculinity in ancient Israel and the ancient Near East, see Chapman, *The Gendered Language of Warfare*. These ideas will be discussed fully in Chapter 5.

7 Darius makes similar boasts of his palace at Susa, built using materials from distant countries and people from those countries. See DSf §3e.22–3k.55. For translations, see Amélie Kuhrt, *The Persian Empire: A Corpus of Sources from the Achaemenid Period* (New York: Routledge, 2007), 492; Roland G. Kent, *Old Persian: Grammar, Texts, Lexicon* (New Haven: American Oriental Society, 1950), 144.

8 Compare Clines, "David the Man," 221–223; idem., "Dancing and Shining at Sinai: Playing the Man in Exodus 32–34," in Creangă, *Men and Masculinity in the Hebrew Bible and Beyond*, 54–64; Stuart Macwilliam, "Ideologies of Male Beauty and the Hebrew Bible," *BibInt* 17 (2009): 265–87. See Chapter 7 for discussion.

9 Numerous scholars note the configuring of knowledge or writing as power in the court tales of Daniel without addressing gender. See Philip R. Davies, "Reading Daniel Sociologically," in *The Book of Daniel in the Light of New Findings*, ed. A. S. van der Woude (Leuven: University Press, 1993), 354–355; Daniel Smith-Christopher, *A Biblical Theology of Exile*, OBT (Minneapolis: Fortress, 2002), 182–187; Donald C. Polaski, "Mene, Mene, Tekel, Parsin: Writing and Resistance in Daniel 5 and 6," *JBL* 123 (2004): 649–69; Anathea Portier-Young, *Apocalypse Against Empire: Theologies of Resistance in Early Judaism* (Grand Rapids: Eerdmans, 2011), 235–242; Newsom, *Daniel*, 73. For the suggestion that knowledge could be configured as masculine elsewhere in the Hebrew Bible, see Jacqueline E. Lapsley, *Whispering the Word: Hearing Women's Stories in the Old Testament* (Louisville: Westminster John Knox, 2005), 107; Hilary Lipka, "Masculinities in Proverbs: An Alternative to the Hegemonic Ideal," in *Biblical Masculinities Foregrounded*, eds. Ovidiu Creangă and Peter-Ben Smit, Hebrew Bible Monographs 62 (Sheffield: Sheffield Phoenix, 2014), 99. I will address these issues in Chapter 6.

10 John J. Collins, *Daniel: A Commentary on the Book of Daniel*, Hermeneia (Minneapolis: Fortress, 1993), 138–9. This scenario fits a model where texts serve the educational enculturation of scribes and for acquiring languages to fulfill scribal duties. See David M. Carr, *Writing on the Tablet of the Heart: Origins of Scripture and Literature* (Oxford: Oxford University Press, 2005).

11 Newsom observes that the description of Daniel and his colleagues is similar to "the ideal scribe in the Egyptian Papyrus Anastasi." See Newsom, *Daniel*, 42–43. On the general importance of scribalism in Daniel, see Davies, "Reading Daniel Sociologically"; Portier-Young, *Apocalypse Against Empire*, 230–231. Scribal masculinity receives minimal attention in scholarship. For the few examples, see Roland Boer, "Too Many Dicks at the Writing Desk, or How to Organise a Prophetic Sausage Fest," *Theology and Sexuality* 16 (2010): 95–108; Claudia V. Camp, *Ben Sira and the Men Who Handle Books: Gender and the Rise of Canon-Consciousness*, Hebrew Bible Monographs 50 (Sheffield: Sheffield Phoenix, 2013). Though not focusing on scribal culture per se, see also Lipka, "Masculinities in Proverbs." These works do not situate the biblical texts in relation to broadly attested scribal concerns in the ancient Near East.

12 See Clines, "David the Man," 219–221; Susan E. Haddox, "Favoured Sons and Subordinate Masculinities," in Creangă, *Men and Masculinity in the Hebrew Bible and Beyond*, 6; Creangă, "Variations on the Theme of Masculinity," 94–95.

13 Newsom, *Daniel*, 50–51.
14 Newsom makes a similar point about the narrative that asks "who 'feeds' Daniel and his friends," though without the connection to masculinity that I am suggesting here. See Carol A. Newsom, "Daniel," in *Women's Bible Commentary, Revised and Updated*, eds. Carol A. Newsom, Sharon H. Ringe, and Jacqueline E. Lapsley, 3rd ed. (Louisville: Westminster John Knox, 2012), 294.
15 Newsom, *Daniel*, 50.
16 Ken Stone, "Lovers and Raisin Cakes: Food, Sex and Divine Insecurity in Hosea," in *Queer Commentary and the Hebrew Bible*, ed. Ken Stone, JSOTSSup 334 (Sheffield: Sheffield Academic, 2001), 116–39.
17 Newsom, "Daniel," 294.
18 Newsom, *Daniel*, 50.
19 Scholars note that later interpreters (e.g., Josephus, *Ant.* 10.188; *b. Sanh.* 93b) connect them with a prophetic word to Hezekiah in Isaiah 39:7. See Collins, *Daniel*, 134–136; Newsom, *Daniel*, 42. The text itself makes no claims on this question. The general parameters for those that are to be brought from Judah is that they must be from either "royal descent or the nobility (מזרע המלוכה ומן הפרתמים)" (1:3). But it is not clear which of these categories applies to Daniel and his colleagues. They are identified only as "from the Judahites (מבני יהודה)" brought to Babylon (v. 6).
20 For a discussion, see Collins, *Daniel*, 135–136. The traditions Collins cites include Josephus *Ant.* 10.10.1; *b. Sanh.* 93b; *Midrash Megillah* 176.
21 Jacob L. Wright, and Michael J. Chan, "King and Eunuch: Isaiah 56:1–8 in Light of Honorific Burial Practices," *JBL* 131 (2012): 99–119.
22 For example, when Arioch introduces Daniel to Nebuchadnezzar it is as a "man" (גבר, 2:25).
23 See Creangă, "Variations on the Theme of Masculinity," 92–93; Mark K. George, "Masculinity and Its Regimentation in Deuteronomy," in Creangă, *Men and Masculinity in the Hebrew Bible and Beyond*, 75.
24 The king's reliance on learned officials could create conflict between king and courtier. See, for example, the ways in which Ashurbanipal boasts of his learnedness to avoid being manipulated by courtiers as discussed in Jeanette C. Fincke, "The Babylonian Texts of Nineveh: Report on the British Museum's 'Ashurbanipal Library Project,'" *AfO* 50 (2003): 121–122; Newsom, *Daniel*, 68–69.
25 See fn. 12 above.
26 Newsom, *Daniel*, 69–70.
27 Collins suggests that the introduction of Dan in 2:14 is from an earlier version of the story in which Daniel was simply a person from the exiles of Judah rather than a courtier, which explains the difficulty of why Daniel was not among those summoned in 2:2–12. See Collins, *Daniel*, 158–160. If Daniel appears as a specifically wise *courtier* at this juncture, it is a result of redactional activity.
28 See also, for example, Newsom, *Daniel*, 59.
29 Louis Hartman makes this observation, but translates the phrase as "Daniel prudently took counsel with Arioch." See Louis F. Hartman, *The Book of Daniel*, AB (Garden City, NY: Doubleday, 1978), 139. In biblical Aramaic, there are two cases in which the root תוב describes a reply (Dan 3:16; Ezra 5:11), both of which use the word פתגם ("word") to form a phrase: "to return a word." Dan 2:14 does not include the word פתגם. Moreover, the sense conveyed in the NRSV requires understanding the nouns עטא וטעם to be functioning as adverbs that characterize the nature of Daniel's reply.
30 See also Newsom, *Daniel*, 73.
31 This possibility is explicitly discounted in Hartman, *Daniel*, 140. Most do not discuss whether the phrase is a hendiadys, but their translation choices suggest that they do not understand it in this way. See, for example, Collins, *Daniel*, 150. Newsom cites Preben

Wernberg-Møller for the claim that the term גבורה in Dan. 2:23 can have "the connotation of intellectual power." But Wernberg-Møller suggests that term is used elsewhere (e.g., Job 12:13; Prov. 8:14) with the root חכם to mean "wondrous, mysterious wisdom" rather than "intellectual power" as Newsom suggests. Compare Newsom, *Daniel*, 63 and 72; Preben Wernberg-Møller, *The Manual of Discipline*, STDJ 1 (Grand Rapids: W.B. Eerdmans, 1957), 74. While Newsom's claim would strengthen my argument, I think the term גבורה in Dan 2:20 has the ordinary connotation of power or might, which is typically displayed through actions involving physical violence, and I do not see evidence of a shift in nuance when Daniel uses the same phrase to describe himself in v. 23. But it is clearly the case, as Newsom and others suggest, that Daniel 2 and other portions of the court tales clearly redefine power as coming through knowledge and wisdom.

32 Portier-Young, *Apocalypse Against Empire*, 239.
33 For some examples, see note 9 above.
34 For a discussion of a similar use of ethnic terms to construct differences in Ruth, see Eunny P. Lee, "Ruth the Moabite: Identity, Kinship, and Otherness," in *Engaging the Bible in a Gendered World: An Introduction to Feminist Biblical Interpretation in Honor of Katharine Doob Sakenfeld*, eds. Linda Day and Carolyn Pressler (Louisville: Westminster John Knox, 2006), 89–101.
35 In the Aramaic portions of Daniel אנש describes something as human, such as eyes or a mind (2:43; 4:13; 5:5; 7:4, 8, 13). It also refers to humankind as a whole (4:14), typically in contrast with animals as a species (2:38; 4:22, 29, 30; 5:21). Finally, the term refers to a single indefinite person in various contexts (2:10; 3:10; 5:7; 6:8, 13). In contrast to אנש which is always found in the singular, גבר is always found in the plural in the court tales of Daniel with two exceptions: 2:25 and 5:11, both of which describe Daniel. At least in the Aramaic of the court tales of Daniel, the pattern is to use אנש for a single indefinite person, but גבר when a group of men is involved (see below). This pattern may not hold for all instances in Aramaic. For example, in Takamitsu Muraoka and Bezalel Portern's study of Egyptian Aramaic, the authors suggest that, "although we lack cases where the persons involved are all women, גבר . . ., like אנש had become a gender-inclusive term." See Takamitsu Muraoka, and Bezalel Porten, *A Grammar of Egyptian Aramaic* (Leiden: Brill, 1998), 174. Likewise, lexicographers include instances outside of the court tales where גבר is used in reference to a single indefinite person. See, for example, J. Hoftijzer, and K. Jongeling, *Dictionary of the North-West Semitic Inscriptions* (Leiden: Brill, 1995), גבר 2:2–3 (211). See also S. J. Vogt, ed., *A Lexicon of Biblical Aramaic Clarified by Ancient Documents*, trans. J. A. Fitzmyer, 2nd ed. (Roma: Gregorian & Biblical Press, 2011), 79–80.
36 Excepting the two instances in which גבר is used to introduce Daniel, the court tales always use the root in conjunction with a modifier, whether a people group (3:8 & 12), the demonstrative אלך (3:12, 13, 21–23, 27; 6:6, 12, 16, 25), a numeral (3:24–5), or a complex adjective construction (3:20). While the term occasionally references a group of indefinite size (3:8, 20, 22), most cases refer to a group of a specified or known number of individuals (3:12, 13, 21, 23–5, 27; 6:6, 12, 15, 25). In all of the latter cases, the term refers to groups of men: Shadrach, Meshach, and Abednego alone or with their companion in the furnace in ch. 3, as well as those that conspire against Daniel in ch. 6. Two points show that the cases in ch. 6 refer to men: 1) They are satraps and their supervisors; 2) The king orders that those who conspired against Daniel along with "their sons and wives (בניהון ונשיהון)" are to be thrown into the pit (v. 24). Even when the term refers to a group of a nonspecific size, it seems that only men are in view. This point is clear for those who bind Shadrach, Meshach, and Abednego and are subsequently killed: they are warriors in Nebuchadnezzar's army (3:20 & 22). With respect to the "Chaldeans" who bring the accusation against Shadrach, Meshach, and

Abednego, the use of masculine verbal forms of which they are the grammatical subjects suggests that this group is comprised exclusively of men (3:8). Moreover, while is not entirely clear that the accusers in 3:8 are the same as the various administrative officials detailed in 3:27, it seems that at least the former are included among the latter. In short, at least in the court tales of Daniel, with the possible exception of 3:8, גבר is always used for groups of men or for Daniel by himself.

37 See note 12 above.
38 Megan Cifarelli argues that similar physical gestures in the reliefs of Ashurnasirpal convey a subordinate position in social hierarchies. See Megan Cifarelli, "Gesture and Alterity in the Art of Aššurnaṣirpal II of Assyria," *Art Bulletin* 80 (1998): 210–28. This convention continued into the Persian period. In the Behistun relief of Darius I, Margaret Cool Root argues that a gesture of bending forward partly conveys the subordination of the conquered. See Margaret Cool Root, *King and Kingship in Achaemenid Art: Essays on the Creation of an Iconography of Empire*, Acta Iranica 19 (Leiden: Brill, 1979), 193–194. While the bound hands and neck of the captives conveys their subordination, these features would only be visible on close examination. But viewed from a distance, the gesture of bending forward before the king is the primary way of constituting their subordination to the king.
39 Collins, *Daniel*, 171–172. Newsom, for example, cites Jerome in suggesting that the text intends to convey "not worship of the human Daniel but of the God whose power has been manifest through him." See *Daniel*, 84. Alternatively, David Valeta suggests that the description creates "a ludicrous image that serves to belittle and make fun of the king" as part of a satirical genre. See *Lions and Ovens and Visions: A Satirical Reading of Daniel 1–6*, Hebrew Bible Monographs 12 (Sheffield: Sheffield Phoenix, 2008), 77. But in light of stories from ancient Egypt in which magicians have offerings made to them as a result of their wonders, Tawny L. Holm suggests that it is not ludicrous in its cultural context. See *Of Courtiers and Kings: The Biblical Daniel Narratives and Ancient Story-Collections*, EANEC 1 (Winona Lake, IN: Eisenbrauns, 2013), 432–436.
40 This point remains even if Nebuchadnezzar is understood to have besieged Jerusalem in his first year as king. For discussion, see Newsom, *Daniel*, 66. While it is not inconceivable that Dan 2 is a story about something that transpired in their training (i.e., a narrative regression), significant internal complications arise in that reading. Their installation in the king's court at the conclusion of their training regimen (1:19) would be superfluous if they had already been installed in high positions of power (2:48–49). Likewise, Nebuchadnezzar's test of Daniel and his colleagues at the end of their training regimen (1:18–20) would be unnecessary if they had demonstrated their knowledge in being able to tell the king both his dream and its interpretation. Finally, Daniel 1 consistently uses the term "boys" (ילדים) to refer to Daniel and his colleagues (vv. 4, 10, 13, 15, 17) whereas Arioch refers to Daniel as a "man" (גבר) in 2:25.
41 See George, "Masculinity and Its Regimentation in Deuteronomy," 75; Creangă, "Variations on the Theme of Masculinity," 92–93, 97, and 104.
42 See, for example, Collins, *Daniel*, 181; Newsom, *Daniel*, 103.
43 Clines refers to an article by Roland Boer. See David J. A. Clines, "Final Reflections of Biblical Masculinity," in Creangă, *Men and Masculinity in the Hebrew Bible and Beyond*, 233; Roland Boer, "Of Fine Wine, Incense and Spices: The Unstable Masculine Hegemony of the Book of Chronicles," in Creangă, *Men and Masculinity in the Hebrew Bible and Beyond*, 20–33.
44 The word for the "image" is צלם (vv. 1–3, 5, 7, 10, 12, 14–15, 18). Unlike יד, another word for statue, צלם is not used as a euphemism for male genitalia. There is no evidence of a lexical link with terminology for an erection. Robert D. Biggs suggests that Akkadian has various terms for an erection, including the noun *tebûtu* and the verb

tebû (to "rise" or "throb") as well as *nīš libbi* ("rising of the heart"). For his complete work with translations of the potency incantation texts, see Robert D. Biggs, *Šà.zi.ga: Ancient Mesopotamian Potency Incantations*, TCS 2 (Locust Valley, NY: J. J. Augustin, 1967). See idem., "The Babylonian Sexual Potency Texts," in *Sex and Gender in the Ancient Near East: Proceedings of the 47th Rencontre Assyriologique Internationale, Helsinki, July 2–6, 2001*, eds. S. Parpola and R. M. Whiting (Helsinki: The Neo-Assyrian Text Corpus Project, 2002), 71–78. Shalom Paul extends Biggs's work, suggesting that the Hebrew equivalent to the Akkadian *tebû* ("to rise") is עור, pointing to Song 2:7 and 3:15 (*sic*) as evidence. Shalom M. Paul, "The Shared Legacy of Sexual Metaphors and Euphemisms in Mesopotamian and Biblical Literature," in Parpola and Whiting, *Sex and Gender in the Ancient Near East*, 498–490. Paul likely intends Song 3:5 rather than 3:15. Curiously, Paul does not cite Song 5:2 in his discussion, though it is closer to the Akkadian idiom as לבי (my heart) is the subject of עור (to arise or stir). In Hebrew, קום is used in one instance that may suggest arousal: "I arose to open for my beloved (קמתי אני לפתח לדודי)" (Song 5:5). But this example could simply be a reference to getting up and need not refer to arousal. Finally, I am not aware of any uses of קום in Aramaic that suggest a connection to arousal or an erection.

45 Describing what unfolds as a "ritual of subordination" borrows phrasing from Erving Goffman, *Gendered Advertisements* (New York: Harper and Row, 1974), 40. For Goffman, gender involves "ritual-like" behavior displays, which do not simply express a preexisting social relation but "in part constitutes it" (8). In Goffman's analysis of advertisements, one example he describes is "the ritualization of subordination," which involves the lowering of one's body in some way vis-à-vis another (40ff.). West and Zimmerman critique Goffman's terminology of gender as "display" because they think it "relegates it [gender] to the periphery of interaction." See West and Zimmerman, "Doing Gender," 127. The criticism is a correction of a *possible* implication of Goffman's terminology rather than a disagreement with the idea of display as activity that produces social relationships. Drawing from a different theoretical trajectory, similar ideas about the "productive" power of rituals to constitute relationships of inequality emerge in biblical studies in Saul M. Olyan, *Rites and Rank: Hierarchy in Biblical Representations of Cult* (Princeton: Princeton University Press, 2000). Olyan writes: "Ritual, in my view, is not simply a reproductive activity in which social distinctions are mirrored, but also a productive operation in which social difference is realized" (4). Likewise, William K. Gilders, in a study of rituals of blood manipulation in the Hebrew Bible, suggests that while rituals may express messages, "these messages also affect status and identity." See William K. Gilders, *Blood Ritual in the Hebrew Bible: Meaning and Power* (Baltimore: Johns Hopkins University Press, 2004), 3. These scholars share a common point regarding the ability of rituals to produce social relationships that do not simply preexist the ritual itself.

46 It is not clear what the statue represents. See John Goldingay, *Daniel*, WBC (Dallas: Word Books, 1989), 73. Occurring after the dream of four metals in Dan 2, some suggest that the statute represents Nebuchadnezzar himself or his kingdom. See Choon Leong Seow, *Daniel*, WC (Louisville: Westminster John Knox, 2003), 52–53. But later in the story, Shadrach, Meshach, and Abednego are accused of failing to "serve" the king's gods and for failing to "prostrate" themselves before the golden image (3:12). Some suggest that this accusation reveals that the image represents Nebuchadnezzar's gods. See Collins, *Daniel*, 182; Newsom, *Daniel*, 103. While this explanation is the most compelling, a single image representing multiple gods remains conceptually challenging (e.g., Exod 32:4). Regardless of what the statue represents, the relationship of inequality between Nebuchadnezzar and his subjects is (re)produced primarily through their submission to his command to participate in the ritual of subordination. This point is not contingent on any one understanding of what the image represents.

47 See note 45 above for further discussion.
48 Holm suggests that while death by burning is rare in Mesopotamia, when it does occur, "it seems to be a penalty particularly suitable for crimes against a hierarchical superior." See Holm, *Of Courtiers and Kings*, 439. From this perspective, the fiery furnace may be fitting, especially in light of my suggestion that the refusal of Shadrach, Meshach, and Abednego to participate in the ritual of subordination threatens Nebuchadnezzar's power. Holm prefers an Egyptian origin for this motif (439–448), but others favor a Mesopotamian background. See Paul-Alain Beaulieu, "The Babylonian Background of the Motif of the Fiery Furnace in Daniel 3," *JBL* 128 (2009): 273–98.
49 For this idea, see Chapter 3, where I discuss a sociological approach to gender.
50 See Robert Alter, *The Art of Biblical Narrative* (New York: Basic Books, 1981); David Gunn, and Danna Nolan Fewell, *Narrative in the Hebrew Bible* (New York: Oxford University Press, 1993); Shimeon Bar-Efrat, *Narrative Art in the Bible* (Sheffield: Almond Press, 1989).
51 A similar exchange occurs in third Isaiah. In an oracle to eunuchs, the prophet promises "a memorial and a name (ושם) better than sons and daughters" (Isa 56:5). Devotion to Yahweh through keeping Sabbath or holding fast to his covenant accomplishes this work (v. 4).
52 Framing the point in this way draws from Stone, "Lovers and Raisin Cakes"; idem., "Queer Reading Between Bible and Film: Paris Is Burning and the 'Legendary Houses' of David and Saul," in *Bible Trouble: Queer Reading at the Boundaries of Biblical Scholarship*, eds. Teresa J. Hornsby and Ken Stone, SemeiaSt 67 (Atlanta: Society of Biblical Literature, 2011), 75–98.
53 Newsom, "Daniel," 296.
54 Newsom's point may suffer from a lack of specificity about the type of tree. Paul Collins argues that in Neo-Assyrian art the fruiting date palm was feminine while the conifer was masculine. See Paul Collins, "Trees and Gender in Assyrian Art," *Iraq* 68 (2006): 99–107. As the tree is nondescript in Dan 4 (an אילן, v. 7), it may hinder the ability to determine whether the tree itself has the associations with femininity Newsom finds. If Newsom's point holds, it would not challenge the main point I am suggesting: the concerns raised by the tree imagery appear thoroughly rooted in ancient configurations of masculinity. Newsom notes these concerns in her own analysis, but without suggesting a connection to masculinity.
55 On the relation of territorial and geographical conquest to masculinity for Neo-Assyrian kings, see Michelle Marcus, "Geography as Visual Ideology: Landscape, Knowledge, and Power in Neo-Assyrian Art," in *Neo-Assyrian Geography*, ed. Mario Liverani (Rome: Universita di Roma, 1995), 193–208.
56 See Stone, "Lovers and Raisin Cakes."; Chapman, *The Gendered Language of Warfare*.
57 I am not suggesting that the dream *reflects* Nebuchadnezzar's anxiety. In the passage, God sends the dream to Nebuchadnezzar as a message (cf. Gen 45:25). While the tree is the dreamer and the significance of the dream is about the dreamer (Dan 4:17–19), the status of the dream as a mechanism of divine communication (esp. v. 21) problematizes referring to the dream as "reflecting" anxiety.
58 Christopher B. Hays, "Chirps from the Dust: The Affliction of Nebuchadnezzar in Daniel 4:30 and Its Ancient Near Eastern Context," *JBL* 126 (2007): 324.
59 This hierarchy is assumed earlier in the court tales of Daniel. When Daniel gives the interpretation of Nebuchadnezzar's earlier dream, he begins by telling the king that God has "*placed* (יהב) the animals of the field and the birds of the air *into your hand* (בידך)" (2:38). Being "placed into a hand" conveys control and dominance. A similar phrase describes what Yahweh does to Jehoaikim: "The Lord put (ויתן) Jehoakim into his [Nebuchadnezzar's] hand (בידו)" (1:2).
60 For a discussion of how Persian period iconography extends and nuances this conclusion, please see my forthcoming article on the topic.

61 Newsom argues that the stories about Nebuchadnezzar in Dan 1–4 are shaped to provide "a story of his education" in which he learns that his rule is delegated by God, the true sovereign. See *Daniel*, 33. Newsom argues that it is in Dan 4 that Nebuchadnezzar finally understands the nature of his rule (149). But as she notes, Nebuchadnezzar's earlier failures to understand his sovereignty become evident in the next story (see esp. 33–35). Accordingly, it is hard to evaluate whether his confession in Dan 4, while differing in some ways from earlier ones, is not yet another misunderstanding.

62 Dan 4 may have originally featured Belteshazzar, who was not the same as Daniel, as the hero. See Newsom, *Daniel*, 134. In each case Dan 4 mentions the hero's name, a gloss clarifies that it is Daniel, who is called *Belteshazzar*, after which the text uses Belteshazzar (vv. 5–6, 15, 16). Dan 1 anticipates this issue (v. 7), a feature designed to account for attributing this earlier story about Belteshazzar to Daniel when it was joined with the other stories. Moreover, Dan 4 describes Belteshazzar as "the chief magician" (v. 6) and in this story the "magicians" are a subcategory of the wise (vv. 3–4). In Dan 2, Daniel rules over the province of Babylon and is "chief prefect over all the wise men of Babylon" (v. 48). The two stories assume that the hero is in different positions of rank, which lends credence to the idea that the stories originated separately and that Dan 4 was not originally about Daniel. As Newsom suggests, this story supplants the original hero's name while interested in how a name could be memorialized through an ironic twist that raises questions about narrative ethics (134).

63 Julie Kelso notes that the beginning of the son's story is the end of the father's story in Chronicles. See Julie Kelso, *O Mother, Where Art Thou? An Irigarayan Reading of the Book of Chronicles* (London: Equinox, 2007), 207. The issue of the way that the son carries on the legacy of the father is central to Camp, *Ben Sira and the Men Who Handle Books*. The Hebrew Bible contains other stories of fathers having problematic sons, such as David and Absalom or Solomon and Rehoboam.

64 As the person called "queen (מלכתא)" in Dan 5:10 knows about events in the reign of Nebuchadnezzar, some suggest that she is a queen mother (i.e., Belshazzar's mother or grandmother) rather than Belshazzar's wife. See Collins, *Daniel*, 248; Newsom, *Daniel*, 172. The OG and the MT, moreover, present this individual in different ways, most notably that she is summoned by Belshazzar in the OG, but comes on her own amidst the confusion of the king and his wise men in the MT. As Newsom suggests, the queen (mother) in the MT thereby functions to underscore the helplessness of Belshazzar (172). Feminist scholarship related to Daniel has focused on Susanna, a Greek addition to Daniel. See Jennifer A. Glancy, "The Accused: Susanna and Her Readers," in *A Feminist Companion to Esther, Judith, and Susanna*, ed. Athalya Brenner (Sheffield: Sheffield Academic, 1995), 288–302; Amy-Jill Levine, " 'Hemmed in on Every Side': Jews and Women in the Book of Susanna," in Brenner, *A Feminist Companion to Esther, Judith, and Susanna*, 303–23. One could also include Toni Craven's contribution to the first edition of the *Women's Bible Commentary* as a focus on Susanna. Later editions reprint it in the Apocrypha section while Newsom contributes a new piece on Hebrew and Aramaic Daniel. See Toni Craven, "Daniel and Its Additions," in *The Women's Bible Commentary*, eds. Carol A. Newsom and Sharon H. Ringe (Louisville: Westminster John Knox, 1992), 191–94; Newsom, "Daniel,"

65 Athalya Brenner, "Who's Afraid of Feminist Criticism? Who's Afraid of Biblical Humour? The Case of the Obtuse Foreign Ruler in the Hebrew Bible," in *A Feminist Companion to Prophets and Daniel*, ed. Athalya Brenner (Sheffield: Sheffield Academic, 2001), 240.

66 Athalya Brenner, "Self-Response to 'Who's Afraid of Feminist Criticism?'" in Brenner, *A Feminist Companion to Prophets and Daniel*, 245–46.

67 See Newsom, *Daniel*, 163–164; Collins, *Daniel*, 32–33.
68 For additional discussion of the father and son dynamics, see Danna Nolan Fewell, *Circle of Sovereignty: Plotting Politics in the Book of Daniel* (Nashville: Abingdon, 1991), esp. 95–101.
69 Newsom, *Daniel*, 178. This suggestion receives support from a recent study of feasting, which is often a memorialization of military success in the ancient Near East. See Jacob L. Wright, "Commensal Politics in Ancient Western Asia: The Background to Nehemiah's Feasting (Part I)," *ZAW* 122 (2010): 212–33; Jacob L. Wright, "Commensal Politics in Ancient Western Asia: The Background to Nehemiah's Feasting (continued, Part II)," *ZAW* 122 (2010): 333–52. As Wright puts it: "By raising the victory cup, one performed the role of victor and thereby communicated to others who lost the battle" (347).
70 See Kelso, *O Mother, Where Art Thou?*
71 See Camp, *Ben Sira and the Men Who Handle Books*.
72 Polaski, "Mene, Mene, Tekel, Parsin," 653–654.
73 Ibid., 659.
74 Scholars rightly point out the difficulties in the text: "Darius the Mede" is not attested. The Babylonian kingdom fell to a Persian named Cyrus. See, for example, Collins, *Daniel*, 30–32.
75 Newsom, for example, suggests that even as the stories in Dan 5 and 6 "might seem redundant," they develop the theme of the nature of human sovereignty by contrasting Belshazzar and Darius with Nebuchadnezzar. See Newsom, *Daniel*, 158.
76 Scholars propose numerous theories to describe the process by which the court tales of Daniel were shaped, but there is agreement on the idea that many or most of the stories were independent and secondarily joined together. Compare, for example, Collins, *Daniel*, 24–38; Newsom, *Daniel*, 6–11. For an especially exhaustive study, see Holm, *Of Courtiers and Kings*. Holm proposes a new macro-genre of the "story collection" for Daniel 1–6, noting that other examples of this genre, though generally drawn from later stories (e.g., Grimms's *Fairy Tales*), include the same story multiple times (315).
77 This basic plot is integral to the court contest genre. See Newsom, *Daniel*, 13.
78 This difficulty only emerges when stories that were originally independent were joined by a compiler. Still, the portrait of Daniel as a loyal court official is a consistent element of the other stories that feature him as the hero. Indeed, Daniel's loyalty to the king is assumed in this story by itself as well.
79 For the suggestion that these confessions may be redactional links to unify the originally independent stories, see Collins, *Daniel*, 35.
80 See note 9 above for how scholars note this theme without connecting it to gender.

5

A PREDOMINANT MASCULINITY AND THE COURT TALES OF DANIEL

The masculinity of the ancient was measured by two criteria: (1) his prowess in battle, and (2) his ability to sire children.
—Harry A. Hoffner[1]

After valor in fighting, the goodness of a man is most signified in this: that he can show a multitude of sons.
—Herodotus *Hist.* 1.136[2]

5.1 Introduction

Reading the court tales of Daniel in light of what scholars associate with masculinity in other texts from the Hebrew Bible, I noted several issues to investigate: (1) physical violence, (2) producing sons to perpetuate the father's name, and (3) protection and provision. At the outset of the stories, for instance, Nebuchadnezzar achieves a military victory and God fails to protect Judah (1:1–2), which introduces a recurring narrative question regarding who truly protects and provides for Daniel and his colleagues. The issue of sons perpetuating a father's name surfaces when Belshazzar tarnishes his father's name while Daniel and his colleagues never seem to become fathers.

This chapter will assess the relevance of these three activities for the court tales of Daniel in light of culturally proximate sources. While the evidence differs in quality and quantity in each case, I suggest that each of these three activities were important to a culturally predominant masculinity in the historical context. To convey the interrelatedness of physical violence, producing sons, and protecting and providing for subordinates for a culturally predominant masculinity, I will refer to these as "threads," each of which is "hegemonic" in the ways that they (re)produce male dominance. In describing this masculinity as "predominant," I intend to suggest that it was culturally idealized and influential.[3] After arguing for these points, I will revisit some of the hypotheses I proposed in Chapter 4 of this study: (1) that Daniel and his colleagues depart from a culturally predominant masculinity and (2) that the relationship between God and the foreign kings engages these threads in a struggle for a dominantly masculine position.

5.2 Sources for testing the hypotheses

Sources from the cultural group that composed the court tales of Daniel, namely other portions of the Hebrew Bible, provide the best evidence for the goal of this chapter. As the stories were not composed in a cultural vacuum, gender in the dominant socio-cultural group also needs attention. The broadly defined time frame within which the court tales of Daniel emerged (i.e., late Persian or early Hellenistic era) presents a problem in this respect.[4] I will focus on ancient Near Eastern sources because of the general consensus that the court tales of Daniel originated in the eastern diaspora and Hellenistic influences on the stories are minimal.[5] Unfortunately, Persian period sources are not always forthcoming. Accordingly, I will discuss some material from other ancient Near Eastern cultural groups in earlier time periods. I am not suggesting that assumptions about masculinity were monolithic among different cultural groups that exercised dominance in the ancient Near East at various time periods.[6] But while gendered norms *can* change over time and across cultures, sometimes they are especially slow to change.[7]

5.3 A culturally predominant masculinity

5.3.1 Violence, power, and masculinity

While Harry A. Hoffner makes no reference to Herodotus's claim in this chapter's epigraph, he offers a nearly identical assessment of the importance of two activities for an ancient Near Eastern masculinity: martial prowess and producing sons. This section considers the former issue, and I will address the latter in the next section. Despite the minimal presence of violence and war in the court tales of Daniel, their importance for a culturally predominant masculinity in the cultural context is hard to overstate, and abundant evidence exists to sustain this connection.

Noted in the earliest scholarship on masculinity in the Hebrew Bible, a link between masculinity and violence has remained a persistent topic in subsequent research.[8] Several relatively explicit statements about masculinity in the Hebrew Bible directly address this issue (Judg 8:20–1; 1 Sam 4:9; 17:33; 1 Kgs 2:2; Jer 50:37; 51:30; Nah. 3:13).[9] Most of these statements compare a male character to a culturally idealized male or exhort him in relation to that male, producing a culturally specific idea about masculinity in the process. After catching the Midianite kings, Gideon instructs his son Jether to kill them and the narrator explains Jether's unwillingness to kill: "for he was afraid, for he was still a boy (כי ירא כי עודנו נער)" (Judg 8:20). That the claim needs no justification reveals that the narrator thinks an audience will not question the explanation of Jether's unwillingness to kill, which conveys its status as a taken-for-granted cultural assumption. While being positioned as a "boy" may not be unmasculine for Jether, the narrator's explanation equates an absence of fear and the willingness to kill with an adult male status.[10] The Midianite kings make this gendered norm explicit when they taunt Gideon to kill them himself: "As a man is so is his strength (כי כאיש גבורתו)" (Judg 8:21). This statement equates a normative adult male status with strength and killing, an equation clearly undergirding Saul's comments to David: "You are not able to go to this Philistine to make war with him *because you are a boy* (כי־נער אתה)" (1 Sam 17:33). Just as the narrator explained Jether's unwillingness to kill, Saul argues that David's status as a נער renders him unsuitable for war. Earlier in Samuel, the Philistines express the other side of this idea: "Strengthen yourselves and become[11] men (התחזקו והיו לאנשים), O Philistines, lest you serve the Hebrews just as they have served you. Become men and engage in battle (והייתם לאנשים ונלחמתם)" (1 Sam 4:9). This rallying cry directly equates activities, "being strong" (חזק) and "engaging in battle" (לחם), with producing themselves as "men" (אנשים). Similarly, David's final words to Solomon also configure strength as masculine: "Display strength and become a man (וחזקת והיית לאיש)" (1 Kgs 2:2). Displaying "strength" (חזק) for Solomon involves killing Joab and Shimei (vv. 5–9). These relatively explicit statements about gender clearly configure violence, displays of strength, and warfare as masculine in the Hebrew Bible.[12] Each statement occurs in the Deuteronomistic History, which matches the relationship of war to masculinity in Deuteronomy.[13]

Texts comparing men to women for being defeated in war provide additional relatively explicit statements about the gendering of physical violence, displays of strength, or killing in a martial context in the Hebrew Bible.[14] In an oracle of Jeremiah, the prophet proclaims a sword against Babylonian personnel with significant implications for the soldiers: "they will become women (והיו לנשים)" (50:37). Similarly, after stating that the warriors of Babylon have ceased engaging in war and that their strength has dried up, Jeremiah asserts: "they have become women (היו לנשים)" (51:30). In both cases, failing to do masculinity in accordance with cultural norms involving martial strength and success results in the subjects being constituted as feminine. These ideas about gender illumine a taunt from the prophet Nahum, who, after describing a devastating martial defeat of Nineveh, states: "Look at your army, they are women among you (הנה עמך נשים בקרבך)" (3:13). While these texts suggest that experiencing martial defeat makes men become women, Isaiah describes Egyptians as "like women (כנשים)" simply because they will "tremble and be afraid (וחרד ופחד)" before Yahweh's raised hand (19:16). As Cynthia Chapman argues, references like these in the Hebrew Bible are similar to curses of feminization in Neo-Assyrian vassal treaties, which leads her to conclude that these sources share an ideology of gender "wherein masculinity and femininity function as metaphors for military victory and defeat respectively."[15] Cumulatively, these relatively explicit statements about gender establish that a thread of a predominant masculinity in the Hebrew Bible involved displays of strength, violence, or killing. Construing masculinity as

A PREDOMINANT MASCULINITY

physical strength or victory in war and femininity with a lack of strength or defeat in war is "hegemonic" because of the way that it legitimates male dominance.

Two lines of evidence show that a predominant masculinity in the dominant socio-cultural group when the court tales of Daniel emerged involved violence as well: (1) the bow in visual and textual sources from the Persian period and (2) the heroic encounter motif in Persian period visual media.

Despite the trend in Persian period iconography away from the gory violence in Neo-Assyrian images, the bow features prominently in Persian period visual media.[16] For instance, Darius holds a bow at his side in the Behistun relief (fig. 5.1) as does Xerxes at Naqsi-Rustam (fig. 5.2).

Figure 5.1 Behistun relief of Darius[17]

Figure 5.2 Tomb of Xerxes at Naqsi-Rustam[18]

Concerning such images, Margaret Cool Root argues that "the bow must be a symbol of the king's military and hunting prowess."[19] She even suggested a specifically gendered aspect of the bow in Persian iconography: "In the Elamite culture, with which the Achaemenids had such strong ties, the bow seems to have had an especially clear symbolic association with the warrior's manhood and personal identity."[20] As a multivalent cultural symbol, the bow evokes violence in war and providing food through hunting, both of which were part of a predominant configuration of masculinity.

Persian period cylinder seals, such as the seal of Darius (fig. 5.3), and coinage, contain an abundance of archer imagery. The coins, attested from early in the Persian empire through the end of fourth century BCE, are more easily discussed because the seals featuring humans have not been fully published.[22] There are four basic types of archer coins: (1) a waist-up archer; (2) a full-bodied archer kneeling with bow drawn; (3) a full-bodied archer kneeling with bow in one hand and a spear in the other; and (4) a full-bodied archer kneeling with bow in one hand and a dagger in the other (fig. 5.4 a–d).[23]

Amidst these subtle variations, the common features include a bearded and crowned individual who holds a bow. Root argues that these archer coins conveyed "the physical prowess and military power of the Persian king."[25] In this respect, the social significance of the bow was its ability to construct the wielder as a warrior. Likewise, concerning the type I style of coins, Cindy Nimchuk argues that "the bow and arrows are part of this message of order, in that military strength is required to establish and protect order; the military power is suggested by the quiescent aspect of the bow and arrows."[26] In a slightly different respect, Nimchuk suggests that the kneeling archer (type II) conveys hunter and heroic imagery, even arguing that "the two roles merge, since a hunter (like a hero) often fulfills simultaneous missions as agent against threatening forces and protector of the weak."[27] Mark B. Garrison argues that the kneeling archer evokes "protection imagery" on the basis of a comparison with similar scenes in seal imagery that show a kneeling archer protecting a weaker animal from the attack of a more powerful animal.[28] Most recently, Ryan P. Bonfiglio finds aspects of both Nimchuk's and Garrison's proposals compelling, seeing in type II coins "hunter and protector" imagery.[29] Each scholar identifies important resonances of the imagery. But no single option fully explains the significance of the bow in these coins, especially when the coins lack a larger visual context within which to situate the use of the bow (i.e., in war as martial imagery, while pursuing an animal as hunter or provider imagery, or while defending an animal as protection imagery). Instead, the bow in this coinage may be explained as a multivalent cultural symbol capable of simultaneously evoking multiple threads of a predominant masculinity: physical violence, protection, and provision.[30] Although the importance of protection and provision for a predominant masculinity has not yet been established, I will develop this point below.

Using the bow as a symbolic object to construct masculinity in the Persian period fits trends in the ancient Near East. Hoffner adduced substantial evidence

Figure 5.3 Seal of Darius[21]

Type I Type II Type III Type IV

Figure 5.4a–d Selection of Archer Series Coins[24]

for this dynamic in various ancient cultures (Hittite, Ugarit, ancient Greece, and ancient Israel).[31] For instance, in a Hittite ritual text, Pissuwattis describes a procedure for a man who

> possesses no reproductive power or has no desire for women. . . . I shall place a mirror (and) a distaff in the sacrificer's [hand]. He will pass under the gate. When he comes [for]th through the gate, I shall take the mirror (and) the distaff away from him. I shall [gi]ve him a bow [and arrows] and while doing so I shall speak as follows: 'See! I have taken womanliness away from thee and given thee back manliness. Thou has cast off the ways of a woman, now [show] the ways of a man!'[32]

In this ritual text, the construction of gender in social interactions is not an abstract concept because it can clearly be produced through actions and objects:

a male's troubles with gender and sexuality, and the categories overlap significantly in this case, may be addressed by giving him culturally feminine objects (mirror and distaff) and replacing them with masculine ones (bow and arrows). As symbolic objects, the bow and arrows produce what they might claim to express: the wielder as masculine. This masculinizing ritual simultaneously functions to address "reproductive power" or "desire for women." In this sense, this masculinity entails two threads Hoffner identified: martial prowess and producing children. The bow in Persian period visual imagery fits trends throughout the ancient Near East, confirming and extending Hoffner's argument about the bow.[33]

Boasts about an ability to manipulate martial implements occur in various Persian period inscriptions, such as an inscription of Darius at Naqsi-rustam (DNb):

> Moreover this (is) my ability, that my body is strong. As a fighter I am a good fighter . . . I am furious in the strength of my revenge with both hands and both feet. As a horseman I am a good horseman. As a bowman I am a good bowman, both on foot and on horseback. As a spearman I am a good spearman, both on foot and on horseback.
> (2g-h/31–45)[34]

As ideas about royal rule could overlap with configurations of masculinity,[35] these claims contain evidence for masculinity in the Persian period, and the gendered connotations of the spear emerge more explicitly in another inscription from the time of Darius (DNa):

> If now you should think: 'How many are the countries which King Darius held?' Look at the sculptures (of those) who bear the throne, then shall you know, then shall it become known to you: the spear of the Persian man has gone forth far; then shall it become known to you: the Persian man has delivered battle far indeed from Persia.
> (§4, 30–47)[36]

The Old Persian word Kuhrt translates as "man" (*martiya*) does not appear to refer to a person unmarked for gender but rather specific men like Darius in this instance.[37] Darius boasts not just about any Persian person but a specifically Persian *male* who achieves a military victory, a claim that configures warfare as culturally masculine. Visual and textual sources clearly converge: when the court tales of Daniel likely emerged, a predominant masculinity in the dominant cultural group involved violence, especially through the manipulation of martial implements like the bow.

The heroic encounter motif in Persian period visual media provides a second strand of evidence for a link between violence and masculinity.[38] The seals from

Persepolis exclusively feature males as the hero.[39] Two variants exist: "the *control encounter*, where a heroic figure holds an animal/creature to either side of its body" and "the *combat encounter*, where a hero fights an animal/creature."[40] Cylinder seals depict the control encounter (e.g., fig. 5.5) more frequently than the combat encounter, which is more prominent in monumental images.[41] Diversity exists in the depiction of the hero (e.g., as a human male or a hybrid creature) and the creature with which the hero contends (e.g., a bull or various hybrid creatures).[42] Despite the variations in the two main types, both clearly convey the primary idea: a display of power.

Concerning the combat variation of the heroic encounter motif Garrison and Root suggest that

> the heroic combatant ... represents the specific ideological construct of a "Persian Man," as articulated in several monumental inscriptions alluding metaphorically to the far-flung military power of the Achaemenid Empire. In this case, the hero of Achaemenid monumental art could be read as a generic figure symbolizing the collective force of Persian power.... This may help explain the importance of rendering the monumental hero figures with ambiguous identity: kingly but not precisely the king and able to be contemplated as a flexible entity with which every person of Persian identification could associate himself. It is important to consider that the capacity of an individual to identify with the Persianness of the "Persian Man" may not have been limited to those of Persian blood lineage.[43]

Even as Garrison and Root address social identity, they omit gender from their otherwise incisive analysis. Their "every person of Persian identification," who initially masquerades as unmarked for gender, becomes masculinized with the reflexive pronoun "himself." But it is not clear whether they intend to gender a "generic" Persian or default to gendered biases in some usages of English, which perpetuates the invisibility of masculinity. Moreover, a gendered component of the construct of "the Persian *man*" provides a crucial mechanism to explain why others of non-Persian identity could identify with it: shared ideas about masculinity. While not framed in gendered terms, Garrison and Root identify these elements when they contend that the combat motif conveys protection or defense of the empire and "as an alternative to literal representations of military combat."[44] In this sense, the combat variant of the heroic encounter motif presents various threads of a culturally predominant masculinity: power, especially in acts of physical violence in war, whether to construct or defend the empire.

Concerning the control motif (e.g., fig. 5.5), Garrison and Root suggest that the image conveys "a balancing of forces – that is really quite different from the combat encounter, with its suggestion of aggression either held at bay or actively

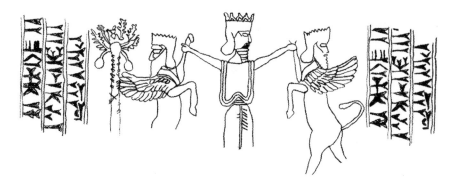

Figure 5.5 PFS 113*; cylinder seal impression from Persepolis[45]
Courtesy of the Oriental Institue of the University of Chicago

thwarted through the imminent or realized smiting of the hero's antagonist."[46] The point that the image primarily conveys "a balancing of forces" distinguishes it from the combat motif as the hero holds the hybrid creature rather than stabbing it as in the combat motif. But it should not obscure the extent to which the control motif imagines power as masculine. The control and combat motifs share a cultural equation in which masculinity entailed power, whether in the violence of warfare or the control of chaotic forces, motifs that often overlap in significant ways in the ancient Near East.[47]

While caution is necessary in utilizing Greek characterizations of Persian culture, Herodotus's assessment of a predominant Persian masculinity clearly fits the argument above: "After valor in fighting, the goodness of a man [ἀνδραγαθία] is most signified in this: that he can show a multitude of sons. To him who can show most, the King sends gifts every year. For multitude, they think, is strength" (*Hist.* 1.136).[48] The key term ἀνδραγαθία, "the goodness of a man," conveys culturally specific ideas about masculinity and provides a relatively explicit statement about the gendering of war as masculine in the process. As important as valor in war was to masculinity, Herodotus identifies another: producing numerous sons. Indeed, the two are not unrelated. Pierre Briant puts it well: "To protect their military and political power in the Empire, the Persians had to maintain a large population on which the king could draw to provide his elite cavalry and to serve as a breeding ground for officers and administrators."[49] A convergence of Persian sources suggest that Herodotus's claims about a predominant Persian period masculinity was not simply a mirror for Hellenistic values.

The court tales of Daniel emerged in a context wherein a culturally predominant masculinity involved physical violence and power, especially in a martial context.[50] The ubiquity of this cultural norm will allow some conclusions about the court tales of Daniel. Because this culturally predominant masculinity entailed additional threads, some of which have already come into view, I will develop these connections first.

5.3.2 Producing sons, names, and masculinity

Producing sons to perpetuate a father's name has surfaced as a second point of agreement between Herodotus and Hoffner about masculinity in the ancient Near East. This section shows that even as a name could be made through martial prowess, producing sons to perpetuate the father's name was central to a culturally predominant masculinity.[51]

A recent article by Jacob L. Wright demonstrates that making a name through martial prowess could be part of an ancient Near Eastern masculinity.[52] Wright begins with the words of Shamsi-Adad, an eighteenth-century B.C.E. Assyrian king, to his son:

> Here your brother won a victory, but there you lie among women! Now, when you march with your army to Qatna, be a man (*lū awīlāt*). As your brother has 'established a great name' (*šumam rabêm ištaknu*), you also in your region 'establish a great name.'
>
> (ARM 1.69, rev. 8–16)[53]

In this excerpt, the Akkadian particle *lū* forms a positive injunction in a verbless clause.[54] Accordingly, the phrase *lū awīlāt* amounts to a relatively explicit statement about gender: an individual is commanded to *be* or *become* a male through the performance of particular actions. This statement provides strong evidence that seeking to make a name for oneself, often through martial prowess, was an integral component to some ancient constructions of masculinity.[55] While Wright devotes attention to comparative sources, he focuses on biblical texts, which he contends: "assign priority and primacy to *procreation* as a means of making and perpetuating one's name. While they countenance and even condone name-making through *martial valor*, they cast aspersions on *heroic death*."[56] Even as Wright may inadvertently imply that biblical texts are unique in advocating procreation as the culturally predominant way of making a name, caution is needed on this point. Elsewhere Wright notes that the cultural norm throughout the ancient Near East was "that men should ideally marry and procreate before embarking on dangerous campaigns."[57] Accordingly, biblical texts differ from other ancient Near Eastern sources primarily on the valorization of heroic death in war rather than procreation being a predominant way of making a name.

The possibility of making a name through war in the Hebrew Bible is especially clear in texts like 2 Sam. 22:8–39, which recounts the names of David's warriors and their exploits, as well as in the song of the women in 1 Sam. 18:7: "Saul has slain his thousands, and David his ten thousands."[58] But Wright argues that other "texts complicate the masculine ambition to make a name for themselves in battle," pointing to the ways that "women deflect honor away from men" in Judges (Deborah, Jael, and Abimelech's unnamed killer) as evidence.[59] Yet these texts can also be read as underscoring the failures of the male characters in gendered terms, which, rather than complicating a configuration of masculinity as name making through war, rely upon and reinforce it to challenge the masculinity of individuals in Judges. Likewise, while Yahweh's name may be preserved through violence (e.g., Exod. 9:16), this point need not complicate the masculine ideology of name making through war.[60] The example assumes and reproduces the norm, creating a hierarchy of masculinities. While these examples attest to the possibility of name making through war in the Hebrew Bible, they are less clear about the priority of procreation in making a name.[61]

Deuteronomic legal traditions provide the most compelling evidence for the prioritization of name making through procreation rather than war in the Hebrew Bible. Independent from Wright, Mark K. George proposes that the importance of producing a son to preserve a man's name explains the possibility of exemption from military service for an engaged male (Deut 20:7) or a recently married male (24:5).[62] Wright also suggests that the textual reason provided for military exemption (i.e., "to make his wife happy") is "likely a euphemism for impregnation."[63] Even if the phrase is not a euphemism, it is hard to imagine that producing a child, ideally a son within the context, is not a goal of this exemption. As exemption from such a culturally predominant masculine activity as warfare could be granted to produce a child, it is crucial for masculinity in Deuteronomy. Indeed, these provisions seem to assume that name making either does not come through war or that it is not as desirable as procreation. In either case, the texts elevate making a name through sons as a predominant cultural practice rather than martial prowess.

Other texts in the Hebrew Bible share similar concerns with producing sons to perpetuate the father's name. George suggests that Deuteronomy contains a pervasive concern with name making beyond the warfare exemptions texts cited above: "Deuteronomy's representation of what it means to be a man in Israel is perhaps best encapsulated with having a name in Israel."[64] For instance, the law of levirate marriage ensures that the name of the deceased brother will continue if he dies without a child (Deut 25:5–10).[65] Instructions to teach children, an important motif in Deuteronomy (e.g., 11:19), require and assume that one will have produced children who can be taught.

Priestly traditions also share a concern for the production of sons to perpetuate the father's name. Sandra Jacobs concludes that in priestly material, "the ideal conception of masculinity . . . is its ability to reproduce prolifically."[66] As evidence, Jacobs points to God's promise of offspring to Abraham (e.g., Gen 15:5–6) and that the idea of an "everlasting covenant" (Gen 17:7) presupposes descendants.[67] While deuteronomic and priestly traditions[68] in the Hebrew Bible may not agree on all points, there was apparently no disagreement on the importance of producing children, especially sons to perpetuate the father's name, for a predominant ancient Israelite masculinity.[69]

Focusing on the silence of women in Chronicles, Julie Kelso argues that women's absence only partly explains their silence, which is better described as a silencing of women through the disavowal and repression of maternal origins in order "to enable the phantasy of mono-sexual production."[70] Kelso describes the logic and tension of Chronicles as follows: "The father must produce a son so that the patrilineal machinery keeps moving. However, in producing a son, he guarantees the eventual ending of his own story, his own eventual silence."[71] In this description, Kelso accounts for important concerns of a culturally predominant masculinity entailing the production of sons to perpetuate the father's name in two respects: this gendered norm at once addresses the son who becomes a father as well as that son's father whose name he perpetuates. This father-son succession introduces an important dynamic discussed below: what the son did with the father's name and reputation mattered significantly. Though the Chronicler may go beyond other biblical traditions with respect to what Kelso describes as a masculine phantasy of "mono-sexual reproduction," the equation of masculinity with producing sons to perpetuate the father's name is clearly (re)produced.

Producing sons to perpetuate the father's name as part of a predominant masculinity in the Hebrew Bible had potential for difficulties. The capacity of sons to affect the name or legacy of their fathers meant they could improve or damage it. As Claudia Camp argues, a concern about a son ruining a father's reputation pervades the slightly later text of Ben Sira, who ultimately seeks a way to preserve a name apart from the unpredictability of sons.[72] I will develop the significance of Ben Sira's response to this issue in Chapter 6. For now, it suffices to note his concern about what a son may do to his father's name. As important as it was to produce sons to perpetuate a male's name, doing so was not without the potential for complications. Likewise, it had significant implications for the son, who was at once expected to produce sons and to build up rather than harm the name of his father. Similar concerns are discernable throughout the Hebrew Bible, especially in the Deuteronomistic history where father-son relationships can be especially bad (e.g., Solomon and Rehoboam, Hezekiah and Manasseh).

Sources describing the Persians also attest to the importance of producing sons to perpetuate the father's name.[73] Recall the previously discussed assessment of Herodotus that, "after valor in fighting, the goodness of a man [ἀνδραγαθία] is most signified in this: that he can show a multitude of sons" (*Hist.* 1.136).[74] Herodotus's claim that a predominant Persian masculinity entailed producing sons may reflect his own Hellenistic cultural values. But that his assessment of the importance of martial prowess for masculinity in the Persian period was congruent with other sources suggests that his claim about sons was not just a mirror for his own values. Two related pieces of evidence that intersect with issues discussed above confirm this point: (1) the presentation of royal lineage as an exclusively male chain of father-son successions and (2) various kings construct an image of themselves as a good son, faithfully carrying on the work of their father and his name.

Persian period inscriptions portray royal lineage as an exclusively male chain of father-son successions. For example, on the Behistun relief, Darius claims:

> I am Darius the Great King, King of Kings, King in Persia, King of peoples/countries, son of Vishtaspa (Gr. Hystaspes), grandson of Arshama (Gr. Arsames), an Achaemenian. Darius the king proclaims: my father is Vishtaspa; Vishtaspa's father is Arshama (Gr. Arsames); Arsamah's father is Ariaramna (Gr. Ariaramnes); Ariaramna's father is Cishpish (Gr. Teispes); Cisphish's father is Hakhaimanish (Gr. Achaemenes).
>
> (DB I 1.1–6)[75]

Lineage matters in this self-presentation of Darius, who goes beyond mentioning his father and grandfather to include a longer genealogy of men that mentions no women. An attempt to legitimate his rule on the basis of biological descent partly motivates this self-presentation. Alongside his biological argument, Darius relies upon and (re)produces a thread of a culturally predominant masculinity in order to legitimate his rule. Darius produces an image of himself as a good son, who faithfully perpetuates the name of his father and his father's father and so on.

A tablet describing the accession of Xerxes (XPf) provides a clear case of a king seeking to construct himself as a good son who adds to the name and work of his father. Xerxes includes genealogical information: "My father (was) Darius; the father of Darius (was) Hystaspes by name; the father of Hystaspes was Arsames by name" (XPf §3.15–27).[76] As Xerxes continues, the importance of what he does with his father's reputation and what has been handed down to him takes the focus: "When I became king, much that (is) superior I built. What had been built by my father, that I took into care and other work I added" (XPf §3.27–43).[77] While being the son of Darius matters to Xerxes, what he does as Darius's son with what his father has passed down is equally important: Xerxes protects and adds to what his father built. In this way, Xerxes presents himself as a good son of Darius, carrying on what his father began, including his name. Xerxes acknowledges that he has brothers, but asserts that Darius made him "greatest," following what Ahuramazda desired (XPf §3.27–43). His building project extends this cultural work of producing an image of himself as conforming to a gendered expectation that he should be a good son in a way that reflects positively on his father, whose name he perpetuates, and himself in the process.

Especially for the dominant cultural group at the time the court tales were composed and compiled, the issue of producing sons to perpetuate a father's name lacks the quantity and quality of evidence as the topic of physical violence. But a convergence of sources suggests that producing sons to perpetuate the father's name was an integral thread of a predominant masculinity in the socio-historical context of the court tales of Daniel. I will address the significance of this claim for the court tales of Daniel after considering a third thread of that masculinity: protection and provision.

5.3.3 Protection, provision, and masculinity

While acting to protect or provide for others surfaced above as a thread of a predominant masculinity in the socio-historical context of the court tales of Daniel, this section focuses on that issue. The cumulative evidence reveals that the concepts of protection and provision were a third thread of a culturally predominant masculinity in the socio-historical context of the court tales of Daniel.[78]

Important dynamics associated with this issue emerge in Cynthia Chapman's work on masculinity in Neo-Assyrian sources. Concerning the title "shepherd (re'û)," which various Neo-Assyrian kings utilized in self-descriptions, Chapman argues that the term "covers the king's role as protector of and provider for his people."[79] These roles are interconnected with a king's ability to demonstrate martial prowess, especially that he is " 'without rival' on the battlefield."[80] Indeed, this overlap surfaced in considering the heroic encounter motif in Persian period iconography.[81] As Chapman describes the cultural logic of a royal masculinity: "In order to assume the role of shepherd over the four corners of the universe, a king first had to win the masculine contest in the battlefield so completely as to prove he had no rival."[82] In this respect, martial prowess and the protection of one's people are interwoven ideas.

Chapman contends that the primary social setting wherein a masculinity involved protection and provision was a familial context of a husband's relation to his wife and children and that it was subsequently mapped onto the king vis-à-vis his people.[83] In relation to this familial setting, Chapman finds compelling evidence: ancient Near Eastern legal collections.[84] For instance, a Middle Assyrian law states that:

> If a woman is residing in her father's house, or her husband settles her in a house elsewhere, and her husband then travels abroad but does not leave her any oil, wool, clothing, or provisions, or anything else, and sends her no provisions from abroad – that woman shall still remain (the exclusive object of rights) for her husband for five years, she shall not reside with another husband.
>
> (MAL 36)[85]

Chapman is not suggesting that this law provides evidence of practices in the ancient Near East, especially when the three key items of food, clothing, and oil are not mentioned in legal records.[86] But the legal tradition constructs cultural values or assumptions, especially in the way they stipulate (un)acceptable actions in terms of gender. This law juridically circumscribes masculinity as providing for a wife.

While the Middle Assyrian Laws are earlier than Chapman's focus on Neo-Assyrian sources, they were found in the library of Assurbanipal (seventh century B.C.E.) and other legal collections from the ancient Near East contain similar laws. Because scholars mention these laws in relation to some biblical texts for this issue, which I discuss below, they merit consideration. Though not making reference to the trio of items, LI 28 and LH 148 both obligate a husband who takes a second wife to provide for the first wife.[87] Concerning these cases, Shalom Paul shows that the trio of food, clothing, and oil were invoked as symbols for the provision of "the basic necessities of life."[88] While these relationships are always hierarchical, they are not just husband-wife relationships as Chapman implies.[89] Each case typically involves a dominant male providing for a subordinate or dependent female.[90] Paul even adduced a handful of documented legal contracts obligating children to provide the trio for their parents, which initially appears to reverse the typical gender hierarchy.[91] But each of these cases specifically obligate *sons* to provide for their parents, seemingly at a point where the father is unable (e.g., old age or death). As the father establishes the contracts while he still lives, they are his attempt to provide for his household, ensuring that another male will assume his place if he is no longer able. Even as these examples extend beyond a husband-wife relationship, they clearly construe providing for the subsistence of others as masculine. One case Paul mentions departs from this pattern entirely: a woman acquires a slave, who had belonged to her father-in-law after he failed to provide the trio of items. In this instance, a class hierarchy (i.e., slave versus non-slave status) enables this mobility. These cases suggest that Chapman may overstate the extent to which provisioning, especially the three items of food, clothing, and oil, were construed as a husband's obligations to a wife. But Chapman's main point that provisioning is generally construed as masculine in the ancient Near East remains compelling.[92]

While no relatively explicit statements about gender in the Hebrew Bible address this issue, the ancient Near Eastern legal texts considered above are often invoked in considering Exod 21:10, which the NRSV translates: "If he takes another wife to himself, he shall not diminish the food (שארה), clothing (כסותה), or marital rights (וענתה) of the first wife." The last term is a *hapax*, which Paul proposes to translate as "oil" on the basis of the trio of food, clothing, and oil found throughout Mesopotamian sources, though there is no clear lexical link to support the claim.[93] Regardless of what the third term means, this law obligates a male to provide basic elements of subsistence for a wife, juridically circumscribing masculinity as providing for a wife.

The legal tradition in Exod 21:10 and similar ones in the ancient Near East clearly illumine Hos 2, which invokes the trio of items in a dispute between God and Israel, presented as a husband and wife.[94] God accuses Israel of thinking,

"Let me go after my lovers, the ones who have given my bread and my water, my wool and my linen, my oil and my ointment" (v. 7). Yet Hosea's God claims to the contrary: "I myself gave to her the grain, the wine, and the oil" (v. 10). Moreover, Yahweh claims that "I will return and take my grain in its time and my wine at its appointed time. I will take away my wool and my linen, which had served to cover her nakedness" (v. 11). Some scholars have made the gendered logic of this passage explicit. In Ken Stone's assessment, this rivalry between Yahweh and Baal for credit as Israel's provider is a masculine one.[95] Stone's evidence that masculinity in ancient Israel entailed agricultural provision is Gen 3:17–19, the ideology of which he contends is mapped onto expectations for Israel's male deity.[96] Susan Haddox comes to similar conclusions about the gendering of the concept of provisioning for this masculine rivalry from the legal parallels discussed above.[97]

Two additional lines of evidence suggest that protection and provision were part of a predominant masculinity in the dominant cultural group at the time the court tales of Daniel likely emerged. The first surfaced in the discussion of bow imagery in Persian period iconography. As argued above, the bow appears in various contexts, including hunting, in Persian period iconography. To be sure, hunting can be a social activity construed primarily as "sport" wherein the production of food is not a primary concern. Still, the role of hunting in food production suggests that the use of the bow in this iconographic context construes food provisioning as a part of a predominant masculinity. Likewise, one of the variations of the combat version of the heroic encounter motif depicts the archer utilizing his bow for the specific purpose of protecting a weaker animal from the attack of a more powerful one. In this visual context, the archer may use a bow to inflict harm on an animal, but the purpose is to protect a weaker animal. In these ways, the bow in Persian period visual sources suggests that the concepts of protection and provision were part of a predominant masculinity.

A second strand of evidence from the Persian period about the importance of protection and provision for a predominant masculinity emerges in the phenomenon of banqueting and feasting, a well-noted interest of classical authors who wrote about the Persians.[98] Previous scholars have also noted the social implications of feasting. As Briant summarizes: "It is not surprising that royal dinners were not confined to taking nourishment. They made an important social and political statement and had much symbolic value. The king's table, truly a symbol of the king's power, was the preeminent place of gift giving and royal largesse."[99] Briant's otherwise insightful comment lacks specificity regarding the extent to which this activity was integral to ancient constructions of masculinity, a point that Wright's survey of feasting in the ancient Near East makes clear. According to Wright, feasting could serve various social functions, including promoting the cohesion of a social group and commemorating military success.[100] Concerning the latter, Wright argues that "by assuming the head seat at the table, hosting a resplendent banquet, and engaging in rituals of triumph, the champion converted a short-lived moment of success into valuable long-lasting symbolic capital."[101] Extending Wright's conclusion, it is possible to be more specific about that "symbolic capital." The overwhelming evidence that martial prowess was integral to a predominant masculinity reveals that the symbolic capital is masculinity. Indeed, feasting brings together two important threads of a culturally predominant masculinity discussed in this chapter: commemorating a military success and the protection of people by providing food.

While Persian period sources are not abundant for this issue, the cumulative evidence reveals that the court tales of Daniel emerged in a social context in which a predominant masculinity involved protecting and providing for subordinates. Even as I have presented each of the three threads of a predominant masculinity in separate sections in this chapter, there have been clear connections and overlap between them.

5.4 Conclusions

This cultural background enables an evaluation of some of my proposals about masculinity in the court tales of Daniel. First, Daniel and his colleagues deviate from the three threads of a culturally predominant masculinity described in this chapter.[102] They belong to a socio-cultural group that suffered defeat in war. None of them seem to produce sons, which would create difficulties for perpetuating their own names. Moreover, rather than protecting or providing for wives or children, they are themselves vulnerable and often need protection in a foreign court. Likewise, their well-being depends on the provisioning of the foreign king, most dramatically in Dan 1. Second, God's initial failure to protect his own people raises questions about God's masculinity in this cultural context.[103] But after this opening, the court tales of Daniel present God with numerous occasions to address his initially inadequate performance. God provides knowledge to Daniel and his colleagues. Likewise, the text implies that God ensures that their alternate diet results in them looking better than others. God clearly protects Daniel and his colleagues in other ways as well: from execution in ch. 2, from death in the fiery furnace in ch. 3, and from being consumed by lions in ch. 6. In this respect, the court tales seem anxious to assert God's ability to protect and provide for his own in spite of initial appearances to the contrary. Third, the tensions between God and the various kings (re)produce threads of a predominant masculinity in the socio-historical context. The narrative implicitly asks who is better at playing the dominant male, and it asserts that their God is able to emerge on top of the foreign ruler. Fourth, attentiveness to these threads of a culturally predominant masculinity heighten the clearly negative portrayals of foreign kings, such as when Nebuchadnezzar's ritual of subordination goes awry and when Belshazzar tarnishes his father's name. These conclusions begin to show the extent to which the court tales of Daniel engage and (re)produce configurations of masculinity attested elsewhere in the socio-historical context even though this cultural work never rises to the foreground in these stories.

Notes

1 Harry A. Hoffner, "Symbols for Masculinity and Femininity: Their Use in Ancient Near Eastern Sympathetic Magic Rituals," *JBL* 85 (1966): 327.
2 David Grene, trans., *The History: Herodotus* (Chicago: University of Chicago Press, 1987), 97.
3 For further discussion of these key terms and the sociological scholarship influencing my use, see Chapter 3 of this book.
4 See discussion in Chapter 1.
5 For instance, Collins notes that there are a far greater number of Persian or Akkadian loan words than Greek loan words in Daniel. See John J. Collins, *Daniel: A Commentary on the Book of Daniel*, Hermeneia (Minneapolis: Fortress, 1993), 18–20. A recent notable exception that prefers an Egyptian origin for the court tales of Daniel is Tawny L. Holm, *Of Courtiers and Kings: The Biblical Daniel Narratives and Ancient Story-Collections*, EANEC 1 (Winona Lake, IN: Eisenbrauns, 2013). For arguments in favor of the dominant position of a Mesopotamian origin, see Collins, *Daniel*, 47–50; Carol A. Newsom, *Daniel: A Commentary*, OTL (Louisville: Westminster John Knox, 2014), 6–12. Even if Holm proves persuasive, the basic point that ancient Near Eastern rather than Hellenistic sources are the most relevant for the court tales remains.
6 See Diane Bolger, ed., *Gender Through Time in the Ancient Near East* (Lanham, MD: AltaMira Press, 2008).
7 See Cecilia L. Ridgeway, *Framed by Gender: How Gender Inequality Persists in the Modern World* (New York: Oxford University Press, 2011).
8 For early work in addition to Hoffner, see John Goldingay, "Hosea 1–3, Genesis 1–4, and Masculist Interpretation," *HBT* 17 (1995): 37–44; David J. A. Clines, "David the Man: The Construction of Masculinity in the Hebrew Bible," in *Interested Parties: The Ideology of Writers and Readers of the Hebrew Bible*, 2nd ed. (Sheffield: Sheffield Academic, 2009), 212–43. For subsequent work, see Cynthia R. Chapman, *The Gendered Language of Warfare in the Israelite-Assyrian Encounter*, HSM 62 (Winona Lake, IN: Eisenbrauns, 2004); David J. A. Clines, "He-Prophets: Masculinity as a Problem for the Hebrew Prophets and Their Interpreters," in *Sense and Sensitivity: Essays on Reading the Bible in Memory of Robert Carrol*, eds. Alastair G. Hunter and Philip R. Davies, JSOTSup 348 (Sheffield: Sheffield Academic, 2002), 311–28; idem., "Dancing and Shining at Sinai: Playing the Man in Exodus 32–34," in *Men and Masculinity in the Hebrew Bible and Beyond*, ed. Ovidiu Creangă, The Bible in the Modern World 33 (Sheffield: Sheffield Phoenix, 2010), 54–63; Ovidiu Creangă, "Variations on the Theme of Masculinity: Joshua's Gender In/stability in the Conquest Narrative," in Creangă, *Men and Masculinity in the Hebrew Bible and Beyond*, 83–109; Brian Charles DiPalma, "De/Constructing Masculinity in Exodus 1–4," in Creangă, *Men and Masculinity in the Hebrew Bible and Beyond*, 36–53; Carole R. Fontaine, "'Be Men, O Philistines' (1 Samuel 4:9): Iconographic Representations and Reflections on Female Gender as Disability in the Ancient World," in *This Abled Body: Rethinking Disabilities in Biblical Studies*, ed. Hector Avalos, Sarah J. Melcher, and Jeremy Schipper, SemeiaSt 55 (Atlanta: Society of Biblical Literature, 2007), 61–72; Mark K. George, "Masculinity and Its Regimentation in Deuteronomy," in Creangă, *Men and Masculinity in the Hebrew Bible and Beyond*, 64–82; Deryn Guest, "From Gender Reversal to Genderfuck: Reading Jael Through a Lesbian Lens," in *Bible Trouble: Queer Reading at the Boundaries of Biblical Scholarship*, eds. Teresa

J. Hornsby and Ken Stone, SemeiaSt 67 (Atlanta: Society of Biblical Literature, 2011), 9–44; Susan E. Haddox, "Favoured Sons and Subordinate Masculinities," in Creangă, *Men and Masculinity in the Hebrew Bible and Beyond*, 2–19; Dennis T. Olson, "Untying the Knot? Masculinity, Violence, and the Creation-Fall Story of Genesis 2–4," in *Engaging the Bible in a Gendered World: An Introduction to Feminist Biblical Interpretation in Honor of Katharine Doob Sakenfeld*, eds. Linda Day and Carolyn Pressler (Louisville: Westminster John Knox, 2006), 73–86; Ken Stone, "Gender Criticism: The Un-Manning of Abimelech," in *Judges & Method: New Approaches in Biblical Studies*, ed. Gale A. Yee, 2nd ed. (Minneapolis: Fortress, 2007), 183–201; idem., "Queer Reading Between Bible and Film: Paris Is Burning and the 'Legendary Houses' of David and Saul," in Hornsby and Stone, *Bible Trouble*, 75–98; Harold C. Washington, "Violence and the Construction of Gender in the Hebrew Bible: A New Historicist Approach.," *BibInt* 5 (1997): 324–63; idem., "'Lest He Die in the Battle and Another Man Take Her': Violence and the Construction of Gender in the Laws of Deuteronomy 22," in *Gender and Law in the Hebrew Bible and the Ancient Near East*, eds. Victor H. Matthews, Bernard M. Levinson, and Tikva Frymer-Kensky (New York: T&T Clark, 2004), 185–213.

9   As explained in Chapter 3, relatively explicit statements about gender equate an activity or characteristic with being or becoming (היה or היה with ל) or being like (with כ) a male or a female.

10 See also Stone, "Gender Criticism."

11 On the use of a form of היה with the preposition ל and the possible translation of "become," cf. *BDB* "היה" II.2.d-h, p. 226; *HALOT* "היה" 7c, p. 244; *DCH* v. 4 "ל" 3c, p. 481.

12 This point is not to suggest the female characters do not engage in violence in warfare (e.g., Jael in Judg 4–5 and the unnamed woman in Judg 9:53). For analysis of these stories, see Guest, "From Gender Reversal to Genderfuck"; Stone, "Gender Criticism."

13 See George, "Masculinity and Its Regimentation in Deuteronomy," George suggests that "work remains to be done on the relationship of Deuteronomy's representation of masculinity to that of the other books in the Deuteronomistic history" (81). On the issue of physical violence and war, there appears to be a strong unity between the construction of masculinity in the legal portions of Deuteronomy and DtrH.

14 To keep the analysis focused, I do not include the comparisons of men in war to women giving birth in the analysis above (e.g., Jer 30:5–7). Concerning these statements, Claudia Bergman contends that the authors "aim at invoking the reader's feeling of sympathy and esteem for the one suffering a crisis like no other. Being in crisis and being (like) a woman giving birth is something to be honored rather than ridiculed." See Claudia D. Bergmann, "'We Have Seen the Enemy, and He Is Only a She': The Portrayal of Warriors as Women," in *Writing and Reading War: Rhetoric, Gender, and Ethics in Biblical and Modern Contexts*, eds. Brad E. Kelle and Frank Ritchel Ames, SymS 42 (Atlanta: Society of Biblical Literature, 2008), 121. A closer consideration, however, reveals that even in these cases, non-exemplarily male behavior in war is described as feminine, whether in relation to women in general or specifically women in labor. For a fuller discussion, see my forthcoming article.

15 Chapman, *The Gendered Language of Warfare*, 141.

16 For a recent discussion, upon which this discussion relies, see Ryan P. Bonfiglio, "Archer Imagery in Zechariah 9:11–17 in Light of Achaemenid Iconography," *JBL* 131 (2012): 507–27. On the trend away from the violence of earlier visual imagery, see Margaret Cool Root, *King and Kingship in Achaemenid Art: Essays on the Creation of an Iconography of Empire*, Acta Iranica 19 (Leiden: Brill, 1979). For analyses of masculinity and martial violence in visual material from earlier time periods, see Irene J. Winter, "Sex, Rhetoric, and the Public Monument: The Alluring Body of Naram-Sîn

of Agade," in *Sexuality in Ancient Art: Near East, Egypt, Greece, and Italy*, ed. Natalie Boymel Kampen (Cambridge: Cambridge University Press, 1996), 11–26; Zainab Bahrani, *Rituals of War: The Body and Violence in Mesopotamia* (New York: Zone Books, 2008); Michelle Marcus, "Geography as Visual Ideology: Landscape, Knowledge, and Power in Neo-Assyrian Art," in *Neo-Assyrian Geography*, ed. Mario Liverani (Rome: Universita di Roma, 1995), 193–208; Cynthia R. Chapman, "Sculpted Warriors: Sexuality and the Sacred in the Definition of Warfare in the Assyrian Palace Reliefs and in Ezekiel 23:14–17," in *The Aesthetics of Violence in the Prophets*, eds. Chris Franke and Julia M O'Brien, LHBOTS 517 (New York: T&T Clark, 2010), 1–17.

17 This image is a cropped derivative of "Stone Record at Behistun" by dynamosquito available online at https://commons.wikimedia.org/wiki/File:Stone_record_at_Behistun.jpg licensed under https://creativecommons.org/licenses/by-sa/2.0. See also Brent A. Strawn, "'A World Under Control': Isaiah 60 and the Apadana Reliefs from Persepolis," in *Approaching Yehud: New Approaches to the Study of the Persian Period*, ed. Jon L. Berquist, SemeiaSt 50 (Atlanta: Society of Biblical Literature, 2007), 114, fig. 15. Cf. Root, *King and Kingship in Achaemenid Art*, pl. 6; Pierre Briant, *From Cyrus to Alexander: A History of the Persian Empire*, trans. Peter T. Daniels (Winona Lake, IN: Eisenbrauns, 2002), 125, fig. 8.

18 This image is a cropped derivative of "Xerxes tomb at Naqsh-e Rostam- upper register (4614878357).jpg" by dynamosquito available online at https://commons.wikimedia.org/wiki/File:Xerxes_tomb_at_Naqsh-e_Rostam-_upper_register_(4614878357).jpg licensed under https://creativecommons.org/licenses/by-sa/2.0/deed.en. For a similar example of Darius, see Amélie Kuhrt, *The Persian Empire: A Corpus of Sources from the Achaemenid Period* (New York: Routledge, 2007), 500, 11.14. Cf. Root, *King and Kingship in Achaemenid Art*, pl. XIIIa; Briant, *From Cyrus to Alexander*, 211, fig. 16.

19 Root, *King and Kingship in Achaemenid Art*, 164.

20 Ibid., 165.

21 "Illustrerad Verldshistoria band I Ill 055.jpg" by Ernst Wallis et al available online at https://commons.wikimedia.org/wiki/File%3AIllustrerad_Verldshistoria_band_I_Ill_055.jpg. Image is in the public domain. See also Edith Porada, *The Art of Ancient Iran: Pre-Islamic Cultures* (New York: Crown Publishers, Inc., 1965), 176, fig. 89. Cf. Bonfiglio, "Archer Imagery," 516, fig. 3; Briant, *From Cyrus to Alexander*, 232, fig. 29a.

22 For a sampling of these seals, see Mark B. Garrison, "Achaemenid Iconography as Evidenced by Glyptic Art: Subject Matter, Social Function, Audience and Diffusion," in *Images as Media: Sources for the Cultural History of the Near East and the Eastern Mediterranean (1st Millenium BCE)*, ed. Christoph Uehlinger, OBO 175 (Fribourg: University Press, 2000), 115–63.

23 For this typology and the subtypes of types three and four, see David Stronach, "Early Achaemenid Coinage: Perspectives from the Homeland," *IrAnt* 24 (1989): 259. For a discussion of the chronology of these coins, see ibid., 258–262, esp. fig. 2. Types three and four were in use for the longest period of time, including through the end of the fourth century BCE.

24 After Stronach, "Early Achaemenid Coinage," 260, figs. 1.1–3 and 7. Used with author's permission. Cf. Bonfiglio, "Archer Imagery," fgs. 1, 4–6; Mark B. Garrison, "Archers at Persepolis: The Emergence of Royal Ideology at the Heart of Empire," in *The World of Achaemenid Persia: History, Art and Society in Iran and the Ancient Near East*, eds. John Curtis and St John Simpson (New York: I. B. Tauris, 2010), 338, 32.1.

25 Margaret Cool Root, "From the Heart: Powerful Persianisms in the Art of the Western Empire," in *Asia Minor and Egypt: Old Cultures in a New Empire. Proceedings of the Groningen 1988 Achaemenid History Workshop*, eds. Heleen Sancisi-Weerdenburg and Amélie Khurt, Achaemenid History 6 (Leiden: Nederlands Instituut voor het Nabije Oosten, 1991), 17.

26 Cindy L. Nimchuk, "The 'Archers' of Darius: Coinage or Tokens of Royal Esteem?" *Ars Orientalis* 32 (2002): 65–66.
27 Ibid., 66.
28 Garrison, "Archers at Persepolis," 352–55.
29 Bonfiglio, "Archer Imagery," 516.
30 For a similar suggestion about the bow in earlier periods in the ancient Near East, see Susan E. Haddox, *Metaphor and Masculinity in Hosea*, StBibLit 141 (New York: Peter Lang, 2011), 84.
31 Hoffner, "Symbols for Masculinity and Femininity,".
32 "Ritual Against Impotence," trans. Albrecht Goetze (*ANET*, 349).
33 For other recent examples, see Chapman, *The Gendered Language of Warfare*, 47 & 51–58; Haddox, "Favoured Sons and Subordinate Masculinities," 8.
34 Trans. Kuhrt, *The Persian Empire*, 504–5. Cf. Roland G. Kent, *Old Persian: Grammar, Texts, Lexicon* (New Haven: American Oriental Society, 1950), 140.
35 See, for instance, Stone, "Queer Reading Between Bible and Film."
36 Trans. Kuhrt, *The Persian Empire*, 503. See also, Kent, *Old Persian*, 138.
37 Kent's lexicon defines the word as "man" without suggesting it refers to a person in a gender-neutral fashion. Given the date of publication, Kent may be using "man" to refer to a person, but when glossing a related Avestan word (*marəta*) Kent defines it as "mortal, man." See Kent, *Old Persian*, 203.
38 For a summary of the motif prior to the rise of the Persians, see Mark B. Garrison, "The Heroic Encounter in the Visual Arts of Ancient Iraq and Iran C. 1000–500 B.C.," in *The Master of Animals in Old World Iconography*, eds. D. B. Counts and B. Arnold (Budapest: Archaeolingua, 2010), 151–74.
39 Mark B. Garrison, and Margaret Cool Root, *Seals on the Persepolis Fortification Tablets, Volume I: Images of Heroic Encounter*, OIP 117 (Chicago: Oriental Institute of the University of Chicago, 2001), 42–43.
40 Garrison, "Achaemenid Iconography," 126–27. Emphasis mine to identify the two key types.
41 Mark B. Garrison, "Royal Achaemenid Iconography," in *The Oxford Handbook of Ancient Iran*, ed. D. T. Potts (Oxford: Oxford University Press, 2013), 582.
42 For a concise summary, see Garrison, "The Heroic Encounter," 165–67.
43 Garrison and Root, *Seals on the Persepolis Fortification Tablets, Volume I*, 57. This idea was originally suggested in Root, *King and Kingship in Achaemenid Art*, esp. 305–307.
44 Garrison and Root, *Seals on the Persepolis Fortification Tablets, Volume I*, 59.
45 Line drawing is after ibid., 88. Image is used Courtesy of the Oriental Institute of the University of Chicago. See also Garrison, "Achaemenid Iconography," 130, fg. 3.
46 Garrison and Root, *Seals on the Persepolis Fortification Tablets, Volume I*, 59.
47 On the portrayal of war as controlling chaos in Egyptian iconography, see Joel M. LeMon, "Yahweh's Hand and the Iconography of the Blow in Psalm 81:14–16," *JBL* 132 (2013): 871 and 877.
48 Trans. Grene, *The History*, 97.
49 Briant, *From Cyrus to Alexander*, 337.
50 For Hellenistic sources, see Ada Cohen, *Art in the Era of Alexander the Great: Paradigms of Manhood and Their Cultural Traditions* (Cambridge: Cambridge University Press, 2010). For a discussion of the way that the link between control over others and masculinity becomes configured as self-control in Greek sources, see Stephen D. Moore and Janice Capel Anderson, "Taking It Like a Man: Masculinity in 4 Maccabees," *JBL* 117 (1998): 249–73.
51 Motifs of (in)fertility and motherhood are important for femininity in the Hebrew Bible. See Susanne Scholz, *Introducing the Women's Hebrew Bible* (New York: T&T

Clark, 2007), 66–70. As Esther Fuchs argues, biblical texts depicting motherhood positively are invested in continuing the male name. See Esther Fuchs, *Sexual Politics in the Biblical Narrative: Reading the Hebrew Bible as a Woman*, JSOTSup 310 (Sheffield: Sheffield Academic, 2000). In her words, "motherhood is indeed extolled in the Hebrew Bible, but it is extolled to the extent that it validates the father's authority and consolidates the son's right to security and prosperity. The mother is a means to an end, she is necessary and therefore validated. But her validation functions ultimately as the validation of the patriarchal hierarchy" (90).

52 Jacob L. Wright, "Making a Name for Oneself: Martial Valor, Heroic Death, and Procreation in the Hebrew Bible," *JSOT* 36 (2011): 131–62.
53 Trans., ibid., 132.
54 John Huehnegard, *A Grammar of Akkadian* (Winona Lake, IN: Eisenbrauns, 2000), 223.
55 Wright, "Making a Name for Oneself," 132.
56 Ibid., 132–33.
57 Ibid., 137.
58 Ibid., 149.
59 Ibid., 146.
60 Ibid., 146–47.
61 For a juxtaposition of sons and martial implements without the explicit focus on making a name, see Psalm 127. The psalmist describes sons as "like arrows in the hand of a warrior" (v. 4). While not claiming that sons are *better than* a warrior's arrows, the two are comparable. The psalmist suggests that "happy is the man (הגבר) who has filled his quiver with them (מלא את־אשפתו מהם)" (v. 5). Given the centrality of martial activities for a culturally predominant masculinity, placing sons rather than arrows in the man's quiver grants a parallel importance of producing sons for a predominant masculinity in the Hebrew Bible. Though obscured in some translations (e.g., the NRSV), the man is the active subject of מלא, who "fills" his quiver, or produces sons. These sons enable defense against enemies in the gate (v. 5). While this psalm does not mention the idea of "name making," the comparison of producing sons with military activities suggests that the two were similarly important for a predominant masculinity.
62 George, "Masculinity and Its Regimentation in Deuteronomy," 74.
63 Wright, "Making a Name for Oneself," 150.
64 George, "Masculinity and Its Regimentation in Deuteronomy," 67.
65 Ibid., 74. Wright suggests that this text be read in light of the exemptions from warfare, but the law in Deut. 25:5 does not specify whether it is only the situation of a man dying in war without having produced sons when the law applies. See Wright, "Making a Name for Oneself," 151. See Gen 38 and the book of Ruth where this concern emerges in narratives. About Tamar and Ruth, Esther Fuchs concludes that "it is the heroines' exceptional performance as wives and mothers and their relentless allegiance to patriarchy that the text stresses as their most exalted properties." See Esther Fuchs, "Status and Role of Female Heroines in the Biblical Narrative," in *Women in the Hebrew Bible: A Reader*, ed. Alice Bach (New York: Routledge, 1999), 79. The aspect of patriarchy with which Fuchs is concerned is the perpetuation and preservation of the father's name by producing sons.
66 Sandra Jacobs, "Divine Virility in Priestly Representation: Its Memory and Consummation in Rabbinic Midrash," in Creangă, *Men and Masculinity in the Hebrew Bible and Beyond*, 150.
67 Ibid., 149–50.
68 For a discussion of the issue of the perpetuation of the father's name in priestly genealogies in Genesis, see also Ingeborg Löwisch, "Gender and Ambiguity in the Genesis

Genealogies: Tracing Absence and Subversion through the Lens of Derrida's Archive Fever," in *Embroidered Garments: Priests and Gender in Biblical Israel*, ed. Deborah W. Rooke (Sheffield: Sheffield Phoenix, 2009), 60–73.

69. The extent to which this sort of ideology is assumed elsewhere in the Hebrew Bible can be seen in a text like Gen. 48:16, in which the elderly Israel/Jacob offers this blessing for Joseph's sons: "May my name be proclaimed through them (ויקרא בהם שמי) and the name of my ancestors, Abraham and Isaac." In this case, the text assumes that having a great number of descendants would be a typical way of ensuring that an ancestor's name would be preserved. Similarly, in an oracle against Babylon in Isaiah, Yahweh declares that he will cut off "name and remnant, offspring and posterity" (14:22). In this case, offspring is presented as parallel to name, or the means by which the name would have been continued.

70. Julie Kelso, *O Mother, Where Art Thou? An Irigarayan Reading of the Book of Chronicles* (London: Equinox, 2007), 165. Kelso's basic argument is reiterated in more recent scholarship that heavily depends upon it. See Christine Mitchell, "1 and 2 Chronicles," in *Women's Bible Commentary, Revised and Updated*, eds. Carol A. Newsom, Sharon H. Ringe, and Jacqueline E. Lapsley, 3rd ed. (Louisville: Westminster John Knox, 2012), 184–91. Given that Kelso's work is more thorough than what is possible in Mitchell's brief contribution to *Women's Bible Commentary*, I focus the discussion on Kelso.

71. Kelso, *O Mother, Where Art Thou?* 207.

72. Claudia V. Camp, *Ben Sira and the Men Who Handle Books: Gender and the Rise of Canon-Consciousness*, Hebrew Bible Monographs 50 (Sheffield: Sheffield Phoenix, 2013).

73. For discussion of other ancient Near Eastern cultural groups and some classical sources, see Wright, "Making a Name for Oneself." Various treaty curses from the Neo-Assyrian empire provide additional evidence about this topic. For discussion, see Chapman, *The Gendered Language of Warfare*. She argues that some of the "curses draw on culturally specific masculine anxieties" by "forcing an enemy king to jeopardize his masculine role as warrior-protector and shepherd-provider of his people" (41). While Chapman focuses on violence in war, protection, and provision, she eclipses a relevant thread of that masculinity in her insightful analysis: producing sons to perpetuate the name of the father. Various lines in Esarhaddon's Succession Treaty rely upon this idea: "May Zarpanitu, who grants name and seed, destroy your name and your seed from the land" (line 433). Trans. Simo Parpola, and Kazuko Watanabe, eds., *Neo-Assyrian Treaties and Loyalty Oaths*, SAA 2 (Helsinki: Helsinki University Press, 1998), 46. Similarly, line 537 reads: "Just as a m[ule has n]o offspring, may your name, your seed, and the seed of your sons and your daughters disappear from the land" (51). Discussing a curse in a treaty between Mati-ilu and Aššurnerari that wishes Mati-ilu would have the sex life of a mule (lines 8–15), Chapman connects the curse to an anxiety about an "inability to produce an heir" (49–50), but does not develop the importance of producing sons to perpetuate the name of the father. For additional instances that mention the destruction of a name, see lines 138, 153, 243, 302, 524, and 660. The concern may also be mentioned in a treaty between Assurbanipal and some Babylonian allies as suggested by Parpola and Watanabe's restoration of the damaged line 21 (for their restoration and translation, see 68). Likewise, stele II from Sefire contains the following: "If you say in your soul and think in your mind, ['I am an ally, and I shall obey Bir-Ga'yah] and his sons and his offspring,' then I shall not be able to raise a ha[nd against you, nor my son against your son, nor my offspring against your offspring], neither to strike them, nor to destroy their name" (face B, lines 5–7). Trans. Joseph A. Fitzmyer, *The Aramaic Inscriptions of Sefire* (Rome: Pontifical Biblical Institute, 1967), 81.

74 Trans. Grene, *The History*, 97. Emphasis mine.
75 Trans. Kuhrt, *The Persian Empire*, 141. Cf. Kent, *Old Persian*, 119.
76 Trans. Kuhrt, *The Persian Empire*, 244. See also Kent, *Old Persian*, 150.
77 Ibid.
78 This argument is not to suggest that women were not significantly involved in producing things necessary for subsistence and survival in ancient Israel or that the motif of provisioning might not also be part of some representations of femininity. Scholars argue that women were significantly involved in the production of key items necessary for subsistence in ancient Israel, especially bread and clothing, two things that will feature in the discussion below. See Carol L. Meyers, *Discovering Eve: Ancient Israelite Women in Context* (Oxford: Oxford University Press, 1988); Jennie R. Ebeling, *Women's Lives in Biblical Times* (New York: T&T Clark, 2010). For a critique of this sort of scholarship, with a sustained focus on Meyers's earlier work, see Esther Fuchs, "The History of Women in Ancient Israel: Theory, Method, and the Book of Ruth," in *Her Master's Tools? Feminist and Postcolonial Engagements of Historical-Critical Discourse*, eds. Caroline Vander Stichele and Todd Penner, GPBS 8 (Atlanta: Society of Biblical Literature, 2005), 211–31. Fuchs's critique went unanswered in an updated version of Meyers's work. See Carol L. Meyers, *Rediscovering Eve: Ancient Israelite Women in Context* (Oxford: Oxford University Press, 2012).
79 Chapman, *The Gendered Language of Warfare*, 21.
80 Ibid., 59.
81 For a discussion of the related image of a human archer defending a weaker animal from a stronger animal, see Garrison, "Achaemenid Iconography," 135–38.
82 Chapman, *The Gendered Language of Warfare*, 33.
83 Ibid., 29.
84 Ibid., 30.
85 Trans. Martha T. Roth, *Law Collections from Mesopotamia and Asia Minor*, 2nd ed., WAW 6 (Atlanta: Scholars Press, 1997), 165–66. See also, *ANET* 183.
86 Chapman, *The Gendered Language of Warfare*, 30–31, fn. 50.
87 A collection of laws relevant to this issue are presented in Shalom M. Paul, *Studies in the Book of the Covenant in the Light of Cuneiform and Biblical Law* (Leiden: Brill, 1970), 56–61.
88 Ibid., 59.
89 Chapman, *The Gendered Language of Warfare*, 31.
90 In LI 28, a man who has a child with a prostitute because his wife was unable to conceive is obligated to provide grain, oil, and clothing for the prostitute. In LE 32, a man giving his son to a nurse to care for the child is expected to provide barley, oil, and wool for the nurse while the child is under her care. Finally, in LH 178, if the father of various religiously affiliated women dies, her brothers are required to provide food, oil, and clothing to her, effectively assuming the role of the father as her provider.
91 Paul, *Studies in the Book of the Covenant*, 58.
92 Supporting evidence for Chapman's argument emerges from the ability of the idea to explain other aspects of Neo-Assyrian sources. For instance, the idea explains the logic upon which various curses in Neo-Assyrian vassal treaties rely. Chapman, *The Gendered Language of Warfare*, 42–43. Likewise, working with this cultural assumption, Chapman accounts for the general absence of Neo-Assyrian women in iconography (i.e., the victorious Neo-Assyrian king protecting his own women from harm) that is contrasted with the frequent depiction of foreign women in martial settings in visual sources to discredit and emasculate the foreign king for failing to protect his people (46–47).
93 Paul, *Studies in the Book of the Covenant*, 59–60.

94 See Martin J. Buss, *The Prophetic Word of Hosea* (Berlin: Verlag Alfred Töpelmann, 1969), 88; Paul, *Studies in the Book of the Covenant*, 61; Brad E. Kelle, *Hosea 2: Metaphor and Rhetoric in Historical Perspective*, AcBib 20 (Atlanta: Society of Biblical Literature, 2005), 67–68–238.
95 Ken Stone, "Lovers and Raisin Cakes: Food, Sex and Divine Insecurity in Hosea," in *Queer Commentary and the Hebrew Bible*, ed. Ken Stone, JSOTSSup 334 (Sheffield: Sheffield Academic, 2001), 126–27.
96 Ibid.
97 Haddox, *Metaphor and Masculinity in Hosea*, 68–69. In another context, Haddox suggests that protection and provision are important for the patriarchs' masculinity in Genesis, though most often in negatively characterizing them when they endanger their wives (e.g., Sarah) or fail to protect them or their daughters (e.g., Dinah). See Haddox, "Favoured Sons and Subordinate Masculinities," 7. On the importance of food production and provision in Deuteronomy, see George, "Masculinity and Its Regimentation in Deuteronomy," 70. For the suggestion that the inability of the Gibeonites to protect their people (Josh 10) "is tantamount to being emasculated," see Creangă, "Variations on the Theme of Masculinity," 103.
98 For the suggestion that banqueting or feasting is related to the attempts of Neo-Assyrian kings to position themselves as a "provider" in relation to their people and its relevance for their masculinity, see Chapman, *The Gendered Language of Warfare*, 31. On this topic as a noted concern of classical authors, see Jacob L. Wright, "Commensal Politics in Ancient Western Asia: The Background to Nehemiah's Feasting (Continued, Part II)," *ZAW* 122 (2010): 344; Briant, *From Cyrus to Alexander*, 286. For a thorough survey of feasting and its social significance in both visual and textual sources, see Jacob L. Wright, "Commensal Politics in Ancient Western Asia: The Background to Nehemiah's Feasting (Part I)," *ZAW* 122 (2010): 212–33; Wright, "Commensal Politics (Continued, Part II)," esp. 333–348.
99 Briant, *From Cyrus to Alexander*, 293.
100 Wright, "Commensal Politics (Continued, Part II)," 345–46.
101 Ibid., 347.
102 In this respect, I agree with the basic suggestion in T. M. Lemos, "'They Have Become Women': Judean Diaspora and Postcolonial Theories of Gender and Migration," in *Social Theory and the Study of Israelite Religion: Essays in Retrospect and Prospect*, ed. Saul M. Olyan (Atlanta: Society of Biblical Literature, 2012), 81–109. As will become clear in Chapter 6, however, I think that Daniel and his colleagues are differently masculine rather than nonmasculine as Lemos implies even though they deviate from a culturally predominant masculinity.
103 In this respect, the action may be similar to what Haddox describes the patriarchs in Genesis as doing to their wives on repeated occasion. See above for discussion.

6

SCRIBAL MASCULINITY AND THE COURT TALES OF DANIEL

> They gave themselves [the scroll as lector-]priest, the writing-board as loving son. Instructions are their tombs, the reed pen is their child, the stone-surface their wife.
> —"The Immortality of Writers" 2.5[1]

6.1 Introduction

Belonging to a people group that has suffered defeat in war, Daniel and his colleagues deviate from a culturally predominant masculinity, especially because a foreign king has taken them as exiles to serve in his court. Moreover, they do not clearly have wives or produce sons to perpetuate their names. But I proposed that the court tales of Daniel may depict Daniel and his colleagues as negotiating with a culturally predominant masculinity to produce a masculinity that was less common in the cultural context. Testing this idea requires a discussion of scribal masculinity, which appeared important when the narrator explained why Nebuchadnezzar brought Daniel and his colleagues to Babylon: "to teach them the literature and language of the Chaldeans (ללמדם ספר ולשון כשדים)" (Dan 1:4). This training is a scribal education for service as officials in the king's court.[2]

This chapter considers Daniel and his colleagues in terms of a scribal masculinity in the ancient Near East. With the phrase "scribal masculinity," I include masculinity among scribes narrowly: those who read and wrote as a profession as a result of training in these skills. I also include those who progressed into official positions for which a scribal training was a prerequisite.[3] The phrase "scribal masculinity" may obscure hierarchical differences between lower-ranking scribes and higher-ranking officials. Still, I use the phrase "scribal masculinity" to convey the common gendered dynamics, concerns, and practices that emerge among scribes and those who progressed into higher positions as officials because of that scribal training. With the label "scribal masculinity," I include practices in addition to a basic ability to read and write, such as displays of knowledge or wisdom, producing literature, and offering counsel or advice.

While an exhaustive study of scribal masculinity in the ancient Near East is desirable, it will not be undertaken here.[4] Instead, I will discuss the dynamics of an ancient Near Eastern scribal masculinity that illumine the court tales of Daniel. I will show that rather than displaying power through violence, scribal masculinity displays power through knowledge. Similarly, rather than producing sons to perpetuate one's name, a scribal masculinity could perpetuate a name through producing literature, displaying knowledge, or faithful service to the king. In both cases, a negotiated exchange, which accepts a part of a predominant masculinity while substituting a different configuration of practices, produces a scribal masculinity. While scribal masculinity was complicitly subordinate to a culturally predominant masculinity, it did not entail a relatively powerless or unimportant position. Instead, scribal masculinity typically involved a high socio-economic and professional status in a royal hierarchy. From this perspective, I will argue that Daniel and his colleagues are differently masculine in the cultural context.

6.2 Scribal masculinity in the ancient near East and the Hebrew Bible

While some evidence suggests that elite women from the ancient Near East occasionally possessed basic scribal training, scribes were predominantly men, especially those who obtained a mastery of the writing system and progressed into positions as court officials.[5] Just as professions in the modern world become gendered (e.g., nurses and doctors), a scribe was stereotypically male in the ancient Near East. But how scribes in the ancient Near East responded to a predominant configuration of masculinity remains an undeveloped topic in scholarship.

Texts from ancient Egypt provide the most thorough evidence for the construction of a scribal masculinity in an ancient Near Eastern context. A section of a papyrus manuscript from the New Kingdom era known as the "Immortality of Writers" opens with a mention of "learned scribes of the time that came after the gods" whose "names have become everlasting" (2.5).[6] The speaker challenges expectations that these scribes achieved everlasting names in culturally typical ways: "They did not make for themselves tombs of copper, with stelae of metal from heaven. They know not how to leave heirs, children [of theirs] to pronounce their names" (2.5).[7] Beginning in this way, the text acknowledges the importance of producing sons to perpetuate a father's name for a culturally predominant masculinity.[8] The claim that these renowned scribes "knew not how to leave heirs" creates tension with the idea that scribes often had children and that the scribal trade in ancient Egypt was typically hereditary.[9] The text may imagine a different situation for these ancient scribes or simply creates the scenario for emphasis. As the text continues, these scribes still make an everlasting name for themselves without children: "they made heirs for themselves of books, of instructions they had composed" (2.5).[10] This assertion exchanges books and instructions for children to preserve the scribe's name and numerous similar transactions occur as the text continues: "They gave themselves [the scroll as lector-]priest, the writing-board as a loving-son. Instructions are their tombs, the reed pen is their child, the stone-surface their wife" (2.5).[11] In these ways, the text substitutes scribal implements or products for the more expected way of preserving a name: producing male children. This negotiated exchange (re)produces an association of masculinity with preserving a name but through practices rooted in scribal activities that were less-common in the cultural context. The author of "The Immortality of Writers" even asserts the superiority of his way over more expected ways of preserving a name: "*Better* is a book *than* a graven stela, *than* a solid [tomb-enclosure] . . . *better* is a book *than* a well-built house, *than* tomb-chapels in the west; *better than* a solid mansion, *than* a stela in the temple" (3.1).[12] In this text, accepting a part of a culturally predominant masculinity (i.e., preserving a name) while asserting a less-recognizable way of achieving it (i.e., scribal activities) produces a scribal masculinity. The need to justify scribal activities as adequate or superior to other gendered practices suggests that scribal masculinity was subordinate to a culturally predominant masculinity. But the text's claim that these scribes had "mansions" (2.5) constructs this masculinity as one with a high professional and socio-economic status.

Other Egyptian texts, especially "The Satire on the Trades," compare the scribal profession with other occupations.[13] Framed as a father's advice to his son, this text praises the scribal profession as superior to all other professions, which it ridicules at length. For example, the father claims: "I have seen the metal worker at the mouth of his furnace. His fingers were somewhat like crocodiles; he stank more than fish-roe" (4.5).[14] Likewise, the father denigrates a builder because "he is dirtier than vines or pigs, from treading under his mud. His clothes are stiff with clay; his leather belt is going to ruin" (5.5).[15] Diatribes against other professions criticize the masculinity of those occupying them. The father claims that the embalmer and the laundry worker alike cannot "oppose his (own) daughter" (8.1).[16] This criticism relies on a configuration of gender holding that a father should be stronger than his own daughter. After concluding his criticisms of the other professions, the father extols the scribal profession: "Behold, there is no profession free of a boss – except for the scribe: he is the boss" (9.1).[17] While clearly a hyperbolic claim, it reveals a concern for dominating others. According to this text, the scribal profession leads to power over others. In addition to a general claim about things being "better" for scribes, the father makes this bold claim about scribal work: "the eternity of its work is (like that of) the mountains" (9.1).[18] As in the "Immortality of Writers," this speaker seeks to produce something enduring, but rather than produce sons, a scribe can produce literature. Like a culturally predominant masculinity, this text seeks power over others and to leave behind something enduring, but it asserts that scribal practices[19] are the best way to achieve those goals. The conclusion to the text clearly conveys the professional and socio-economic status of this masculinity in relation to others: "Behold, there is no scribe who lacks food, from the property of the house of the king – life, prosperity, and health" (11.1).[20] Even as this scribal masculinity appears complicitly subordinate to a culturally predominant one, it entails a high socio-economic status and professional occupation.

Scribal exercises from ancient Egypt frequently exhort the reader, who is the implied trainee, to pursue a scribal profession. But rather than comparing several professions as in "The Satire on the Trades," other examples of this motif compare only two occupations: a soldier and a scribe. In light of the well-attested importance of martial prowess for a culturally predominant masculinity, these comparisons implicitly negotiate with gendered norms to produce a scribal masculinity. While many examples of this motif exist in papyri from ancient Egypt,[21] I confine the discussion here to the most developed one in a section of Papyrus Lansing, which dates to the 20th dynasty (12th-11th c. BCE). The others are highly repetitive, and this text contains numerous relevant themes, such as the appearance of the scribe and the socio-economic status of this masculinity. The repetitiveness of these motifs in scribal training literature suggests that the authors were especially concerned to naturalize and normalize a scribal masculinity as they negotiated with a culturally predominant masculinity.

P. Lansing contains instructions of the superior Nebmare-nakht to his apprentice Wenemdiamun. Just before comparing the lot of a scribe with a soldier, the physical fitness of the scribe in training enters the gaze of the superior who critiques the trainee: "For there is not the bone of a man in you. You are tall and thin" (7.5).[22] While describing the trainee as "tall and thin" may not unambiguously invoke gendered norms, the accusation that "there is not the bone of a man in you" brings gender to the foreground.[23] The superior continues his critique: "If you lifted a load to carry it, you would stagger, your legs would tremble. You are lacking in strength; you are weak in all your limbs; you are poor in body" (7.5–8.1).[24] In a social context where a predominant masculinity required physical strength, this assessment of the trainee's physical abilities amounts to a specifically, though entirely implied, gendered criticism of him. But rather than rejecting a configuration of strength as masculine, the superior provides another way to do masculinity: "Set your sight on being a scribe; a fine profession that suits you. You call for one; a thousand answer you. You stride freely on the road. You will not be like a hired ox. You are in front of others" (8.1).[25] The claimed advantages of the scribal profession include a lack of being supervised by others (i.e., "you stride freely on the road. You will not be like a hired ox") and being in positions of dominance over others (i.e., "You call for one; a thousand answer you").[26] The gendered argument of the superior is that while the trainee lacks physical strength, the scribal profession will accomplish this same goal in other ways. This argument (re)produces a link between strength and masculinity while asserting a less-recognizable way to do masculinity.

When the superior in P. Lansing turns to compare the scribal profession with the role of a soldier, he begins with the finer things a scribe can expect: a powerful position, supervising when treasuries or granaries are opened, being trusted by the king, having a fine house, and possessing various slaves (8.8–9.2).[27] The teacher subsequently describes a profession he considers far less desirable: "Come, <let me tell> you the woes of a soldier" (9.1–5).[28] The woes are many: having numerous superiors, being forced to rise early in the morning, working into the night, constantly being hungry, and long marches with foul water to drink (9.5–10.2).[29] Moreover, the teacher asserts that a soldier's commanders tell him: "'Quick, forward, valiant soldier! Win for yourself a good name'" (10.1).[30] In this claim, the teacher acknowledges a culturally particular way of making a name: martial prowess. But he claims that contrary to what his apprentice expects, when the soldier dies, "there is none to perpetuate his name" (10.5).[31] The teacher concludes: "Be a scribe, and be spared from soldiering" (10.5).[32] More than being spared the woes of a soldier's life, the teacher provides an additional motivational element: "You call and one says: 'Here I am'" (10.5).[33] In other words, the teacher claims that a scribe can expect power over others such that when he calls, others will answer him. The teacher accepts part of a predominant cultural masculinity but reframes it for his trainee in a way that involves less-common practices.

In these Egyptian texts, accepting a thread of a culturally predominant masculinity and reframing it so that scribal activities become an equal or superior way of meeting gendered expectations produces scribal masculinity. This negotiation involves two basic dynamics: (1) rather than exercise power through martial prowess or physical fitness, the scribe accomplishes this goal through scribal activities, like writing; and (2) scribal products or implements can preserve a name for oneself independent of the production of sons. While scribal masculinity does gender differently, it (re)produces hegemonic aspects of a culturally predominant masculinity. Evidence from cultural groups more proximate to the socio-historical context in which the court tales of Daniel emerged reveal similar dynamics in the production of a scribal masculinity.

Scribes do not appear in visual sources from the Neo-Babylonian or Persian periods, but they are depicted in Neo-Assyrian wall-reliefs. These scribes occur exclusively in martial scenes depicting the aftermath of battle. A wall-relief from the central palace at Nimrud dating to the reign of Tiglath-Pileser III provides an early depiction of scribes in Neo-Assyrian iconography (fig. 6.1). This relief

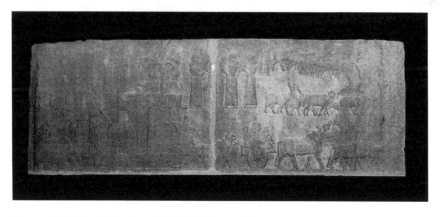

Figure 6.1 Wall relief; reign of Tiglath-Pileser III[36]
Image is © The Trustees of the British Museum. All rights reserved.

depicts two beardless scribes, who stand attentively as they take orders from an official outside a conquered city.[34] Several factors convey that the battle for this city is over: there are no longer any inhabitants in the city walls, the battering rams at the base of the walls are unmanned, prisoners of war are being led from the city, and no soldiers are assaulting the city. Accordingly, while the scribes appear in a scene depicting the aftermath of battle, it remains a context connected to warfare. This visual context is crucial because the battlefield was a primary arena on which a predominant masculinity was contested and produced.[35] In this image, the officer directing the scribes has a more stereotypical martial implement at his side (i.e., a sword). But the scribes also have their own martial implements, namely scribal instruments, including a tablet, a scroll, a stylus, and a pen. Unlike soldiers and officials who enter a martial scene through engaging in acts of war with instruments of war, scribes enter as subjects through engaging in scribal activities with their own unique tools for war.

Numerous wall reliefs from the northwest palace of Ashurbanipal depict scribes in a similar visual context. As an illustrative example, I discuss one of these reliefs, which was located in room F of the palace (fig. 6.2). This image is split into two main registers. The upper register depicts an ongoing siege of a city whereas the lower register shows the aftermath. In this respect, the relief depicts both the active assault against the city as well as its aftermath. In the upper register, soldiers scale the city walls while others assault the walls from below. Enemy

Figure 6.2 Wall relief; northwest palace of Ashurbanipal[38]
Image is © The Trustees of the British Museum. All rights reserved.

soldiers fall from the walls while others float in the river below. The lower register depicts captives and goods from the defeated city processing toward the king, who sits on top of the large horse just outside the image. The scribes are located in the top portion of this lower register in front of the king. These two scribes, who are counting the captives, stand at the front of the procession. Accordingly, they remain connected to a martial scene but exist on the periphery of the battle itself, a pattern that holds in numerous other examples of Neo-Assyrian marital images.[37]

In these reliefs, unlike the Assyrian soldiers and officials, who almost always appear with a martial implement (e.g., spear, sword, dagger, shield, bow), scribes never appear with these tools of war. But neither are the scribes empty-handed. Scribal implements are their tools of war. The most common configuration of scribes depicts one with a tablet and the other with a scroll (e.g., fig. 6.1). But there are a few instances of both scribes with tablets (e.g., fig. 6.2).[39] While the scribal pair usually consists of one bearded scribe and one non-bearded scribe (e.g., fig. 6.2), examples exist of two bearded scribes[40] and two non-bearded scribes (e.g., fig. 6.1). The most common configuration of a bearded and non-bearded scribe typically depicts the bearded one with a tablet and the non-bearded one with a scroll.[41] But instances of the reverse (i.e., bearded scribe with scroll and non-bearded scribe with tablet) also exist.[42] These variations complicate any conclusions about the significance of scribes with a beard and those that lack a beard. But some consistency clearly emerges: scribes enter a martial image through scribal activity and implements alongside the soldiers who enter through acts of warfare and martial implements.

The masculinity of scribes in Neo-Assyrian wall-reliefs clearly departs from a culturally predominant one. Scribes are always on the periphery of battle, appearing only in scenes depicting the aftermath of the battle. Moreover, soldiers vastly outnumber scribes, a point that is especially clear in fig. 6.2. In most cases, scribes are easy to miss amidst the chaotic battle and rhythmic procession of captives. Julian Reade even suggests that "these scribes do not seem particularly important individuals . . . they are merely *ṭupšarrē* [scribes]."[43] While Reade's observation presents a marked contrast with the self-aggrandizing Egyptian sources, it is noteworthy that scribes appear at all in these images. Scribal activities may not have been a culturally typical way of doing masculinity in a martial context, but they remained a way, one that enabled them to emerge as masculine in the scene. Scribes also had a part to play in producing masculinity on the battlefield.

The "Words of Ahikar" contain additional evidence for the construction of a scribal masculinity in an ancient Near Eastern context. Though the narrative mentions the Neo-Assyrian kings Sennacherib and Esarhaddon, it was likely composed later. The earliest manuscript is in Aramaic from a Jewish settlement at Elephantine and dated to the late fifth century BCE.[44] At a crux for one of the issues considered here, the Aramaic has not survived well. But A. Cowley suggests a compelling restoration of the lacuna in lines 3–4: ואמר אנ[ה לם בנן ל[א ועל עטתי] ומלי הוה שנחאריב מלך אתור.[45] In line three, Cowley restores the preposition על on the basis of parallels in lines 43 and 61, both of which are better preserved.[46] The key phrase involves the preposition על with a form of the

89

verb הוה, woodenly translated as "to be upon." Cowley suggests the phrase means "to rely upon," which seems intended even if it might not be an idiom, and offers this translation: "I indeed had no sons and on my counsel and words Sennacherib king of Assyria used to rely."[47] Following this translation, Ahikar seeks to enhance his credibility as a royal official: lacking sons, Ahikar would be inclined to advance the king's own interests rather than his own in that hope that the king would reward him.[48] In this way, Ahikar implicitly acknowledges his departure from an aspect of a culturally predominant masculinity (i.e., that he produce sons) while putting forward another practice as compensatory (i.e., loyal and faithful service in offering counsel as an official). J. M. Lindenberger's translation makes this implied exchange more explicit with a disjunctive conjunction: "'I] may not have any sons, *but* Sennacherib, king of Assyria, relies [on my counsel] and advice.'"[49] Ahikar's adoption of his nephew Nadin could be read as an acknowledgment that his duties as a scribal official do not fully compensate for his lack of sons. Yet assuming the proposed restoration is accurate, Ahikar positions his service as a court official as at least partially commensurate to meeting the culturally gendered expectation that he produce sons. Even as Ahikar's masculinity may not be culturally predominant, his position as the king's seal bearer reveals the extent to which he occupied a profession with a high socio-economic status in a royal hierarchy.

While it may not be surprising to find a saying in Ahikar extolling words as powerful, it reveals the process involved in constructing a scribal masculinity. Saying 16 of Ahikar reads: "For an ambush of the mouth is stronger than an ambush in battle."[50] Rather than contest the association of violence with a predominant masculinity, this saying negotiates with it in a way that preserves a link between strength and masculinity while asserting a less-common way of demonstrating strength in the cultural context. This transaction produces a masculinity that deviates from a predominant one, but that is no less motivated by a preservation of a cultural equation of masculinity with power.

A final source I will consider before turning to the Hebrew Bible is Sirach. According to Claudia Camp, Ben Sira composed the core of the book in the early second century, and his grandson translated it into Greek with a prologue around 130 BCE, placing it slightly later than Daniel.[51] But Sirach provides additional evidence for the construction of a scribal masculinity in an ancient Near Eastern context and reveals the consistency of the dynamics that can shed light on the court tales of Daniel. Moreover, even though Sirach is slightly later, it provides important evidence for this topic because it is from the larger socio-cultural group that produced the court tales of Daniel.

Camp argues that Ben Sira lived in a world in which "both money and women are overdetermined symbols of male honor, which has to do . . . with the need for external signs of control: they are the sigla of manliness."[52] While Ben Sira desired an immortal name (e.g., Sir 37:26; 38:24–39:11), the possibility of shame if he could not control a wife or his sons greatly bothered him.[53] To deal with this concern, Ben Sira turns to wisdom, producing literature, and his students. For instance, Ben Sira asserts: "Children and the building of a city establish one's name, but better than either is one who finds wisdom" (40:19).[54] In this saying, Ben Sira acknowledges a culturally predominant way of establishing one's name (i.e., the production of sons and city-building) while exchanging a practice he views as superior (i.e., wisdom). While Ben Sira's claim is not explicitly framed as dealing with gender, he negotiates with a culturally predominant masculinity to produce a scribal masculinity. A similar negotiation emerges when Ben Sira asserts that "One who is wise among his people will inherit honor, and his name will live forever" (37:26). Likewise, Ben Sira writes about a scribe:

> Many will praise his understanding; it will never be blotted out. His memory will not disappear, and his name will live through all generations. Nations will speak of his wisdom, and the congregation will proclaim his praise. If he lives long, he will leave a name greater than a thousand, and if he goes to rest, it is enough for him.
> (39:9–11)

According to Camp, there are two reasons that Ben Sira seeks to preserve his name through scribal activities rather than a culturally predominant way of producing sons:

> First, unlike women or God, they are to a large degree under the control of their producer. Second, they offer the glory of a lasting name: Ben Sira's students will carry his memory into the next generation and – the ultimate prize – his book will carry it into all eternity.[55]

In other words, because of his anxieties about having his name preserved in ways that were typical in his cultural context (i.e., a wife and male children), Ben Sira turns to scribal activities (i.e., the production of literature and the teaching of students) to preserve his name. Camp summarizes Ben Sira's response to his dilemma: "to trade penis for pen, sons for books."[56] While concisely accounting for Ben Sira's production of a scribal masculinity, describing this exchange as a "trade" should not be construed so as to suggest that Ben Sira abandons a quest for masculinity in the preservation of his name. Quite to the contrary, Ben Sira accepts a part of a culturally predominant masculinity but asserts another way to do gender, a dynamic I have described in other ancient Near Eastern examples.[57] In a rather fortuitous twist for Ben Sira, his own grandson preserves his name and his book. Apparently, Ben Sira has the best of both worlds, literature and a good grandson, to preserve his name.

As displays of knowledge and offering counsel to kings were integral to scribal masculinity, Ben Sira also reflects on the power of words. In a saying that is similar to one in Ahikar, Ben Sira asserts: "The blow of a whip raises a welt, but a blow of the tongue crushes the bones. Many have fallen by the edge of the sword, but not as many as have fallen because of the tongue" (Sir 28:17–18). Though specifically referring to slander, comparing words with the sword suggests that Ben Sira views words as powerful, and the emphasis falls on their destructive potential. As Ben Sira continues, he asserts that those who manage to avoid being the recipient of such violent and destructive words are happy (28:19–26). Comparing words with swords or whips (re)produces an equation of power with masculinity. While Ben Sira focuses on the danger of such destructive words in this verse, elsewhere he acknowledges the productive power of words: "If you blow on a spark, it will glow; if you spit on it, it will be put out; yet both come out of your mouth" (28:12). In this instance, Ben Sira argues that words coming from one's mouth can make a situation worse or better. In both cases, words are powerful, more powerful than a double-edged sword (see also 5:12–13).

Ben Sira's reflection on the conditions necessary for one to become a scribe makes the socio-economic and professional status of the scribe abundantly clear:

> The wisdom of the scribe depends on the opportunity of leisure; only the one who has little business can become wise. How can one become wise who handles the plow, and one who glories in the shaft of a goad, who drives oxen and is occupied with their work, and whose talk is about bulls?
>
> (38:24–25)

The relative social prominence of the scribe in Ben Sira's view emerges again as he describes things that are unavailable to various artisans and workers (e.g., the seal carver or the smith): "Nor do they attain eminence in the public assembly. They do not sit in the judge's seat . . . they are not found among the rulers" (38:32–33). Ben Sira claims the scribe has a different experience: "He serves among the great and appears before rulers; he travels in foreign lands" (39:5). Even as this scribal masculinity was complicitly subordinate to a culturally predominant one, it entailed a high socio-economic and professional status in the historical context.

In light of this consistent pattern in the construction of a scribal masculinity in ancient Near Eastern sources, I now consider the most culturally proximate sources for understanding the court tales of Daniel. In the Hebrew Bible, two relatively explicit statements about gender address the power of knowledge generally without a direct connection to scribalism narrowly construed (Job 38:3; 40:7). God commands Job: "Gird your loins like a warrior (אזר־נא כגבר חלציך)" (38:3; 40:7). David J. A. Clines suggests that the activity of loin-girding is generally related to "some strenuous male activity, fighting, running, travelling, or showing off."[58] Attending to the specific activities for which Job must gird his loins as a warrior provides some relatively explicit evidence about gendered norms. As Clines argues, these verses suggest that displays of strength are integral to a masculinity.[59] While the masculine contest between God and Job involves words, which could lead to the conclusion that it is about "persuasion," it is as much or more about the power of knowledge. In Job 38:3, God asks, "Who is this darkening counsel with speech lacking *knowledge* (דעת)?" After God commands Job to gird his loins, the reason is given: God will question (שאל) Job, and it will be Job's responsibility to instruct (*hiph.* of ידע) God (v. 3). God desires to test Job's knowledge more than his ability to duel with words. God's taunting commands to Job hammer the importance of knowledge in this wrestling match: "Declare it, if you are *knowledgeable* (אם־ידעת בינה)" (v. 4); "Declare it, if you *know* all of it (אם־ידעת כלה)" (v. 18). God even ridicules Job's lack of knowledge: "You *know* (ידעת) for you were born at that time" (v. 21). God's use of questions, the answers to which Job cannot know, emphasizes Job's lack of knowledge and God's own superior knowledge. While this metaphorical loin-girding is a battle that uses words, it is best described as a battle of wits.[60] In this respect, displays of knowledge clearly could be a way of doing masculinity in an ancient Israelite context. While these relatively explicit statements about gender in the Hebrew Bible lack a connection to "scribalism" narrowly construed, other examples from the Hebrew Bible reveal dynamics that are entirely consistent with the patterns sketched above.

Ezekiel 9 juxtaposes the activities of a scribe with the activities of the overseers of Jerusalem and presents important evidence about scribal masculinity in the Hebrew Bible. Yahweh instructs the scribe to move through the city and mark the heads of those whom Yahweh will spare (vv. 3–4). The overseers follow the scribe, killing those who lack the mark (vv. 5–6). Each of the destroyers holds a "weapon of destruction" (v. 1) and the scribes also have their own specific tools. Roland Boer proposes that the *hapax legomena* קסת in the phrase קסת הספר במתניו (vv. 2–3, 11) is the scribal tool or writing utensil and translates the phrase as "the scribal pen(is) on his testicles."[61] Boer's stated desire to objectify and sexualize men's bodies in texts to disempower them, just as male scholars have done to female bodies in texts, motivates this translation.[62] While some will quibble with this choice, it leads to insights about scribal masculinity. Boer suggests that the text portrays the scribe as "far more powerful than the others, for his tool is not a simple weapon of annihilation but a scribal pen(is) firmly based on his testicles. With that pen(is), he designates salvation and destruction – his dong is the key of heaven, if you will."[63] Boer may again overstate the point. Ezekiel 9 does not clearly portray the scribal tool as *more powerful than* the overseers' tools. Rather, the scribal tool has *as much power as* the tool of the overseers. Fulfilling Yahweh's commands requires both the tools of the scribe and the overseers. While other texts from the ancient Near East boast that scribal activities or tools are *superior to* or *more powerful than* others, including martial ones, Ezekiel 9 is not one of them. Despite this point of contention, Boer's conclusion that for scribes "masculinity and power are determined by one's phallic ability to write" remains compelling.[64] In Ezekiel, masculinity entails acts of power for the scribe and the overseers alike. For the scribe, power is not constituted through the sword but through a scribal activity (i.e., writing) and implement (i.e., his tool or קסת).[65] This negotiation produces a scribal masculinity easily intelligible in terms of other examples from the ancient Near East. The scribe's clothing ("linen"), which is mentioned repeatedly (9:2, 3, 11; 10:2, 6–7), suggests that the scribe has a higher socio-economic or professional status than the destroyers even though he is outnumbered six-to-one.[66]

Proverbs also describes a similar dynamic in the production of a scribal masculinity.[67] For example, Proverbs 21:22 states: "A wise man went up against a city of warriors and brought down the strength of its confidence (עיר גברים עלה חכם וירד עז מבטחה)." The saying juxtaposes a city of warriors (גברים) and a single wise man (חכם) who goes up against them. In the process, the saying inverts a cultural expectation assuming that pitting even a single warrior against several wise men would result in the warrior emerging on top. Although this saying does not explain how the wise man emerges victoriously, it imagines a situation in which a wise man has more power or strength than a city full of warriors. Given the clear importance of violence for a culturally predominant masculinity, this saying produces another masculinity by accepting a predominant cultural norm (i.e., a configuration of masculinity as entailing strength) while putting forth a less-common way of doing so (i.e., wisdom rather than swords). On the basis of examples like this one, Hilary Lipka concludes that "Proverbs presents a viable alternative for men who do not feel affinity for the hegemonic ideal."[68] Lipka's conclusion needs refinement on two points. First, the masculinity in Proverbs may be an "alternative" to a culturally predominant masculinity for those who are unable to live up to its demands regardless of whether they feel any affinity for it.[69] Second, the masculinity in Proverbs is not necessarily equal to a culturally predominant masculinity.[70] Describing it as "an alternative" is not to suggest that these masculinities are socially equal. In light of the patterns discussed above, this scribal masculinity was likely subordinate to a culturally predominant masculinity even as it involved a high socio-economic and professional status. While Lipka does not situate Proverbs in an ancient Near Eastern context, scribal masculinity in Proverbs entails a dynamic I have described in other examples from this socio-cultural milieu: a link between masculinity and power is (re)produced in arguing that wisdom is more powerful than martial prowess.

Qohelet recounts a story that reverses aspects of the previously discussed pithy saying in Proverbs even as it (re)produces similar gendered dynamics. He begins with "a small city in which there were only a few men (עיר קטנה ואנשים בה מעט)" (9:14). Against this small city, a "great king (מלך גדול)" comes and lays "great siegeworks (מצודים גדלים)." Characterizing the city as "small" with only a "few" men that faces the "great" siege works of a "great" king sets up a clear expectation of the outcome: the great king will win. Qohelet continues: "Yet a poor wise man was found in it and he himself saved the city by means of his wisdom" (v. 14). In this way, the story pits the power of wisdom against the power of the sword. While it was not clear how the wise person triumphed in Prov 21:22, Qohelet's story leaves less ambiguity: it was "by means of his wisdom (בחכמתו)" (Eccl 9:15). The story portrays wisdom as powerful as, or perhaps even more powerful than, the martial onslaught of a great king. While this outcome elevates a less-stereotypical way of achieving power or dominance (i.e., "wisdom" rather than a "sword"), it (re)produces a link between power and masculinity. Qohelet's own appraisal of this dynamic comes through as he continues: "But no one remembers this poor man"

(v. 14). While elevating wisdom, Qohelet claims that this wisdom may not lead to a socially predominant position: "Better is wisdom than might. But the wisdom of the poor is spurned and his words are not heeded . . . Better is wisdom than battle implements and yet one who sins will destroy much good" (vv. 16 and 18).

Considering these sources from the ancient Near East and the Hebrew Bible, a consistent dynamic emerges in the production of a scribal masculinity. Accepting part of a predominant masculinity while substituting a different configuration of practices produces a scribal masculinity. These practices could include various activities rooted in scribalism, such as reading and writing, displaying knowledge or wisdom, offering counsel or advice, or being a loyal official. Assessing whether the court tales of Daniel present Daniel and his colleagues as intelligible in terms of a culturally particular masculinity clearly requires moving beyond thinking about masculinity as a singular construct.[71] Before offering some conclusions concerning the court tales of Daniel in light of this argument, the relationship of this scribal masculinity to the culturally predominant one with which it negotiates needs specific attention.

Because scribal masculinity accepts basic equations that are integral to a culturally predominant masculinity while asserting less-recognizable ways of doing gender, it produces a complicitly subordinate relationship to this predominant masculinity. Indeed, that scribes assert and argue that their practices are equally valid or superior to more widespread configurations of practices in the cultural contexts suggests that their masculinity was not as idealized. Sociologist R. W. Connell describes a "complicit" relationship as one that is "constructed in ways that realize the patriarchal dividend, without the tensions or risks of being the front-line troops of patriarchy."[72] While scribal masculinity appears consistently subordinated to a culturally predominant masculinity, it would be a mistake to conclude that this relationship subverts the predominant ideal. One of the primary reasons multiple masculinities often emerge is that few are able to consistently meet a predominant norm with any sort of consistency.[73] Instead, these masculinities exist in an unequal yet mutually necessary and beneficial relationship. Moreover, while scribal masculinity may be subordinate to a culturally predominant masculinity, this conclusion is not to suggest that it lacked dominance vis-à-vis numerous other masculinities in its context. Nor is it to suggest that a scribal position entailed a low socio-economic or professional status within the cultural context. To the contrary, numerous examples considered above provide compelling evidence that scribal masculinity typically involved a relatively high-status profession in a royal hierarchy. Similarly, scribal masculinity should not be understood as any less invested in the (re)production of gendered inequality. Indeed, it is especially interested in perpetuating the association of power with masculinity. Likewise, seeking alternative ways to perpetuate one's name apart from the production of sons further marginalizes women. In this respect, these aspects of scribal masculinity are also hegemonic in the way that they (re)produce gendered inequality.

6.3 Conclusions

On the basis of the evidence presented above, I will now revisit some of my proposals about masculinity in the court tales of Daniel. The court tales of Daniel present Daniel and his colleagues in a manner that is intelligible in light of the dynamics of a scribal masculinity in the ancient Near East and the Hebrew Bible. In Dan 1, Daniel and his colleagues alike publicly display their knowledge in a way that creates social differences between them and the other males of their class. In Dan 2, Daniel's powerful knowledge in the form of dream interpretation, which was determined in consultation with his colleagues, leads to the king performing gestures of subordination before Daniel. In Dan 4, Daniel's interpretation of the king's dream is so potent that it leads to Daniel's name being memorialized in a letter sent throughout the empire. Finally, in Dan 5, Daniel's interpretation of the mysterious writing leads to his own advancement in the court, and Belshazzar is dead at the end of the story. Likewise, the court tales of Daniel imagine a situation in which Daniel's faithful service to the king, which involves interpreting the king's dream, results in his name being memorialized throughout the empire in a royal letter (ch. 4). In a similar respect, Shadrach, Meshach, and Abednego preserve names for themselves in a royal decree promulgated throughout the empire as a result of their devotion to God (ch. 3), though this clearly marks a shift in that their primary loyalty and devotion is to their God rather than the king, which is a pattern that recurs in Dan 6.[74] Daniel and his colleagues may not conform to a culturally predominant masculinity, but they (re)produce a scribal masculinity that is complicitly subordinate to it. In this respect, Daniel and his colleagues are differently masculine within the cultural context. Although it might seem that the masculinity of Daniel and his colleagues subverts gendered norms within the cultural context in a way that may appeal to modern readers, this argument suggests otherwise: their construction of a scribal masculinity remains differently invested in the (re)production of gendered inequality with similar results. Indeed, excepting the Queen's rebuke of Belshazzar in Dan 5:10–12, women are entirely absent from the court tales of Daniel, and even this one woman is nameless. This argument presents further evidence about how the court tales of Daniel are (re)producing cultural configurations of masculinity attested elsewhere in the cultural context.

Notes

1 Trans. Miriam Lichtheim, *Ancient Egyptian Literature: A Book of Readings*, vol. 2 (Berkeley: University of California Press, 1976), 176. This volume is abbreviated *AEL* in subsequent citations.
2 John J. Collins, *Daniel: A Commentary on the Book of Daniel*, Hermeneia (Minneapolis: Fortress, 1993), 138–39. For further discussion, see Chapter 4.
3 See note 5 below.
4 There are some studies of scribal masculinity in the Hebrew Bible that I discuss below, including Roland Boer, "Too Many Dicks at the Writing Desk, or How to Organise a

Prophetic Sausage Fest," *Theology and Sexuality* 16 (2010): 95–108; Hilary Lipka, "Masculinities in Proverbs: An Alternative to the Hegemonic Ideal," in *Biblical Masculinities Foregrounded*, eds. Ovidiu Creangă and Peter-Ben Smit, Hebrew Bible Monographs 62 (Sheffield: Sheffield Phoenix, 2014), 86–103. Boer's article was republished as the fifth chapter in Roland Boer, *The Earthy Nature of the Bible: Fleshly Readings of Sex, Masculinity, and Carnality* (New York: Palgrave Macmillan, 2012). Scribal masculinity also emerges in a recent study of Ben Sira. See Claudia V. Camp, *Ben Sira and the Men Who Handle Books: Gender and the Rise of Canon-Consciousness*, Hebrew Bible Monographs 50 (Sheffield: Sheffield Phoenix, 2013). None of these scholars situate their arguments in relation to an ancient Near Eastern context.

5 Christopher A. Rollston, *Writing and Literacy in the World of Ancient Israel: Epigraphic Evidence from the Iron Age*, ABS 11 (Atlanta: Society of Biblical Literature, 2010), 126; Karel van der Toorn, *Scribal Culture and the Making of the Hebrew Bible* (Cambridge: Harvard University Press, 2007), 55; David M. Carr, *Writing on the Tablet of the Heart: Origins of Scripture and Literature* (Oxford: Oxford University Press, 2005), 11–12; Dominique Charpin, *Reading and Writing in Babylon*, trans. Jean Marie Todd (Cambridge, MA: Harvard University Press, 2010), 63–64; Edward F. Wente, "The Scribes of Ancient Egypt," in *Civilizations of the Ancient Near East*, ed. Jack Sasson et al., vol. IV (New York: Charles Scribner's Sons, 1995), 2214–2215; Laurie E. Pearce, "The Scribes and Schools of Ancient Mesopotamia," in Sasson, *Civilizations of the Ancient Near East*, 2265–66. For a discussion of evidence for literate women from New Kingdom Egypt, see Betsy Bryan, "Evidence for Female Literacy from Theban Tombs of the New Kingdom," *Bulletin of the Egyptological Seminar* 6 (1985): 17–32. Based on the presence of a scribal palette under the chairs of five women, Bryan suggests there were some literate women in the period of the New Kingdom. But her conclusion is tempered in the acknowledgment that the scribal palette is primarily a symbol of elite status and does not permit any conclusions about the profession of the person with whom it is associated (24). For a summary of evidence from ancient Mesopotamia about female scribes that concludes that the scribal profession was overwhelmingly male, see Rivkah Harris, "The Female 'Sage' in Mesopotamian Literature (With an Appendix on Egypt)," in *The Sage in Israel and the Ancient Near East*, eds. John G. Gammie and Leo G. Perdue (Winona Lake, IN: Eisenbrauns, 1990), 3–18. On the topic of wise women in ancient Israel, see Claudia V. Camp, "The Female Sage in Ancient Israel and in the Biblical Wisdom Literature," in Gammie and Perdue, *The Sage*, 185–204.

6 Trans. *AEL* 2:176. Cf. "In Praise of Learned Scribes," trans. John A. Wilson (*ANET*, 431–432).

7 *AEL* 2:176.

8 For a discussion of this point, see the analysis in Chapter 5 of a predominant masculinity in the socio-historical context of the court tales of Daniel.

9 Carr, *Writing on the Tablet of the Heart*, 65–66; Toorn, *Scribal Culture*, 67.

10 *AEL* 2:176

11 Ibid.

12 *AEL* 2:177. Emphasis is mine.

13 Quotations and page references come from trans. John A. Wilson (*ANET*, 432–434).

14 Ibid., 432–433.

15 Ibid., 433.

16 Ibid., 433. The same phrasing is used for both.

17 Ibid., 434.

18 Ibid.

19 "The Satire on the Trades" generally omits specific scribal practices other than writing and contains only general exhortations to "be a scribe." The vagueness of this phrase

"scribal practices," which could include any number of things, seeks to avoid going beyond the clear textual claims.
20 Ibid.
21 Similar material can be found in P. Anastasi III 5.5–6.10; P. Anastasi IV 9.4–10.1; P. Anastasi V 10.3–11.1; P. Sallier I 3.5–11; P. Turin C 1.1–2.2. For translations, see Richard A. Caminos, *Late-Egyptian Miscellanies* (London: Oxford University Press, 1954).
22 *AEL* 2:171 See also Caminos, *Late-Egyptian Miscellanies*, 395–400.
23 While some scribes in Egyptian visual sources are lean, many are depicted as pudgy to varying degrees, with noticeable skin folds above the stomach. See, for example, *ANEP* fg. 230. For side-by-side examples of a pudgier and leaner scribe, see Christiane Ziegler, *Les Statues Égyptiennes de l'Ancien Empire* (Paris: Réunion des Musées Nationaux, 1997), 36–37.
24 *AEL* 2:171.
25 Ibid.
26 Visual depictions of scribes often locate them in similar positions of prominence, especially in supervising a variety of agricultural or martial activities. See Patrizia Piacentini, "Scribes," in *OEAE* 3:190. For some examples, see *ANEP* fgs. 3, 133, and 231.
27 For a trans., see *AEL* 2:171. See also Caminos, *Late-Egyptian Miscellanies*, 400–401.
28 *AEL* 2:172.
29 For a trans., see ibid.
30 Ibid.
31 Ibid.
32 Ibid.
33 Ibid.
34 Though the Neo-Assyrians made use of eunuchs in various ways, beardlessness alone cannot be taken as evidence that these scribes were eunuchs. See Jacob L. Wright, and Michael J. Chan, "King and Eunuch: Isaiah 56:1–8 in Light of Honorific Burial Practices," *JBL* 131 (2012): 104–5.
35 See Chapter 5's discussion of Cynthia R. Chapman, *The Gendered Language of Warfare in the Israelite-Assyrian Encounter*, HSM 62 (Winona Lake, IN: Eisenbrauns, 2004).
36 Image is © The Trustees of the British Museum. All rights reserved. See also Richard David Barnett, *The Sculptures of Aššur-Nasir-Apli II, 883–859 B.C., Tiglath-Pileser III, 745–727 B.C. [and] Esarhaddon, 681–669 B.C., from the Central and South-West Palaces at Nimrud* (London: British Museum, 1962), pgs. III and V. Cf. ANEP pl. 367; Paul Collins, Lisa Baylis, and Sandra Marshall, *Assyrian Palace Sculptures* (Austin: University of Texas Press, 2009), 69.
37 Scribes are similarly located in room M from the northwest palace of Ashurbanipal. In the upper register of slabs 12–13, the Assyrian army surrounds a city while the lower register depicts the aftermath in which captives and goods are processed towards the king. Two scribes stand opposite a pile of the severed heads and martial implements of those killed. A similar example from the northwest palace of Ashurbanipal is room V¹/T¹ slabs A and B. The scene is highly fragmentary and most of the originals are lost, which leaves only line drawings for analysis. Some battle or conflict is suggested in the upper-left hand corner because various soldiers (charioteer, horseman, and foot-soldiers) face the fragmentary edge of the relief with bows drawn. As in other scenes, two scribes face a group of captives led by Assyrian soldiers, some of whom hold severed heads. Again, the scribes are located in registers after the battle is over. For line drawings of the now lost originals, see Barnett, *Sculptures from the North*, plate LXVII. Numerous additional examples that follow this pattern can be found in the southwest palace of Sennacherib at Nineveh. Plates referenced are in Richard David Barnett, *Sculptures from the Southwest Palace of Sennacherib at Nineveh* (London: British Museum, 1998). See Room V, slab 7 (plate 56); Court VI, slab 11 (Plate 83);

Room VII, s 14 (plate 132); Room X, s 11 (plate 143); Room XIV, s 13 (plate 174); Room XVII, s? (plate 186); Court XIX, s 19 (plate 195); Court XIX, s 11 (plate 213); Court XIX, fragment (plate 222); Room XXVIII, s 6 (plate 245); Room XXVIII, s 9–10 (plate 252); Room XXXVIII s 15 (plate 363); Room LI, s? (plate 426).

38 Image is © The Trustees of the British Museum. All rights reserved. See also Barnett, *Sculptures From the North Palace of Ashurbanipal at Nineveh (668–627 B.C.)*, plate XVII.
39 See also Barnett, *Sculptures from the Southwest Palace of Sennacherib at Nineveh*, plate 222. This image is a fragment from court XIX.
40 Ibid., plate 174.
41 From the southwest palace of Sennacherib at Nineveh, see (plate numbers are from Barnett, *Sculptures from the Southwest Palace of Sennacherib*) Court VI, slab 11 (Plate 83); Room VII, s 14 (plate 132); Room X, s 11 (plate 143); Court XIX, s 19 (plate 195); Court XIX, s 11 (plate 213); Room XXVIII, s 6 (plate 245); Room XXVIII, s 9 (plate 252); Room XXXVIII, s 15 (plate 363).
42 From the southwest palace of Sennacherib at Nineveh, see (plate numbers are from Barnett, *Sculptures from the Southwest Palace of Sennacherib*) room V, slab 7 (plate 56); Room XVII, s? (plate 186); Room XXVIII, s 9 (plate 252).
43 Julian E. Reade, "The Neo-Assyrian Court and Army: Evidence from Sculptures," *Iraq* 34 (1972): 97.
44 J. M. Lindenberger, "Ahikar: A New Translation and Introduction," in *The Old Testament Pseudepigrapha*, ed. James H. Charlesworth, vol. 2 (Garden City, NY: Doubleday, 1985), 479–82.
45 A. E. Cowley, *Aramaic Papyri of the Fifth Century* (Oxford: Clarendon, 1923), 212.
46 Ibid., 227 and 231–232.
47 Ibid., 220.
48 My thanks to Joel M. LeMon for suggesting this possibility (personal conversation). On these dynamics for a childless official like a eunuch, see Wright and Chan, "King and Eunuch."
49 Lindenberger, "Ahikar: A New Translation and Introduction," 2:494. Emphasis mine.
50 Translation mine. James Lindenberger transcribes the Aramaic as follows: "כי עזיז ארב פם מן ארב מלחם." Even though Lindenberger acknowledges that ארב is more literally "ambush" and that עזיז means "strong," he nevertheless translates the saying as: "For the treachery of the mouth is more dangerous than the treachery of battle." See James M. Lindenberger, *The Aramaic Proverbs of Ahiqar* (Baltimore: Johns Hopkins University Press, 1983), 77–78. H. L. Ginsberg, however, reads ארב rather than ארב, translating the line as: "The instruction of the mouth is stronger than the instruction of war" (*ANET* 428). Consulting photographs of the manuscripts proves inconclusive due to the similarity of ד and ר. See E. Sachau, *Aramäische Papyrus Und Ostraka Aus Einer Jüdischen Militär-Kolonie Zu Elephantine*, vol. 2 (Leipzig: Hinrichs, 1911), tafel 45. Sachau reads ארב (163–164). Most translations follow Sachau's original proposal. For example, P. Grelot translates the relevant saying: "car une ruse de bouche est plus forte qu'une ruse de guerre." See Pierre Grelot, *Documents Araméens D'Égypte* (Paris: Les Éditions du Cerf, 1972), 436. Likewise, M. Wiegl translates the saying as, "Denn der Hinterhalt eines Mundes ist stärker als der eines Krieges," See Michael Weigl, *Die Aramäischen Achikar-Sprüche Aus Elephantine Und Die Alttestamentliche Weisheitsliteratur*, BZAW 399 (Berlin: Walter de Gruyter, 2010), 101.
51 Camp, *Ben Sira and the Men Who Handle Books*, 2–3. In this study, I adopt Camp's convention of referring to the book as Sirach and its author as Ben Sira (2, fn. 5).
52 Ibid., 80.
53 Ibid., 38–81.
54 All translations of Sirach are NRSV unless otherwise noted.
55 Camp, *Ben Sira and the Men Who Handle Books*, 154.

56 Ibid., 172.
57 While I am largely in agreement with Camp's reading of Ben Sira, my argument suggests Ben Sira is less innovative than Camp implies.
58 David J. A. Clines, "Loin-Girding and Other Male Activities in the Book of Job," 4, http://academia.edu/2469762/Loingirding_and_Other_Male_Activities_in_the_Book_of_Job.
59 Ibid., 13–14.
60 Battles of wit can also be seen in later Ahikar traditions, such as the Armenian version. For a translation of the relevant portion that depicts battles of wit and riddles between Ahikar and the king of Egypt, see F. C. Conybeare, J. Rendel Harris, and Agnes Smith Lewis, *The Story of Aḥikar From the Aramaic, Syriac, Arabic, Armenian, Ethiopic, Old Turkish, Greek and Slavonic Versions* (Cambridge: Cambridge University Press, 1913), 47–50. My thanks to Carol Newsom (personal conversation) for calling this text to my attention.
61 Boer, *The Earthy Nature of the Bible*, 60.
62 Ibid., 59.
63 Ibid., 61.
64 Ibid.
65 Other texts in the Hebrew Bible clearly represent writing and written words as so powerful that they can be a life and death matter or even sufficient to ensure the flourishing or destruction of a kingdom. See, for example, Exod 24:3–8; Deut 28:58–68; 30:1–10; Josh 1:8; 23; 1 Kgs 2:3; 2 Kgs 22; Is 30:8; 34:16; Jer 8:8; 36:1–32; 51:59–64; Ezek 3; Ezra 4–6; 2 Chr 25:4. In texts such as these, Boer correctly observes that the references to writing are autoreferential, wherein scribes reflect on the power of their own craft (64–65).
66 For additional discussion of the "class dynamics" of scribal masculinity, though without this specific suggestion about the clothing of the scribes in Ezekiel 9, see ibid., 66.
67 For a full discussion, see Lipka, "Masculinities in Proverbs."
68 Ibid., 99. In this quote, Lipka uses the term "hegemonic" to describe an idealized or widespread masculinity within a particular context. In keeping with developments in critical studies of masculinity, I prefer to describe this masculinity as a culturally predominant one. For discussion, see Chapter 3.
69 On this point, see my discussion in Chapter 3 of R. W. Connell, *Masculinities*, 2nd ed. (Berkeley: University of California Press, 2005).
70 Lipka does not clearly indicate how she understands the relationship between these two masculinities. Describing the masculinity in Proverbs as a "viable alternative" (94, 99) suggests that Lipka views them as socially equal.
71 For a more thorough consideration of the idea, see Chapter 3.
72 Connell, *Masculinities*, 79.
73 Ibid. In Connell's earlier work, this idea is framed in terms of "hegemonic ideal."
74 Though not making any explicit connections to gender, Josephus suggests a similar dynamic about the book of Daniel itself, which, he argues, functions to memorialize the names or memory of Daniel and his colleagues: "Now it is fitting to relate certain things about this man (Daniel) which one may greatly wonder at hearing, namely that all things happened to him in a marvelously fortunate way as to one of the greatest prophets, and during his lifetime he received honour and esteem from kings and people, and, since his death, his memory lives on eternally. For the books which he wrote and are left behind are still read by us even now, and we are convinced by them that Daniel spoke with God, for he was not only wont to prophesy future things, as did the other prophets, but he also fixed the time at which these would come to pass" (*Ant.* X.267 [Marcus, LCL]). This idea of literature preserving a name is clearly in agreement with the ideologies discussed above that are integral to the production of a scribal masculinity throughout the ancient Near East.

7

BEAUTY, MASCULINITY, AND THE COURT TALES OF DANIEL

7.1 Introduction

The issue of beauty appears for the first time in the court tales of Daniel when the narrator describes those whom the palace master brings from the defeated Israelites to serve in Nebuchadnezzar's court (1:4). This chapter assesses the topic of beauty and masculinity in the court tales of Daniel. I begin by analyzing previous work on the topic of beauty and masculinity in the Hebrew Bible, including two ways scholars have approached this topic: (1) cataloguing beauty as a trait of masculinity[1] and (2) assessing the social consequences of male beauty.[2] After suggesting that a cataloguing approach must lead into a consideration of the social consequences of male beauty, I will discuss evidence about the relationship of beauty to masculinity in an ancient Near Eastern context with a focus on the Persian period. In the final portion of the chapter, I will return to this topic and its relevance for the court tales of Daniel.

7.2 Approaching beauty and masculinity

As with many topics concerning masculinity in the Hebrew Bible, the relationship between beauty and masculinity first receives attention in David J. A. Clines's pioneering study of the stories about David in Samuel. Clines begins with the servant's introduction of David (1 Sam 16:18) and notes descriptions of his physical appearance (16:12; 17:42) as additional pieces of evidence as he builds his case.[3] He notes that some texts describe female characters with terms of beauty that are identical to those used for David but does not address whether this point would complicate his conclusion that beauty "is an aspect of 'real manhood' for which a man can expect praise and admiration."[4] Still, it is clear that although biblical Hebrew does not use distinct roots to differentiate male beauty from female beauty,[5] there were different notions of what constituted male beauty and female beauty in ancient Israel.[6] While Clines makes a critical contribution in putting the topic of beauty and masculinity on the scholarly agenda when analyzing gender in biblical texts, his implicit approach, which catalogs beauty as an aspect or trait of masculinity, needs refinement.

An especially strong piece of evidence in the Hebrew Bible concerning beauty and masculinity is Psalm 45. In this royal psalm, the speaker begins by praising the king as the most beautiful among humans (v. 2). The speaker subsequently associates the king's praiseworthy beauty with favor and divine blessing (v. 2). Moreover, immediately after praising the king for his beauty, the speaker focuses on the king's martial abilities (vv. 3–5), creating clear links between beauty and a masculinity involving military might.

Yet the topic of beauty and masculinity in the stories about David is more complex than in Psalm 45. The narrator mentions David's physical appearance as Samuel seeks a new king among Jesse's sons to replace Saul. Especially in light of ideas about beauty and royal rule attested in the Hebrew Bible (e.g., Ps 45) and the broader ancient Near Eastern context, it is not surprising that physical appearances would arise in this narrative.[7] Indeed, earlier in Samuel, the text specifically notes Saul's attractive appearance and height shortly before his anointing as king (9:2). The first description of David emerges after Samuel has rejected each of Jesse's sons and Jesse mentions that there is one additional son who is הקטן, which may mean "smallest" or "youngest" (16:11). The narrator further describes David as "ruddy, with beautiful eyes, and good-looking" (v. 12). Because Yahweh specifically instructed Samuel *not* to consider the height and appearance of Eliab, whom Samuel had mistakenly thought would be the next king (v. 7), the narrator's description of David's attractive appearance seems surprising at this juncture. But Yahweh's instructions to Samuel do not require the conclusion that Yahweh's choice for Saul's replacement will be unattractive. Quite to the contrary, the text explicitly states that David displays a beauty. The point is that David's beauty is not the same as Eliab's. These points suggest that the text does not envision "male beauty" as a unitary category but rather as one that might entail diverse components when interacting with other social categories like age. The features of these differing notions about beauty are difficult to determine with precision. The only feature the text mentions about Eliab's appearance is "the highness of his height (גבה קומתו)" (v. 7).[8] As noted, David is the son of Jesse who is הקטן, which may mean either "youngest" or "smallest" in size, and there is clear potential for overlap. The multiple meanings associated with הקטן complicate definitive assessments, but suggest that height differentiates the physical appearance of David from Eliab. In this case, Yahweh chooses David for reasons in addition to his beauty that differed from expectations such as those that Samuel held.

Goliath's response to David's beauty adds further complexity to this topic. After Goliath sees the attractive David, he does not praise him. Goliah "despises" David because he is a young man (נער), who is "ruddy, with a beautiful appearance (אדמני עם־יפה מראה)" (1 Sam 17:42). As with the first mention of David's beauty, Goliath's disdain suggests that attractive physical features of a male could differ in significance when interacting with other social categories like age. While Goliath's disdain for David's appearance clearly challenges simplistic acceptance of Clines's assessment about beauty and masculinity, Clines's basic insight bears merit because it remains the case that the attractive individual David manages to triumph over Goliath even if the standards associated with David's beauty are not what Goliath sought. In this respect, even as the text may broaden the range of features associated with a beautiful male, it (re)produces equations forged in other clearer instances, like Psalm 45.

Apart from the points above that add nuance to Clines's conclusion about male beauty, his approach short-circuits a thorough analysis of the textual contexts in which references to male beauty occur. Simply listing beauty as a feature of masculinity does not require substantial discussion beyond observing whether a text describes a character with terms for beauty, which can occlude points such as those suggested above. Indeed, in Clines's study of David, after cataloguing the texts that describe David's appearance, Clines presents his conclusion and finishes the discussion.[9] Similarly, in an article on Moses, after arguing unconvincingly that Moses's shining face is a beautiful face,[10] Clines ends the discussion.[11] For this study's focus on the court tales of Daniel, this approach would only require the observation that Daniel and his colleagues are described with terms of beauty (Dan 1:4). While Clines makes a needed contribution in alerting scholars to consider the role of physical appearances when addressing masculinity, the approach itself constitutes a necessary but insufficient step in addressing this topic.

Stuart Macwilliam extends the study of male beauty beyond simply cataloguing its presence.[12] Focusing on the root יפה, Macwilliam begins with Psalm 45, which he considers typical of ideologies of beauty in the Hebrew Bible: "female beauty operates as the object of male desire, whereas male beauty operates in terms of power and prestige."[13] From a queer theoretical position, Macwilliam argues that the depictions of Joseph, David, and Absalom undermine a link between male beauty and power in the Hebrew Bible.[14] I will consider the three examples Macwilliam discusses to assess his contention and to provide a basis for comparing male beauty in the court tales of Daniel with other texts from the Hebrew Bible.

Concerning David's defeat of Goliath, Macwilliam concludes that: "As a queer theorist, I should hope to be participating in the project of undermining the idealisation of masculinity as power and authoritarianism. . . . What more effective way can there be of forwarding this project than by making a pretty boy the victor?"[15] This conclusion underappreciates the textual context of the clash between David and Goliath, especially the terms on which they confront each other: acts of war in which the victor kills and decapitates the loser. The beautiful youth David succeeds precisely in the masculine arena of war.[16] Even if the text expands the portrait of what a war hero could look like, it is unclear how this text undermines an idealization of masculinity as power when it celebrates David's killing and decapitation of Goliath, which lead to David's rise as king. In discussing Joseph's beauty (Gen 39:6), Macwilliam concedes that "the narrator may well intend us to understand by it a sign of divine favor," but instead thinks that because Joseph's beauty leads to vulnerability, it "undercuts" the positive connotation of divine favor.[17] The relationship between these options need not be one undercutting the other, as Macwilliam contends. The two options may be mutually reinforcing, even partly constitutive of each other: Joseph's beauty leads to danger, but because Yahweh protects and favors him, things go well for Joseph (Gen 39:23). Additional occasions emerge for Yahweh to favor Joseph in the midst of danger, and being the recipient of that favor is advantageous for Joseph. While Macwilliam's description of Absalom as a tragic figure is compelling given the nature of Absalom's death, if Absalom's character remains a tragic one, it is precisely because things do not work out as they *should* or as one might *expect*. In other words, for Absalom's case to be tragic, it relies upon and reinforces a configuration of male beauty as power.

In short, texts in the Hebrew Bible typically associate male beauty with power even when some ambiguity about it exists and some texts envision a broader range of features that comprise male beauty. Still, Macwilliam's approach to this topic makes a critical contribution in progressing beyond simply cataloguing instances of male beauty, though that is an obvious first step. His approach asks additional questions about the representation of male characters as beautiful, such as: With what is male beauty associated? What does being beautiful enable? Is it an asset, a liability, a sign of divine favor? In raising these questions, Macwilliam's approach pushes the discussion beyond an observation that a character is beautiful to considering the social significance of that beauty.

Turning to assess the socio-historical context in which the court tales of Daniel likely emerged, some of the clearest evidence concerning male beauty and physical appearances in a Persian setting emerges in Greek sources. Based on these sources, Pierre Briant concludes that the accounts of the physical attractiveness and beauty of Persian kings in connection with their royal status are "obviously *a posteriori* justifications: a man did not become king because he was handsome or a battle-hardened lancer; it was because of his position as king that a man was automatically designated handsome and courageous."[18] Briant suggests that because royal ideology in the Persian period demanded beauty, a king would be understood as beautiful regardless of his physical appearance. Indeed, the portrayal of male beauty in various classical sources as indicative of royal, high status or otherwise powerful males contains critical evidence for assumptions about male beauty in the Persian period. I will discuss these classical sources first and subsequently show that they align with similar ideas throughout the ancient Near East, including Persian period visual sources. Xenophon's account of Cyrus introduces the topic of male beauty in a Persian context:

> We have observed in Cyrus that he held the opinion that a ruler ought to excel his subjects not only in point of being actually better than they, but that he ought also to cast a sort of spell on them. At any rate, he chose to wear the Median dress himself and persuaded his associates to adopt it; for they thought that if any one had any personal defect, that dress would help to conceal it, and that it made the wearer look very tall and very handsome. For they have shoes of such a form that without being detected the wearer can easily put something into the soles so as to make

him look taller than he is. He encouraged also the fashion of pencilling the eyes, that they might seem more lustrous than they are, and of using cosmetics to make the complexion look better than nature made it.

(*Cyr.* 8.1.40–42)[19]

In this passage, Xenophon suggests that physical appearances were so socially important that they should not be left to "nature" alone. Instead, physical beauty should be produced, assisted, and manipulated by various techniques, including clothing styles to conceal undesirable features, shoe inserts to increase one's height, and cosmetics to improve the appearance of one's face. According to Xenophon, the reason for the concern with putting on a "good face" was that it prevented those under their rule from despising them. To occupy a position of dominance in social relations with others, it was perceived as necessary to look the part as well. The ambiguity in the phrase "looking good" in English idiom would not be anachronistic for this point.[20] The phrase can be about physical appearances or social prestige, and this slippage facilitates the equation of physical attractiveness with positions of power or dominance. Xenophon's story (re)produces the idea that a more attractive male will occupy higher positions of power or social standing. This concept applies not only to the king, but also to those under him who are in positions of dominance over others in a complex social hierarchy. Male beauty entailed an extensive hierarchical scale of power wherein the better one appeared with respect to physical appearances, the higher one was assumed to rank in a social hierarchy of dominance.

A story Xenophon recounts about a procession from Cyrus's palace conveys a similar assumption about the relationship of male beauty to power:

Next after these Cyrus himself upon a chariot appeared in the gates wearing his tiara upright, a purple tunic shot with white (no one but the king may wear such a one), trousers of scarlet dye about his legs, and a mantle all of purple. . . . With him rode a charioteer, who was tall, but neither in reality nor in appearance so tall as he; at all events, Cyrus looked much taller. And when they saw him, they all prostrated themselves before him, either because some had been instructed to begin this act of homage, or because they were overcome by the splendour of his presence.

(*Cyr.* 8.3.13–14)[21]

In this instance, a particular garment reserved for Cyrus and selectively pairing[22] Cyrus with a shorter individual makes Cyrus look superior. Again, the appearance of the body is not left to "nature," but manipulated and produced such that the higher-status male is made taller than the other with whom he rides. For this image to be effective in its cultural context, it relies upon and reproduces assumptions about male beauty, height, and power. One may certainly wonder whether any individuals prostrated before Cyrus for any reason other than a direct command. But among the reasons that Xenophon includes as motivating this gesture of submission to the dominant male is the appearance of the king himself that overpowers his subjects. In this respect, Xenophon presents a situation in which others view a male's beautiful physical appearance as indicative of his superior social position and respond to that beautiful male with rituals of subordination.

Later Greek sources also attest to a cultural assumption that the appearance of a male was an indicator of social power. Diodorus recounts a story after Alexander had captured the wife and mother of Darius. Alexander reported to Darius's wife and mother that he would visit them in the morning. Diodorus reports that:

> At daybreak, the king took with him the most valued of his friends, Hephaestion, and came to the women. They both were dressed alike, but Hephaestion was taller and more handsome. Sisyngambris took him for the king and did him obeisance. As the other present made signs to her and pointed to Alexander with their hands she was embarrassed by her mistake and made a new start and did obeisance to Alexander.
> (*The Library of History* 17.37.5–6)[23]

Diodorus tells this story to praise what he considers a virtue of Alexander, showing pity to the conquered (17.38.5–6). For this study, his presentation of the social perception of male beauty is most significant. Diodorus does not state that it was *because* of his superior height and beauty that Sisyngambris mistakes Hephaestion for Alexander. But juxtaposing the description of their appearances with Sisyngamrbis's action implies a causal connection, which suggests that the story assumes a cultural understanding of male beauty in which a taller or better-looking male among two similarly adorned men was thought to hold a higher position of power. What Diodorus implies Quintus Curtius makes explicit: "Though Hephaestion was of the same age as the king, he nevertheless excelled him in bodily stature. Hence the queens, thinking that he was the king, did obeisance to him in their native fashion" (*History of Alexander* 3.12.16–17).[24] This story clearly attests to a widespread cultural belief that a better-looking male will be in a greater position of power.

While it is possible that Greek authors describing male beauty in a Persian context simply project Hellenistic ideas, a common iconographic convention in Persian period visual media attests to similar ideas about male beauty. Concerning the Behistun relief (fig. 7.1), for example, Margaret Cool Root argues that "by the device of graduated scale of height, status differentials are clearly demarcated."[25] The image depicts Darius as the tallest individual in the scene. The attendants standing behind Darius are slightly smaller than the king. The captives processing toward Darius are smaller than both Darius and the attendants. This image relies upon and (re)produces the assumption that a taller male occupies a higher position of power and dominance in social relationships. A hierarchy of scale is also evident in the original central panel of Apadana (fig 7.2).[26] The crown prince is slightly smaller than the seated king, while the attendants behind both are even smaller. Likewise, the official approaching the king is smaller than the king and

BEAUTY, MASCULINITY

Figure 7.1 Behistun relief of Darius[28]

Figure 7.2 Original central panel at Apadana[29]
Courtesy of the Oriental Institute of the University of Chicago

crown prince. While the king and crown prince are larger than the others, they are also on a raised platform, which makes them appear even larger than the others. Physical size constitutes differences in power, and a raised platform further heightens these differences. Several reliefs on doorways from the palace of Darius (e.g., fig. 7.3) rely on this same convention. In this image, the king is much taller than both of the attendants behind him. While simply depicting him in this fashion would convey his social power, having an attendant reach above the king with an arm extended emphasizes the king's height and power. This image also relies on the principle Root describes as a "graduated hierarchy of scale": a taller invidivudal occupies a higher position of power. In short, Greek sources describing Persian ideas about male beauty are not simply a mirror for Hellenistic values. Indeed, the iconographic principle of a hierarchy of scale is not a distinctively Persian convention, but rather a recurring one throughout various ancient Near Eastern cultures.[27]

The way classical sources describe Persian ideas about male beauty fit iconographic conventions in Persian period visual media as well as earlier trends in

Figure 7.3 Relief of king and two attendants[30]
Courtesy of the Oriental Institute of the University of Chicago

the ancient Near East. Likewise, other portions of the Hebrew Bible, the most proximate cultural source for understanding the court tales of Daniel, associate male beauty with power or prestige. A convergence of factors reveals that these short stories were composed and compiled in a social context that typically linked male beauty with positions of power or dominance.

7.3 Beauty and the court tales of Daniel

Even as the lack of specificity in the statements about physical appearances in the court tales of Daniel complicate this analysis, I will show that while the descriptions of a character's physical appearance foster different rhetorical ends in the stories, each (re)produces a cultural equation of male beauty with power.

The list of attributes the king desires among those who will be taken from Judah provides the first mention of beauty (Dan 1:4). In this context, the good looks of Daniel and his colleagues are part of a package that includes other clearly favorable characteristics, including their distinguished knowledge and a prestigious lineage. Yet it is specifically the king who wants them to look good as part of his effort to display his power over foreign lands and people. In this respect, their beauty involves conflicting ideas: it empowers them in a social world that disempowers them.

When Daniel requests a different diet, the physical appearances of Daniel and his colleagues becomes an issue. The palace master fears that if they eat anything less than the best, they will not look their best (1:10). Contrary to his expectations, the alternate diet results in them looking even better than the others (v. 15). In addition to the general statement that they look better than the others, the narrator states that they are "fatter of flesh" (בריאי בשׂר, v. 15), the same description used for one set of cows in Pharaoh's dream (Gen 41:2).[31] As Joseph interprets that dream, the cows "fat flesh" promises years of agricultural prosperity and well-being, which suggests that the image of Daniel and his colleagues is that they are prosperously healthy. Ordinarily, their healthy appearance would be attributable to the consumption of the choicest foods available, and their beauty would reflect positively upon the one who provides for them, the king. Yet even as the vegetables and water must come from the king, the narrative implies that their increased beauty comes from God, their true provider who protects them in this foreign context. Moreover, the narrative correlates their improved physical appearance with an increase in their knowledge, again something that God provides (Dan 1:17). Given the clear association of power with knowledge in the court tales of Daniel, this correlation (re)produces a link between looking better and increased power. As before, this dynamic introduces some ambiguity for Daniel and his colleagues because their increased knowledge and beauty may empower them, but it is in a cultural group that defeated their people and in which they are subordinated.

Concerning their improved appearance, Carol A. Newsom describes a narrative twist wherein "the traditional values are reversed, and it is ostensibly weak foods and the hidden power that they represent that make Daniel and his friends superior to those nourished from the king's table."[32] What is the significance of Newsom's point that their vegetal diet has associations with weakness with respect to their masculinity? While it may initially appear that this twist subverts gendered norms, a series of related points complicates that conclusion. Even as their improved appearance through a weak diet exposes the contingency of cultural norms, the story suggests that God can triumph on behalf of his own because he has such power that he can cause them to look better despite their weak diet. Just as Nebuchadnezzar wants his displays of his power to look as good as possible, so too does God want his displays of power to look their best. Being subjected to this power play between God and Nebuchadnezzar may entail some ambiguities for Daniel and his colleagues. But their improved physical appearance proves advantageous for them. Even as cultural expectations about diet and physical appearances may be challenged in this narrative twist, ideas about gender from the cultural context are (re)produced: the more powerful male still must look better.

Daniel's appearance comes into view again at the conclusion of Dan 5. After interpreting the writing on the wall for the king, the king clothes Daniel in purple and provides him with a gold chain for his neck (v. 29). Although the narrator does not describe Daniel as "beautiful" because of these adornments, improving Daniel's physical appearance is precisely what they accomplish. These beautifying adornments directly accompany a significant increase in rank and power for Daniel: ruling as third in the kingdom (v. 29). The narrative clearly does not suggest that because Daniel looks better, he is granted a higher position of power. However, the story (re)produces the assumption that occupying a higher position of power or dominance in social relations should be accompanied by looking better as well. In this way, the court tales of Daniel (re)produce assumptions about male beauty that equate increased beauty with increased power.

Descriptions of various kings' appearances similarly (re)produce this association between beauty and power, but for different rhetorical goals. A king's physical appearance comes into view at narrative junctures in the court tales of Daniel when a king loses control, power, or social standing. After Shadrach, Meshach, and Abednego refuse to participate in Nebuchadnezzar's ritual of subordination, the narrator reports that the king was "filled with rage and the image of his face turned (צלם אנפוהי אשתנו") (3:19). Their refusal to participate undermines a mechanism that (re)produces the king's power and it is precisely at this point that the narrator describes his appearance, though in a somewhat vague fashion: his face was turned.[33] This description of the king's appearance seems to be a negative one correlated with his loss of control amidst a furious rage, a point that becomes even stronger in considering similar phrases in Dan 5:6 and 9. When Belshazzar sees the hand write on the wall, the narrator reports that "his countenance changed (זיוהי שנוהי) and his thoughts terrified him. The joints of his hips loosened and his knees knocked, this one to that" (5:6). Concerning the king's changed countenance, Newsom writes that

> In some Aramaic and Hebrew dialects, *zîw* ["countenance"] also refers to the blossoms of flowers and as the name of a month in which flowers bloom (1 Kgs 6:1, 37). It thus suggests the normally healthy, glowing appearance of a person, with cheeks suffused with blood like the color of a flower. To say that someone's *zîw* changes is to suggest an unhealthy appearance.[34]

In this case, the king's "changed countenance" accompanies his fear, even to the point of losing control over his own body, clearly not a strong or masculine response. After initial efforts to decipher the writing fail and the situation becomes worse, the narrator again reports that "his countenance turned against him" (5:9). Just as before, a negative physical appearance corresponds with significant fear and loss of control. Similarly, in Dan 4, the king's appearance comes into view after the voice has delivered the divine judgment. As suggested previously, describing the king's appearance with animalic imagery conveys a subordinate social position, at once accompanying and producing a demotion in power and prestige. In short, a consistent pattern emerges: a negative description of the king's appearance occurs in conjunction with a loss of power or threats to it. This repetition (re)produces ideas about male beauty and power attested in the historical context of the court tales of Daniel.

The remaining instances in the court tales of Daniel referring to physical appearances do not address beauty narrowly but a related concept of bodily wholeness. After summoning Shadrach, Meshach, and Abednego from the fiery furnace, the king and his elite note that the three men lack any sort of bodily harm or disfigurement despite having thrown the three men into the fiery furnace (3:27). The story explains that their bodies lack harm because their God protected them. In this way, the narrative associates their bodily wholeness with their faithful devotion to their God. The court tales of Daniel make a similar point about Daniel himself. After Daniel emerges from the pit of lions unscathed, he tells the king that the lions did not "harm" (√ חבל) him because he was "innocent" before both his God and the king himself (Dan 6:23), a point the narrator later affirms (v. 24). Although these statements do not describe Daniel as "beautiful" or "good looking," they associate his bodily wholeness with his faithfulness. Even as these instances are slightly different from those that associate beauty with power, they participate in a similar set of ideas: the appearance of the body conveys something beyond that appearance, whether related to power or moral character.

7.4 Conclusions

The court tales of Daniel (re)produce a cultural equation of male beauty with power in two primary ways depending upon whose beauty is in view. The stories consistently associate the good looks or bodily wholeness of Daniel and his colleagues with displays of power or moral character, though this relationship is not without ambiguities for them at places. Descriptions of the physical appearance of kings also (re)produce these assumptions in a different way. Less than positive descriptions of a king's appearance come into view when his power is undermined, he is forced into a subordinate position, or he is afraid. In these ways, the text associates a loss of power with a negative physical appearance. The court tales of Daniel engage gendered assumptions to differing literary ends, sometimes bettering the image of Daniel and his colleagues while occasionally harming the image of kings. Both rely upon cultural assumptions about male beauty and power, revealing yet another way that this collection of stories (re)produces configurations of masculinity attested elsewhere in the cultural context.

Notes

1. David J. A. Clines, "David the Man: The Construction of Masculinity in the Hebrew Bible," in *Interested Parties: The Ideology of Writers and Readers of the Hebrew Bible*, 2nd ed. (Sheffield: Sheffield Academic, 2009), 212–43.
2. Stuart Macwilliam, "Ideologies of Male Beauty and the Hebrew Bible," *BibInt* 17 (2009): 265–87.
3. Clines, "David the Man," 221–22.
4. Ibid., 223.
5. The root יפה (beauty) followed by either תאר (form) or מראה (appearance) can be used for male characters like Joseph (Gen 39:6) and female characters like Rebekah (Gen 29:17) or Abigail (1 Sam 25:3). Likewise, יפה on its own can be used for male characters like Absalom (2 Sam 14:25) and female characters such as Sarah (Gen 12:14), Tamar (2 Sam 13:1), or Abishag (1 Kgs 1:3). This usage differs from conventions in English where different terms create differences between male beauty (e.g., "handsome") and female beauty (e.g., "pretty"). Some translations of the Hebrew Bible obscure this point when they use specifically gendered terminology in English for characters that are described with similar phrases. For example, when Rachel is described as יפת־תאר ויפת מראה, the NRSV translates this phrase as "graceful and beautiful" and the JPS translates the phrase as "shapely and beautiful" (Gen 29:17). But when Joseph is similarly described as יפת־תאר ויפת מראה, the NRSV translates the phrase as "handsome and good-looking" and the JPS translates the phrase as "well-built and handsome" (Gen 39:6). See also Macwilliam, "Ideologies of Male Beauty and the Hebrew Bible."
6. The point is clear in the Song of Songs when the lovers praise the beauty of each other (Song 4:1–7; 6:4–7; 7:1–9). At times, the lovers praise a part of the other's body using the same or nearly identical language, such as the eyes that each lover compares to doves (4:1; 5:12). At other points, the lovers compare the same body part to different things. For example, he compares her lips to a crimson thread (4:3) while she compares his lips to lilies (6:13). Moreover, each partner devotes attention to parts of the other's body concerning which the other partner omits mention. While the Hebrew Bible does not use distinct terminology to distinguish between male beauty and female beauty, at least in the Song of Songs the lovers have different ideas about what constitutes praiseworthy aspects of the other with respect to their physical attractiveness.
7. This issue will be considered in detail below. On the larger ancient Near East, see Irene J. Winter, "Sex, Rhetoric, and the Public Monument: The Alluring Body of Naram-Sîn of Agade," in *Sexuality in Ancient Art: Near East, Egypt, Greece, and Italy*, ed. Natalie Boymel Kampen (Cambridge: Cambridge University Press, 1996), 11–26; idem., "The Body of the Able Ruler: Toward an Understanding of the Statues of Gudea," in *On Art in the Ancient Near East: Volume II From the Third Millenium B.C.E.*, ed. Irene J. Winter (Leiden: Brill, 2010), 151–66; Zainab Bahrani, *Rituals of War: The Body and Violence in Mesopotamia* (New York: Zone Books, 2008).
8. Saul is also described as very tall, which provides another point of contrast with David (1 Sam 9:2; 10:23).
9. Clines, "David the Man," 221–23.
10. See David J. A. Clines, "Dancing and Shining at Sinai: Playing the Man in Exodus 32–34," in *Men and Masculinity in the Hebrew Bible and Beyond*, ed. Ovidiu Creangă, The Bible in the Modern World 33 (Sheffield: Sheffield Phoenix, 2010), 54–63. Clines focuses on elucidating the significance of Moses face, the skin of which is described as "shining" (√ קרן, Ex. 34:29–30). Clines's argument falters on the question of whether a "shining" face is a beautiful face. Pointing to Ps 104:15, Clines suggests that only those with surplus wealth could use oil as a cosmetic to make one's face shine and "we all know that in many cultures money is a powerful aphrodisiac" (60). Leaving aside the

problematic issue of who is included in Clines's "we," the argument stumbles because the word that the NRSV translates as "shine" in Ps 104:14 is not from the root קרן but rather from the root צהל. Likewise, the other instances Clines cites with respect to a shining face do not use the root קרן (e.g., Ps 80:4). Additionally, Clines understands the description of Moses as a child as טוב (Exod 2:1) to refer to physical beauty, which is not the only possibility. Most problematically, the argument neglects the point that Exodus gives no indication that Moses's face shines because of an oil treatment. The text claims that the skin of Moses's face was shining because he had been speaking with God.

11 Ibid., 59–62.
12 Macwilliam, "Ideologies of Male Beauty and the Hebrew Bible."
13 Ibid., 268.
14 Ibid., 285.
15 Ibid., 278.
16 For discussion of masculinity and violence in a martial context. see Chapter 5.
17 Macwilliam, "Ideologies of Male Beauty and the Hebrew Bible," 275.
18 Pierre Briant, *From Cyrus to Alexander: A History of the Persian Empire*, trans. Peter T. Daniels (Winona Lake, IN: Eisenbrauns, 2002), 225–26.
19 Trans. Walter Miller, LCL.
20 This ambiguity is not restricted to English. A similar issue is discernible in biblical Hebrew as evident in the description of Moses as "good" (טוב) in Exod 2:2, which has been understood as either a comment about his physical beauty or his character or potential for leadership. This ambiguity facilitates the association of physical attractiveness with moral worth or positions of power.
21 Trans. Miller, LCL.
22 Erving Goffman argues that some modern advertisements use a similar strategy of conveying social power and gendered differences in terms of relative physical size. See Erving Goffman, *Gendered Advertisements* (New York: Harper and Row, 1974), 28.
23 Trans. C. Bradford Welles, LCL, 223.
24 Trans. John C. Rolfe, LCL, 141.
25 Margaret Cool Root, *King and Kingship in Achaemenid Art: Essays on the Creation of an Iconography of Empire*, Acta Iranica 19 (Leiden: Brill, 1979), 194.
26 For discussion of the placement, see ibid., 88.
27 See, for instance, Gay Robins, "Some Principles of Compositional Dominance and Gender Hierarchy in Egyptian Art," *Journal of the American Research Center in Egypt* 31 (1994): 33–40. On the presentation of Naram-Sin's body as alluring and well-formed as an integral component to ideologies of royal rule that were closely intertwined with martial prowess, see Winter, "Sex, Rhetoric, and the Public Monument." Winter makes similar arguments regarding the visual appearance of the statues of Gudea. See Winter, "The Body of the Able Ruler." For related arguments regarding the "mantic body" throughout Mesopotamian thought, see Bahrani, *Rituals of War*, 76–98.
28 This image is a cropped derivative of "Stone Record at Behistun" by dynamosquito available online at https://commons.wikimedia.org/wiki/File:Stone_record_at_Behistun.jpg licensed under https://creativecommons.org/licenses/by-sa/2.0. See also Brent A. Strawn, "'A World Under Control': Isaiah 60 and the Apadana Reliefs from Persepolis," in *Approaching Yehud: New Approaches to the Study of the Persian Period*, ed. Jon L. Berquist, SemeiaSt 50 (Atlanta: Society of Biblical Literature, 2007), 114, fig. 15. Cf. Root, *King and Kingship in Achaemenid Art*, pl. 6; Briant, *From Cyrus to Alexander*, 125, fig. 8.
29 Image is Courtesy of the Oriental Institute of the University of Chicago. See also E. F. Schmidt, *Persepolis I*, OIP 68 (Chicago: University of Chicago Press, 1953), pl.

121. Cf. Root, *King and Kingship in Achaemenid Art*, pl. XVII; Briant, *From Cyrus to Alexander*, 218, fig. 20; Strawn, "'A World Under Control,'" 94, fig. 7.
30 Image is Courtesy of the Oriental Institute of the University of Chicago. See Schmidt, *Persepolis I*, pl. 138b. See also Root, *King and Kingship in Achaemenid Art*, XVa-b; Briant, *From Cyrus to Alexander*, 220, fig. 23.
31 John J. Collins, *Daniel: A Commentary on the Book of Daniel*, Hermeneia (Minneapolis: Fortress, 1993), 144; John Goldingay, *Daniel*, WBC (Dallas: Word Books, 1989), 20.
32 Carol A. Newsom, "Daniel," in *Women's Bible Commentary, Revised and Updated*, eds. Carol A. Newsom, Sharon H. Ringe, and Jacqueline E. Lapsley, 3rd ed. (Louisville: Westminster John Knox, 2012), 294.
33 I find no evidence to suggest that this phrase is an idiom for simply "being angry," especially because it would be redundant with the earlier statement that the king was "filled with rage."
34 Carol A. Newsom, *Daniel: A Commentary*, OTL (Louisville: Westminster John Knox, 2014), 169–70. Newsom even suggests translating the phrase "he became deathly pale" (170). While certainly conveying the sense of the text in a concise fashion, I have opted for a more wooden translation above.

8

DISCOURSE, MASCULINITY, AND THE COURT TALES OF DANIEL

8.1 Introduction

Daniel is the first persuasive speaker in the court tales when he persuades the palace master to allow another diet (Dan 1:8–13). But despite the use of the concept of persuasive speech in research on masculinity in the Hebrew Bible, I have already suggested a difficulty with this concept: not all speech fits a category of "persuasion" even as it may be related to gender. This chapter analyzes the role of discourse[1] in constructing masculinity in the court tales of Daniel. Given the prominence of the analytical category of persuasive speech in previous work, I will begin by assessing the limited and ambiguous evidence pertaining to the concept. I also suggest that the category is too narrow for all discourse and too broad for what it purports to cover. Building on these points, I will propose another approach to analyzing the role of all discursive activity, persuasive or otherwise, to gender. Working with this framework, I will describe how characters use discourse to do gender in the court tales of Daniel.

8.2 Beyond persuasion: problems with "persuasive speech"

Biblical scholars have used the concept of persuasive speech for analyzing masculinity in relation to David,[2] the patriarchs in Genesis,[3] Pharaoh and Moses in Exodus,[4] and Joshua.[5] As with many issues concerning masculinity in the Hebrew Bible, David J. A. Clines was the first to suggest a link between masculinity and persuasive speech: "to be master of persuasion is to have another form of power, which is not an alternative to, and far less a denatured version of, physical strength, but part of the repertoire of the powerful male."[6] Even as Clines treats persuasive speech as a discrete category, this statement moves the specific claim that persuasive speech is masculine to a general one: power is masculine while persuasion is a means to such ends. This ambiguity exists in his later study on Moses, in which Clines contends that "persuasive speech was in ancient Israel a typical mark of male behaviour" and that "to be master of persuasion is to have another form of power."[7] Concerning the story about Moses persuading God to spare the people after the incident with the calf (Exod 32:7–14), Clines writes: "Moses' masculine strength shows itself here in a speech of persuasion that has the effrontery to change the mind of *God*."[8] In these instances, it is not clear whether strength or persuasive speech should be understood as masculine.[9] This ambiguity requires assessing the pertinent evidence.

Clines relies on implicit evidence: the description of David as "intelligent of word (נבון דבר)" (1 Sam 16:18) and instances where David persuades others with his words (e.g., 1 Sam 17:34–36).[10] While implicit evidence throughout the Hebrew Bible might be considered, I confine this discussion to the block of literature in which the narratives about David are set: the Deuteronomistic History (DtrH). Working with the criteria proposed in Chapter 2 for analyzing implicit evidence to advance claims about gender (relative consistency, repetition, and ideology), the depiction of numerous male characters meet these criteria. Moses, Joshua, Samuel, and Solomon deliver the "end-of-era reflections," a key piece of evidence for the unity of DtrH.[11] Likewise, prophets in the DtrH are typically male (e.g., Samuel, Nathan, Elijah, Elisha, and Isaiah). But the DtrH mentions some female prophets (Deborah in Judg 4 and Huldah in 2 Kgs 22), and women speak persuasively throughout the DtrH (Rahab in Josh 2, Abigail in 1 Sam 25, the wise woman of Tekoa in 2 Sam 14, and Bathsheba in 1 Kgs 1).[12] Implicit evidence in the DtrH results in an impasse in terms of the criterion of consistency: both male and female characters speak persuasively in the DtrH.

Aware of this type of objection to his claims, Clines responds that "it is precisely because our own culture insists so strongly on defining a man as 'not a woman' that we are tempted to think that anything a woman can do cannot also be characteristically male; but that is a fallacy."[13] In other words, Clines argues that because ancient Israelite norms of masculinity were not defined in an oppositional fashion (i.e., being male = not being female),[14] the presence of persuasive female speakers would not challenge his argument. Alternatively, an explanation for this data could emerge from the idea that gendered norms do not naturally flow from particular bodies but are the result of complex and dynamic cultural processes.[15] From this perspective, one expects to find individuals departing from gendered norms, and such deviations do not always undermine the norm in question. Indeed, sociologists describe females doing masculinity,[16] and persuasive female speakers in the Hebrew Bible, like Abigail, could be described similarly if there was compelling evidence that the Hebrew Bible configures persuasive speech as masculine.[17] Alternatively, persuasive male speakers could be doing femininity. It also remains entirely possible that persuasive speech was not gendered in ancient Israelite contexts. Adjudicating between these possibilities depends on the evidence for the gendering of "persuasive speech," and the implicit evidence appears inconclusive.

A careful consideration of the single relatively explicit statement about gender in the Hebrew Bible related to this issue also results in significant difficulties: Jer 1:6.[18] When Yahweh appoints Jeremiah as a prophet, Jeremiah objects that he does not know how to speak (1:6). While Moses raises a similar objection (Exod 4:10),

Jeremiah attributes his professed lack of knowledge about speaking to his status as a נער (Jer 1:6). Jeremiah does not further explain his excuse, which suggests that he relies upon assumptions about behavior, which was either (in)appropriate or (im)possible for a נער, that were taken for granted in the cultural context. Yet the meaning of this term, which can refer to a young person (e.g., Gen 22:3) or subordinate social status more generally (e.g., Gen 22:12), is difficult to determine. Brent A. Strawn concludes that נער in Jer 1:6 is not primarily related to age but rather an appeal to his "weak and insignificant status in order to summon the Deity's compassion."[19] The two options may be more closely related than Strawn suggests if נער is a social category that is constituted through actions and *related* rather than *essential* to age. In other instances where a character or a narrator uses the term נער to explain an inability to perform an act, abundant evidence reveals that the behavior in question is part of an adult masculinity: violence, killing, or acting as king (Judg 8:20; 1 Sam 17:33, 42; 1 Kgs 3:7). While this point suggests that Jeremiah may construe the ability to speak as an age- or status-based masculine act, the possibility that he simply configures the act as appropriate to an adult or higher status individual without reference to gender cannot be excluded due to the ambiguity of that act. Indeed, the most confounding part about Jeremiah's claim is the nature of the act in question: "I do not know [how] to speak (לא־ידעתי דבר)." As the statement occurs in a dialogue, it cannot be taken literally. With the use of the root ידע (to know) rather than something like יכל (to be able), a skilled or learned speaking seems to be Jeremiah's concern. But it is not clear whether this type of speaking is "persuasive speech." Clines omits a discussion of what is included as "persuasive speech." Based on how scholars use the concept, it refers to influencing others with words.[20] Working with this broad definition of "persuasive speech," is this what Jeremiah intends? If so, it would be ironic that Jeremiah influences Yahweh through these very words.[21] Alternatively, perhaps Jeremiah claims only that he lacks knowledge of prophetic types of speaking for which the category of "persuasion" is not always fitting.[22] At most, Jeremiah's claim may configure a knowledgeable or skillful speaking as an age or status-specific masculine characteristic. But it is not even clear that this type of discourse is "persuasive speech."

With these points in mind, the Hebrew Bible may not contain sufficient or clear evidence to assess whether "persuasive speech" itself was configured as masculine activity. The number of persuasive female speakers in the Hebrew Bible renders the implicit evidence ambiguous at best, especially when construing persuasive speech as broadly as influencing others with words. Jeremiah's protest may suggest that a learned type of speaking was part of a masculinity, though the possibility that Jeremiah configures the act in question as simply adult or high-status behavior cannot be excluded. Nor is it even clear that this type of discourse is persuasive speech. In short, sustaining a narrow and specific claim that the Hebrew Bible, the most proximate cultural evidence for understanding the court tales of Daniel, configures persuasive speech as masculine encounters difficulties.[23]

While utilizing the concept of "persuasive speech" in an extended sense (i.e., that it is a means to power) for analyzing gender may still generate some insights, important issues remain. In particular, the category of persuasive speech proves too narrow for analyzing the relevance of all discourse to gender: not all discourse is oriented toward persuasion. As all discourse has the potential to be a resource for doing gender, some discursive activity would be eclipsed when using persuasive speech as the category. Moreover, the category of "persuasive speech" requires a minimal consideration of the words themselves. For instance, the topic of conversation and the ways in which people speak about it are entirely optional matters. All that must be determined is whether a speaker influences another with words and this criterion short-circuits a detailed analysis of the words while foreclosing other lines of inquiry about the words and their relevance to gender.[24] A final limiting aspect of the concept of persuasive speech is how broadly it is construed in scholarship. It would clearly be possible to delimit persuasive speech further for issues such as who speaks, to whom is one speaking, the context in which the speech occurs, the topic of the speech, and the forms of speech used. But considering these issues moves the analysis in the direction I am arguing is necessary: rather than asking whether or how "persuasive speech" is gendered in the Hebrew Bible, it would be more generative to ask, for instance, whether there are specific ways to speak, persuasively or otherwise, that are gendered.

8.3 Another approach: using discourse to do gender

Scholars widely recognize and discuss the many ways people use discourse in interactions to do gender in many modern contexts.[25] To introduce this concept to biblical scholars, I revisit C. J. Pascoe's study of masculinity in a high school setting. Pascoe argues that in the context she studied, masculinity can be thought of "as a variety of practices and discourses that can be mobilized by and applied to both boys and girls."[26] While "discourses" are "practices," distinguishing the two illumines additional ways gendered and sexualized identities were produced in interactions. One way individuals did gender through discourse was to call someone a "fag," which was "used as a weapon with which to temporarily assert one's masculinity by denying it to others."[27] In this case, the use of an explicitly gendered and sexualized term was a strategy individuals utilized to construct themselves as heterosexual and masculine. A second way that the adolescent boys used discourse to produce a gendered and sexualized self was to talk about sexual activity: "boys talking about heterosexuality are and are not talking about sex. Their talk about heterosexuality reveals less about sexual orientation and desire than it does about the centrality of the ability to exercise mastery and dominance literally or figuratively over girls' bodies."[28] In this case, talking about a particular topic (i.e., heterosexual acts) was a way that many adolescent males sought to demonstrate competence, mastery, and domination, which were crucial for masculinity in that context. By appealing to and invoking these gendered categories in discourse about a topic, the boys sought to constitute themselves as heterosexually masculine. Pascoe's work shows that focusing on the use of discourse, whether related to the use of specific terms or topics of conversations, enables the detection of additional ways that individuals do gender in interactions.

Biblical scholars have long recognized that language use can be constitutive of social differences in texts or in ancient Israel. For example, Judg 12:1–6 dramatizes how differences in the pronunciation of a word (*sh*ibboleth versus *s*ibboleth) could produce tribal differences.[29] Additionally, biblical scholars have discussed how the preservation or collapse of diphthongs can distinguish southern and northern dialects in epigraphic and biblical Hebrew.[30] These examples consider only a small portion of language use (i.e., pronunciation) with respect to producing social differences. But biblical scholars have not typically considered whether the use of discourse could be a way of doing gender in biblical literature.[31] Working from the idea that there were oral traditions or genres distinctly associated with women in ancient Israel, Athalya Brenner and Fokkelien van Dijk-Hemmes initially seek to recover texts in the Hebrew Bible that were authored by or originated from women.[32] But in light of the changes that may occur in transitions from orality to textuality, they shift their goal to detecting "traces of textualized women's traditions," for which they use the term "F voices."[33] Jacqueline Lapsley critiques a methodological problem with this approach: reconstructing women's traditions in ancient Israel relies heavily on the texts themselves, resulting in some circularity.[34] At the same time, Lapsley extends their work in a narrowly textual approach to assessing whether women's actions in Exod 1–4 reflects women's values. Rather than asking whether those textual voices trace back to women's traditions from ancient Israel, Lapsley assesses whether there are differences within the texts between values or voices associated with female characters and male characters.[35]

The primary question I am posing for assessing the relevance of discourse to gender in biblical literature is this: Is discourse used in ways that (re)produce gendered differences? The question is clearly relevant beyond the court tales of Daniel.[36] This basic question draws from sociolinguistics and discourse analysis, approaches often adopted in studies of gender in conversations among people in the modern world.[37] To address the basic question about whether discourse is used to do gender, several factors must be considered. One issue to address is speaker positions: *who* says what to *whom*? A second issue is the content or topic about which someone speaks: *what* is someone speaking about? The third issue to consider is the way or manner in which a person speaks: *how* does the person speak about the topic? The final issue is the social consequences of the speaking: *what does the speaking do*? Especially on this last point, texts may not always present evidence for each question. But the above issues introduce distinctions and categories for assessing whether characters use discourse to do gender in texts. This question integrates each issue above: who says what to whom in what ways to what end? While this approach may be easiest to adopt when studying lengthier texts that contain a larger sample size and with more numerous female characters with which to contrast the male characters (e.g., the Pentateuch or the DtrH), it can also be used in an overwhelmingly male environment like the court tales of Daniel to assess whether discourse produces differences among men.

8.4 Discourse and masculinity in the court tales of Daniel

Working with the framework presented above, this section shows how characters in the court tales of Daniel use discourse to do gender in various ways and to varying degrees. As the primary way characters use discourse to do gender in the court tales of Daniel involves making recourse to configurations of masculinity in the cultural context, I summarize the most important aspects from the outset. A culturally predominant masculinity in the socio-historical context involved three interrelated activities or threads: (1) physical violence, especially in the context of war; (2) producing sons to perpetuate the father's name; and (3) protection and provision. Displays of knowledge and loyalty or faithful service were especially important practices in producing scribal masculinity.

The interpretation of mysterious signs, either dreams or writing, is a primary discursive activity in the construction of masculinity in the court tales of Daniel. These interpretations are the way Daniel demonstrates his knowledge. These interpretations are always presented to a king, typically in the presence of others.[38] The public failures of other court officials differentiate Daniel from them and create hierarchical differences among men in terms of the ability to interpret (2:4–11; 4:3–4; 5:7–8). Moreover, as a result of his interpretations, Daniel is typically elevated to a higher position of power, though it is unclear what happens to him at the conclusion of ch. 4. Additionally, the interpretations themselves prove exceedingly powerful.[39] The successive kingdoms in Nebuchadnezzar's dream in ch. 2 appear to rise and fall as the court tales unfold. Likewise, just as Daniel interprets Nebuchadnezzar's second dream, the king experiences a subordinating sojourn, only to be reinstalled in his former position (ch. 4). Similarly, after Daniel interprets the writing on the wall to mean that the king's days are numbered, Belshazzar dies by the conclusion of the story (5:30–31). The interpretation of mysterious signs is a critical discursive activity in producing masculinity in the court tales of Daniel: they are displays of knowledge, create hierarchical differences among men, and are exceedingly powerful.

A decree is another type of discursive activity used to do gender in the court tales of Daniel (2:5, 13, 15; 3:10, 29; 4:3; 6:8–10, 13–14, 16, 27).[40] While various individuals in the court tales of Daniel refer to or use the terminology of a decree, only a king may issue one. As it seems like this type of speech depends on preexisting relationships of inequality, it appears to have little to do with their creation. But it is also the acceptance of the utterance as speech to which others must give assent that makes it a decree. This acceptance constitutes the speaker as king and those who submit to it as subordinate to him. In this sense, decrees (re)produce social inequality in the court tales. This dynamic is evident in the simplest form in Dan 4. The king decrees that all the wise men should be summoned to tell the king his interpretation (v. 3). Although all except Daniel fail, the basic terms of the decree are met, which (re)produces hierarchical relationships between the king, as one who issues a decree, and the court officials, who submit to that decree. The primary social axis along which decrees produce inequality is royal status. As a type of speech, a decree is gendered in a limited degree in the sense that it is only a king who issues one. As the highest-ranking royal male, a decree is a discursive activity integral to (re)producing his position as dominantly masculine.

The content of some of the decrees becomes a resource for doing masculinity in the court tales of Daniel with some rather subtle twists. Decrees bookend Dan 3. A herald issues the initial decree, which contains the instructions for the ritual of subordination (vv. 4–7). The threat of physical violence against others, which was one of the threads of a predominant masculinity in the socio-historical context of the court tales, implicitly makes recourse to cultural configurations of gender. In this respect, the king attempts to position himself as one who can inflict violence on others and as culturally masculine through discourse. In keeping with the strictest terms of the decree, Shadrach, Meshach, and Abed-nego are thrown into the fire. But they are not killed, which is the clear intent of the decree, and the story calls into question the king's ability to kill those he desires. The king's final decree in Dan 3 prohibits blasphemy against the God of Shadrach, Meshach, and Abed-nego (vv. 28–29). As with the decree in vv. 4–7, the content of this decree engages a thread of a culturally predominant masculinity: Nebuchadnezzar seeks to position himself as one who can *protect* the reputation or status of the *name* of the God of Shadrach, Meshach, and Abed-nego. Yet subtle narrative twists undermine the efficacy of his use of discourse to do masculinity: the decree seeks to compel obedience while celebrating an occasion on which others disobeyed a decree and prospered. Likewise, although Nebuchadnezzar seeks to position himself as one who protects the name of their God, the story shows that this God is quite capable of protecting himself and his own. Even as this story concludes with the king attempting to produce himself as masculine through this discursive activity, subtle narrative ironies undermine the effort.

The decrees in Dan 6 involve similar dynamics. Various officials attempt to use this powerful type of speech to their own ends. While they cannot establish a decree, they exercise their collective influence to convince Darius to issue one. But the outcome they seek is reversed: they are killed while Daniel lives. It is not clear whether their deceptiveness or their attempt to gain access to the power of a decree leads to this result. Either way, the narrative reinforces the idea that a decree is a powerful type of discourse reserved for a king. But in this case, Darius issues a decree that he later does not wish to apply to a particular individual. In this respect, the story portrays a decree as so powerful that it is stronger than its issuer, overpowering a king by his very own words. Darius, in other words, undoes (or over-does?) himself through his decree. Fortunately for Darius and Daniel alike, a more powerful male (i.e., Daniel's God) intervenes and protects his own even against this powerful type of speech. The final decree in Dan 6 seeks to compel others to fear and tremble before Daniel's God (v. 26), which is Darius's attempt to position himself as one who can protect the status of this deity. But the narrative has shown that Darius's decree is unnecessary to protect the reputation of Daniel's God (vv. 25–27). While this decree might have ordinarily been a strategy by which Darius produced himself as masculine through discourse, the text shows that he is in fact the one who needs protection, even from his own decree.

A confession, in which a person acknowledges what God has done, is another type of speech in the court tales of Daniel that is important for gender (2:19–23, 47; 3:28; 4:2–3, 34–37; 6:26–27). This type of speech (re)produces hierarchical relationships between the confessor and the one to whom the confession is offered. For instance, when Daniel praises God for revealing the dream and its interpretation to him, Daniel constructs himself as dependent upon and subordinate to his God. Yet being subordinate to his God is in no way "unmanly" for Daniel. Instead, adopting a subordinate position vis-à-vis his God enables him to receive the empowering knowledge of the dream and its interpretation, which are crucial for Daniel's masculinity in this chapter. In this respect, (re)producing a "proper" place in a hierarchy of masculinities, which Daniel does with this confession, is partly constitutive of his masculinity. Similarly, when Nebuchadnezzar confesses that Daniel's God is "lord of kings (מרא מלכין)," he produces himself as subordinate to Daniel's God (2:47). As with Daniel, the acceptance of a subordinate position in relation to this deity is partly constitutive of his exceedingly powerful position as king. In both cases, the connection to masculinity is that these confessions have the social effect of producing hierarchies among men.

A confession frequently functions to conclude a struggle between God and a foreign king in the court tales of Daniel. In particular, Nebuchadnezzar blesses the God of Shadrach, Meshach, and Abed-nego after he has unsuccessfully tried to kill them and God has successfully protected them from the king (3:28). In this way, the confession marks the conclusion of a struggle between God and the king wherein Nebuchadnezzar admits his defeat. The gendered aspect of this confession is in specific relation to the content of what the king confesses: the king has been unable to kill because God successfully protected his own. Both of these actions (violence and protection) were important concerns of a culturally predominant masculinity. Accepting defeat in this way does not jeopardize his position as king even as he (re)produces himself as subordinate to God with the confession. Daniel 4, itself a lengthy confession because it begins (vv. 2–3) and ends (vv. 34–37) in a confessing mode, entails a similar dynamic. The confession recounts a time when Nebuchadnezzar usurped his subordinate position to God, thinking that the magnificence of his capital city has been his own doing, which leads to him being forced into a submissive position until he accepts it and his eventual restoration as king (vv. 30–36). The confession is a discursive strategy by which the king accepts defeat and produces a hierarchical relationship between himself and God. The final confession in the court tales comes from Darius (6:26–27). Unlike Dan 3, the king and God are not necessarily working toward opposite purposes (killing versus saving the hero or heroes). They are on the same side, or at least desiring the same thing: protecting Daniel from death. Darius's confession acknowledges that Daniel's God has been successful in accomplishing what he was unable to do.

This confession answers the central narrative question of who is able to protect Daniel, a concern that is intelligible in terms of one of the threads of a culturally predominant masculinity. In this light, this confession becomes a discursive strategy by which Darius admits that there is a more masculine individual than himself and to whom Darius is subordinate. While a confession as a type of speech clearly (re)produces hierarchal relations, the content of these confessions is especially relevant to masculinity in the court tales of Daniel when they refer to configurations of masculinity attested in the socio-historical context.

Titles, such as "king" or "servant," are frequently used in discourse to (re)produce relationships of inequality in the court tales of Daniel. These titles always occur in the context of hierarchical relationships. The title that occurs most frequently is "king." The most basic use of this title is when a speaker addresses a king directly with this term. For example, when Daniel transitions to describing the king's dream, he begins: "As for you, *O King* . . . (אנתה מלכא)" (2:29; cf. 2:31, 37; 3:12, 17–18, 24; 4:22, 24, 27; 5:18; 6:7–8, 12 (2x), 13, 15, 22). Closely related to this simple use of the title "king" as a vocative are the numerous instances in which the speaker also expresses the wish that the king would "live forever (לעלמין חיי)" (2:4; 3:9; 5:10; 6:6, 21). Another variation adds "my lord" to further describe the king: "my lord, the king (אדני המלך or מראי מלכא)" (1:10; 4:21). Finally, the king is once referred to simply as "my lord (מראי)" (4:16). In each of these instances, speakers position themselves as subordinate to the king through the invocation of a term denoting rank in a royal hierarchy. In this respect, the primary axis along which the relationships are produced is royal status. Indeed, when the queen speaks to the king in Dan 5:10, she uses one of these phrases ("O King, live forever") to (re)produce her subordination to him. But that the term is not about gender alone does not mean that it is not about gender at all. As a term of royal status and rank, "king" denotes a social position as the culturally dominant male and the term (re)produces a social identity in terms of both royal status and gender. In this respect, the term is one way that characters in the court tales position the addressee as the culturally dominant male and themselves as subordinate to him.

A title that is related to "king" and that occurs repeatedly throughout the court tales of Daniel is "servant(s)" (עבד). Hebrew and other related Semitic languages use distinct terminology to differentiate between a specifically *male* servant (עבד) and a *female* servant (אמה or שפחה).[41] Even as the convention of translating עבד as "servant" avoids specificity in English (e.g., male servant or female servant), it should not obscure the extent to which this term indexes a social identity at once marked for social status (i.e., servant) and gender (i.e., male). The title "servant" can be used in a self-referential manner in the court tales. Daniel, for instance, uses this title to refer to himself and his colleagues when speaking to the palace master (1:12–13). Likewise, when speaking to the king, the wise men refer to themselves as his "servants" (2:4, 7). In these instances, speakers (re)produce an unequal relationship between themselves and the person to whom they are speaking. Moreover, the speakers seek to obtain something from the dominant person with whom they communicate: Daniel desires an alternate diet, and the wise men want to know the dream. Used self-referentially, the title "servant" is part of a request submitted from a subordinate to a superior. While the unequal relationship between them is (re)produced through using this term, it also becomes a way that the speaker attempts to exert pressure or influence on the dominant person. On two occasions, kings use the title "servant" to describe the relationship of either Daniel or his colleagues to their God (3:26; 6:20). With the term "servant," the king positions Daniel and his colleagues as subordinate to their God, a position they have embraced readily. In both cases, the term is used after Daniel and his colleagues refuse to submit to royal decrees. In this respect, the king acknowledges that he is not the most dominant male.

Another title that (re)produces hierarchical differences among men in the court tales of Daniel evokes socio-political status and ethnicity simultaneously: "exiles of Judah (בני גלותא די יהוד)" (2:25; 5:13; 6:13). On one occasion, the term "Judean" is used without reference to their socio-political status as exiles (3:12). Arioch introduces Daniel to Nebuchadnezzar as "a man from among the exiles of Judah" (2:25). This introduction aligns Arioch with Nebuchadnezzar as dominant over Daniel in socio-political and ethnic categories. When Daniel is brought before Belshazzar to interpret the writing, the king describes him as being "from the exiles of Judah" (5:13). Again, this phrase (re)produces hierarchical social differences among men in socio-political and ethnic terms. In both cases, these titles are used to suggest an unlikely source for solving the king's problem, especially when his own Babylonian wise men have failed. Daniel challenges these expectations, showing that he can do better than the Babylonians in what should be their own area of expertise. But hierarchical differences between them are (re)produced through the use of these titles. Likewise, when Shadrach, Meshach, and Abednego refused to participate in the ritual of subordination, their accusers described them as "Judean men (גברין יהודאין)" to the king (3:12). This title aligns the Chaldean accusers with the king against Shadrach, Meshach, and Abed-nego in ethnic terms. Similarly, when the conspirators describe Daniel to the king, he is presented as being "from the exiles of Judah" (6:14). Using this descriptive title for Daniel (re)produces hierarchical differences between these men in ethnic and socio-political terms.

The remaining types of speech in the court tales of Daniel that I will discuss occur only once rather than multiple times in the stories. The queen's words to Belshazzar after the other wise men have failed to read or interpret the writing are an isolated type of speech in the court tales of Daniel: advice. Initially, it appears that her words are a rebuke when she commands the king not to be troubled by his thoughts (5:10). But she does not compare his behavior with others and subsequently explains the reason for her command: Daniel will be able to read and interpret the writing (v. 11). Moreover, she concludes her speech to the king with advice to the king (v. 12). Through her words, the queen positions herself as one who can help solve rather than create a problem for the king. Yet her words pose a significant problem for the king. As discussed previously, Athalya Brenner argues that the queen's advice shows her to be more knowledgeable than the king.[42] The queen's knowledge is not the more contextually valued task of being able to read or interpret the writing, but a more basic one: she knows *about* Daniel, who possesses the knowledge and ability to address the problem. In light of the importance of knowledge for masculinity in the court tales of Daniel, it is striking that the only time a female character appears, she engages in a type of activity that is crucial for masculinity even if it is not the more situationally valued type of knowledge (interpretive prowess). Her advice has significant implications for gender in the court tales of Daniel: they contribute to a specifically gendered critique of Belshazzar, who does not know what to do.

The final instance to consider is Daniel's evaluation of Belshazzar in the form of a critique. Daniel's reading and interpretation of the writing on the wall is confined to 5:25–28. But Daniel begins with a verbal lashing that describes Nebuchadnezzar's example to set the stage for the major blow itself: Belshazzar knew about his father and failed to act rightly in accordance with that knowledge (5:22). Through critiquing the king, Daniel elevates himself to a position from which he can offer an evaluation of the king. This critique, moreover, contributes to the images of Daniel as knowledgeable and Belshazzar as foolish. In light of the gendering of knowledge in the court tales of Daniel and their socio-historical context, the critique clearly has implications for the masculinity of Daniel and Belshazzar. In other words, discourse is again used as a resource for doing gender in the court tales of Daniel.

8.5 Conclusions

Characters in the court tales of Daniel use discourse to do gender in various ways and to varying degrees. Many of these ways (e.g., the use of titles) would have been missed entirely if approached with the conceptual category of "persuasive speech" that previous scholars have used for analyzing masculinity in the Hebrew Bible. While I argued that evidence in support of a specific link between masculinity and persuasive speech is not especially forthcoming, a more important difficulty with this conceptual category is the way that it forestalls a more sustained analysis of all discourse. Indeed, spoken words that are not oriented toward persuasion may still be relevant for gender, a point that I have developed in considering the way that decrees, confessions of God's power, and interpretations of mysterious signs are crucial discursive activities in constructing masculinity in the court tales of Daniel. In this respect, attention to the various ways that characters make recourse to configurations of masculinity in the socio-historical context through discourse reveals another way that the court tales of Daniel (re)produce configurations of masculinity in the cultural context.

Notes

1 I prefer "discourse" over "speech" because the latter is easily linked with persuasive speech. As my goal is to move the analysis beyond persuasive speech, I avoid using "speech" for spoken words.

2 David J. A. Clines, "David the Man: The Construction of Masculinity in the Hebrew Bible," in *Interested Parties: The Ideology of Writers and Readers of the Hebrew Bible*, 2nd ed. (Sheffield: Sheffield Academic, 2009), 212–43.
3 Susan E. Haddox, "Favoured Sons and Subordinate Masculinities," in *Men and Masculinity in the Hebrew Bible and Beyond*, ed. Ovidiu Creangă, The Bible in the Modern World 33 (Sheffield: Sheffield Phoenix, 2010), 2–19.
4 Compare the discussions in David J. A. Clines, "Dancing and Shining at Sinai: Playing the Man in Exodus 32–34," in Creangă, *Men and Masculinity in the Hebrew Bible and Beyond*, 54–63; Brian Charles DiPalma, "De/Constructing Masculinity in Exodus 1–4," in Creangă, *Men and Masculinity in the Hebrew Bible and Beyond*, 36–53.
5 Ovidiu Creangă, "Variations on the Theme of Masculinity: Joshua's Gender In/stability in the Conquest Narrative," in Creangă, *Men and Masculinity in the Hebrew Bible and Beyond*, 83–109.
6 Clines, "David the Man," 220.
7 Clines, "Dancing and Shining at Sinai," 56.
8 Ibid.
9 As Clines introduces this ambiguity and others reproduce it in following Clines as their source, I focus on Clines's work. For instances where this ambiguity is reproduced, see Creangă, "Variations on the Theme of Masculinity." Creangă contends that "persuasion is thus part of the repertory of the hegemonic male" and that exercising power through words can exercise dominance over others just as can be done with swords (95). The issue recurs in Haddox, "Favoured Sons and Subordinate Masculinities." After stating the she will consider "wisdom and persuasiveness" as characteristics of masculinity relevant for the ancestral narratives, Haddox elaborates: "The ability to show good leadership and to persuade others to agree and conform increases a person's power and thus his masculinity" (6). Haddox's specific claim (i.e., persuasive speech is masculine) yields to a general one (i.e., power is masculine).
10 Clines, "David the Man," 219.
11 For a discussion, see Richard Nelson, "The Double Redaction of the Deuteronomistic History: The Case Is Still Compelling," *JSOT* 29 (2005): 320–321.
12 For a discussion of the few female prophets in the Hebrew Bible, which otherwise depicts prophets as male, see Susan Ackerman, "Why Is Miriam Also Among the Prophets? (And Is Zipporah among the Priests)," *JBL* 121 (2002): 47–80. For a discussion of some persuasive and wise women in the Hebrew Bible, see Linda Day, "Wisdom and the Feminine in the Hebrew Bible," in *Engaging the Bible in a Gendered World: An Introduction to Feminist Biblical Interpretation in Honor of Katherine Doob Sakenfeld*, eds. Linda Day and Carolyn Pressler (Louisville: Westminster John Knox, 2006), 114–27.
13 Clines, "David the Man," 220–1.
14 Stephen Moore suggests the precise opposite of Clines's formulation for ancient Israelite gendered norms. See Stephen D. Moore, "Final Reflections on Biblical Masculinity," in Creangă, *Men and Masculinity in the Hebrew Bible and Beyond*, 246. Indeed, Clines's assertion appears questionable in light of the discussion in Chapter 5 of texts that portray men defeated in war as women.
15 See, for example, Cecilia L. Ridgeway, *Framed by Gender: How Gender Inequality Persists in the Modern World* (New York: Oxford University Press, 2011). See also the further discussion of gender in Chapter 3 of this book.
16 C. J. Pascoe, *Dude, You're a Fag: Masculinity and Sexuality in High School* (Berkeley: University of California Press, 2007); James W. Messerschmidt, "Goodbye to the Sex-Gender Distinction, Hello to Embodied Gender: On Masculinities, Bodies, and Violence," in *Sex, Gender, and Sexuality: The New Basics: An Anthology*, eds. Abby L. Ferber, Kimberly Holcomb, and Tre Wentling (New York: Oxford University Press, 2009), 71–88.

17 In this way, the link between men and masculinity would be further separated as some biblical scholars suggest is needed. Deryn Guest, *Beyond Feminist Biblical Studies*, The Bible in the Modern World 47 (Sheffield: Sheffield Phoenix, 2012), 125; Martti Nissinen, "Biblical Masculinities: Musings on Theory and Agenda," in *Biblical Masculinities Foregrounded*, eds. Ovidiu Creangă and Peter-Ben Smit, Hebrew Bible Monographs 62 (Sheffield: Sheffield Phoenix, 2014), 276.
18 I do not consider Job 38:3 and 40:7 relevant. Each time God begins speaking to Job, he tells him to "Gird your loins like a warrior (אזר־נא כגבר חלציך)." Given the prominence of speech in God's response to Job and God's demand that Job answer him, it might seem that these relatively explicit statements about gender deal with persuasive speech. But as argued in Chapter 6, while this metaphorical male activity of loin-girding requires words, the battle is about wits rather than persuasion. Demonstrating knowledge requires words in this contest, but Job's ability to speak persuasively is not the issue.
19 Brent A. Strawn, "Jeremiah's In/Effective Plea: Another Look at נער in Jeremiah I 6," *VT* 45 (2005): 369.
20 Clines even includes David's explanation of why he did not kill Saul as an example of "persuasive speech" (2 Sam 24:10–15). See Clines, "David the Man," 219. As a clearer example, Susan Haddox notes that Abraham persuades God to change his mind regarding Sodom and Gomorrah (Gen 18:16–33). See Haddox, "Favoured Sons and Subordinate Masculinities," 7. Likewise, in a different article, Clines points to the exchange after the golden calf episode when Moses changes God's mind through words (Exod 32:11–13). See Clines, "Dancing and Shining at Sinai," 56–57. I am not suggesting that Abraham or Moses are not persuasive speakers in these cases. My point is that the concept of persuasive speech seems to be any exercising of influence over others through words regardless of other factors.
21 Strawn, "Jeremiah's In/Effective Plea," 377.
22 The difficulty with the category of "persuasion" for analyzing all prophetic speech is that even as prophets can attempt to influence others with their words, prophets do far more than persuade (e.g., Isa 6:9–10; Ezek 3:16–21). Clines argues that prophetic speech is stereotypically masculine in the Hebrew Bible. See David J. A. Clines, "He-Prophets: Masculinity as a Problem for the Hebrew Prophets and Their Interpreters," in *Sense and Sensitivity: Essays on Reading the Bible in Memory of Robert Carrol*, eds. Alastair G. Hunter and Philip R. Davies, JSOTSup 348 (Sheffield: Sheffield Academic, 2002), 311–28.
23 I am not aware of data from Persian sources that suggest a link between masculinity and "persuasive speech." The same cannot be said for Hellenistic sources, where abundant evidence for the association of "persuasive speech" with masculinity exists. But understanding persuasive speech as masculine in a Hellenistic social context presents another set of problems: persuasive speech would need to be defined in such a specific way that it would cease to be discernible in the court tales. Moreover, my primary point is that scholars need to move beyond a narrow approach to analyzing all discourse in terms of "persuasive speech."
24 Using the category of persuasive speech clearly could involve a more substantial consideration of the words themselves, but my contention is that this work is not essential for the concept. For a more helpful deployment of the concept, see Creangă, "Variations on the Theme of Masculinity."
25 For an overview of key debates about language use and gender, see Susan Ehrlich, and Miriam Meyerhoff, "Introduction: Language, Gender, and Sexuality," in *The Handbook of Language, Gender, and Sexuality*, eds. Susan Ehrlich, Miriam Meyerhoff, and Janet Holmes (Malden, MA: Wiley-Blackwell, 2014), 1–20. On the diversity of approaches to analyzing language use and gender, see Jane Sunderland and Lia

Litossetliti, "Current Research Methodologies in Gender and Language Study: Key Issues," in *Gender and Language Research Methodologies*, ed. Kate Harrington et al. (New York: Palgrave Macmillan, 2008), 1–18. On the analysis of language use in relation to historical developments and diverse trajectories of thought within feminist scholarship on gender, see Mary Bucholtz, "The Feminist Foundations of Language, Gender, and Sexuality Research," in Ehrlich, Meyerhoff, and Holmes, *The Handbook of Language, Gender, and Sexuality*, 23–47. For a discussion of how discourse appealing to widespread configurations of masculinity in an American context was part of presidential conventions, see Sheryl Cunningham et al., "Accruing Masculinity Capital: Dominant and Hegemonic Masculinities in the 2004 Political Conventions," *Men and Masculinities* 16 (2013): 499–516. For an analysis of the discursive strategies some gay men employed in a Christian religious context to respond to the stigmatization of homosexuality in ways that often (re)produced gendered inequality, see J. Edward Sumerau, "'That's What a Man Is Supposed to Do': Compensatory Manhood Acts in an LGBT Christian Church," *Gender & Society* 26 (2012): 461–87. For a discussion of the discursive strategies men employed in response to their feminization from having their hair done in a salon, see Kristen Barber, "The Well-Coiffed Man: Class, Race, and Heterosexual Masculinity in the Hair Salon," *Gender & Society* 22 (2008): 455–76.

26 Pascoe, *Dude, You're a Fag*, 9.
27 Ibid., 82.
28 Ibid., 85–86.
29 For discussions, see Robert Boling, *Judges: Introduction, Translation, and Commentary*, AB (Garden City, NY: Doubleday, 1975), 212–213; J. Alberto Soggin, *Judges: A Commentary*, trans. John Bowden, OTL (Philadelphia: The Westminster Press, 1981), 220–222; Susan Niditch, *Judges: A Commentary*, OTL (Louisville: Westminster John Knox, 2008), 137–138.
30 See, for instance, W. Randall Garr, *Dialect Geography of Syria-Palestine, 1000–586 B.C.E.* (Philadelphia: University of Pennsylvania Press, 1985), 38–39 and 233–234; Jo Ann Hackett, "Hebrew (Biblical and Epigraphic)," in *Beyond Babel: A Handbook for Biblical Hebrew and Related Languages*, eds. John Kaltner and Steven L. McKenzie, RBS 42 (Atlanta: Society of Biblical Literature, 2002), 142; Shmuel Ahituv, *Echoes From the Past: Hebrew and Cognate Inscriptions from the Biblical Period* (Jerusalem: Carta, 2008), 4. For additional discussion of possible northern features, see Gary A. Rendsburg, "A Comprehensive Guide to Israelian Hebrew: Grammar and Lexicon," *Orient* 38 (2003): 5–35. This dialectal difference in language use may illumine Amos 8:1–3. After Yahweh shows Amos a "basket" (*qayiṣ*) of summer fruit in a vision (v. 1), Yahweh explains its significance: the "end" (*haqqeṣ*) has come to Israel (v. 2). Shalom Paul explains: "Amos, therefore, while addressing his northern audience, affected their very own dialectical pronunciation in order to heighten the similarity of sounds." See Shalom M. Paul, *Amos: A Commentary on the Book of Amos*, Hermeneia (Minneapolis: Fortress, 1991), 254.
31 The possibility is raised, though not pursued, in Bruce K. Waltke, and M. O'Connor, *An Introduction to Biblical Hebrew Syntax* (Winona Lake, IN: Eisenbrauns, 1990), 3.4.f, 59.
32 Athalya Brenner, and Fokkelien van Dijk-Hemmes, *On Gendering Texts: Female and Male Voices in the Hebrew Bible* (New York: Brill, 1993).
33 Ibid., 7.
34 Jacqueline E. Lapsley, *Whispering the Word: Hearing Women's Stories in the Old Testament* (Louisville: Westminster John Knox, 2005), 130, fn. 73.
35 Ibid., 86. Lapsley may be closer to Brenner and van Dijk Hemmes than initially apparent. As one criterion for detecting an F voice, Brenner and van Dijk Hemmes propose

this criterion: "Is there in it talk of a (re)definition of reality from a female perspective, so that the story Contains defineable differences between the views of the male as against the female figures?" See *On Gendering Texts*, 106. Where Laplsey seems to part ways with Brenner and van Dijk Hemmes is that she is less optimistic about the possibility of recovering women's traditions from ancient Israel within these texts.

36 This type of framework has been profitably used in a study of Homer: Elizabeth Minchin, *Homeric Voices: Discourse, Memory, Gender* (Oxford: Oxford University Press, 2007).

37 For an introduction, see Susan A. Speer and Elizabeth Stokoe, "An Introduction to Conversation and Gender," in *Conversation and Gender*, eds. Susan A. Speer and Elizabeth Stokoe (Cambridge: Cambridge University Press, 2011), 1–28. For another discussion, see Sara Mills and Louise Mullany, *Language, Gender and Feminism: Theory, Methodology and Practice* (New York: Routledge, 2011).

38 Court officials are clearly present in Daniel 2 and 5. Their presence is not explicit in Daniel 4, but at least seems implied given that their failure is noted earlier in the chapter.

39 For additional discussion of the following points, see Chapter 4.

40 I understand a "decree" as a type of speech that seeks to compel others to conform to its terms and intends to produce behavior in the future. In addition, relevant terminology must also accompany this type of speech for it to be a decree. The terminology itself is varied, including "law" (דת, e.g., Dan 2:9), "decree" (טעם, e.g., 3:29), and "interdict" (אסר, e.g., 6:10). I exclude the watcher's judgment of Nebuchadnezzar in Daniel 4. Although common English translations (e.g., NRSV and JPS) of the relevant verses (vv. 14, 21, 28, 30) use versions of the word "decree," they obscure that different terminology is used for the watcher's judgment (root גזר with פתגם) than what is typical of decrees in the court tales (דת, טעם, and אסר). As the watcher's words are oriented toward an evaluation and condemnation of previous actions, they are better described as words of judgment.

41 For Hebrew and Semitic cognates, see BDB and HALOT on עבד, אמה, and שׁפחה. See also the entries on ʻbd₂ and ʼmh₂ in J. Hoftijzer, and K. Jongeling, *Dictionary of the North-West Semitic Inscriptions* (Leiden: Brill, 1995). For specific Aramaic examples, see Ahikar 84 and A. E. Cowley, *Aramaic Papyri of the Fifth Century* (Oxford: Clarendon, 1923), 10.10, p. 30.

42 Athalya Brenner, "Who's Afraid of Feminist Criticism? Who's Afraid of Biblical Humour? The Case of the Obtuse Foreign Ruler in the Hebrew Bible," in *A Feminist Companion to Prophets and Daniel*, ed. Athalya Brenner (Sheffield: Sheffield Academic, 2001), 228–45. Brenner clarifies that this depiction of the queen is not a positive valuation of a female character as the literary goal is to make the king look more foolish: suggesting, as the narrative does, that even a woman knows what to do in this situation is hardly a positive estimation of a female character. See Athalya Brenner, "Self-Response to 'Who's Afraid of Feminist Criticism?'" in Brenner, *A Feminist Companion to Prophets and Daniel*, 245–246.

9

ADVANCING GENDER STUDIES IN THE HEBREW BIBLE

9.1 Introduction

One goal of this study has been to advance gender studies in the Hebrew Bible in light of my arguments about masculinity in the court tales of Daniel, and this chapter addresses that goal directly. I begin with a summary of my arguments and subsequently offer an assessment of the methodological approach I adopted in this study. In the remainder of the chapter, I will discuss three further issues: (1) What happens when a textual character deviates from predominant gendered norms? (2) What are the political implications of a study of masculinity in the Hebrew Bible? (3) Where does a study of masculinity in the Hebrew Bible fit in relation to existing critical approaches?

9.2 Summary of arguments and areas for future research

Through a consideration of the socio-historical context in which the court tales of Daniel emerged, my central argument has been that the court tales of Daniel are androcentric literature beyond the obvious fact that they feature an almost exclusively all-male cast: the stories (re)produce configurations of masculinity attested in the cultural context.

Daniel and his colleagues deviate from a culturally predominant masculinity that involved three interrelated threads: (1) physical violence, especially in war; (2) producing sons to perpetuate the father's name; and (3) protecting and providing for subordinates, especially in a familial context (Chapter 5). Defeated in war and exiled to serve a foreign king, Daniel and his colleagues depart from the first thread. Lacking wives or children, they fall short of the other two. But despite their clear deviance from those aspects of a culturally predominant masculinity, I argued that they are differently masculine when considered in terms of the recurring dynamics of scribal masculinity in the ancient Near East (Chapter 6). A negotiated exchange, which accepts part of a culturally predominant masculinity but entails different practices, produces this scribal masculinity. Specifically, rather than becoming powerful through physical violence, Daniel and his colleagues display powerful knowledge. Rather than producing male children to perpetuate their names, knowledge or faithful service results in the king sending their names throughout the empire. Attention to these cultural dynamics reveals that the competition between other court officials and Daniel and his colleagues involves more than negotiations of ethnic or socio-political status. While the narratives explicitly foreground those social categories on occasion, the court tales of Daniel simultaneously negotiate cultural norms of masculinity. A scribal masculinity that illumines these dynamics was subordinate to a culturally predominant masculinity, but it was not associated with a low socio-economic or professional status. Quite to the contrary, this scribal masculinity entailed high-ranking positions in service of the king in his court. Moreover, even as this scribal masculinity was produced through a configuration of practices that differed from a culturally predominant masculinity, it was no less involved in the (re)production of gendered inequality.

When assessing the kings in the court tales of Daniel in light of configurations of gender in the cultural context, numerous things are visible. In particular, the struggles between God and the foreign kings occur along specifically gendered lines as the narratives ask who truly protects and provides for Daniel and his colleagues. While God initially failed to protect his people from the military prowess of a foreign king, he later successfully intervened on multiple occasions to protect them against the king or other court officials. Likewise, the narrative portrays God as the true provider of the exceptional knowledge of Daniel and his colleagues. When the king accepts his subordination to God, he is not presented with problems. But usurping that position, dramatized mostly clearly in Dan 4, leads to God forcing the king back into a subordinate role, conveyed partly through the animalic imagery in that context. Attentiveness to configurations of gender in the cultural context also sheds new light on the clearly critical depictions of the foreign kings, such as when Nebuchadnezzar's ritual of subordination centered around his erect statue goes awry (ch. 3) and when Belshazzar tarnishes his father's name (ch. 5). Just as with Daniel and his colleagues, the depiction of foreign kings engages and (re)produces configurations of masculinity in the cultural context.

The depiction of physical appearances and beauty in the court tales of Daniel similarly (re)produce a cultural assumption that a better-looking male will occupy a higher position of power. The stories consistently associate the positive appearance of Daniel and his colleagues with their knowledge or moral character. Conversely, negative descriptions of the king's appearance occur when his power is threatened or he is afraid. In these ways, the court tales of Daniel are intelligible in terms of and (re)producing predominant ideas about power and male beauty in the socio-historical context.

Finally, I showed how characters in the court tales of Daniel use discourse to do gender. Interpreting mysterious phenomena is the primary narrative strategy to portray Daniel as differently masculine because of his powerful knowledge. The content of some of the decrees becomes relevant to masculinity when Nebuchadnezzar (3:29) and Darius (6:26) seek to protect God's name and reputation, though subtle ironies undermined these attempts. Similarly, a king's confessions of God's power (2:47; 3:28–29; 4; 6:26–27) marks the conclusion of a struggle between the two wherein the king acknowledges his defeat and (re)produces his subordination to God, the dominant male in the stories.

An important question that emerges as result of my arguments is whether my claims about masculinity in these stories would have been intelligible to the authors or first readers of the court tales of Daniel. Clearly, the topic of masculinity never explicitly surfaces in the court tales of Daniel. But the various relatively explicit statements about gender in the Hebrew Bible suggest that the idea that what a person did in relation to various culturally particular norms could produce someone into different sex categories, which aligns with the sociological concept of gender I have utilized in this study, is not an anachronistic imposition. Indeed, even the ability of people in the modern world to describe the doing of gender in routine interactions would depend on their consciousness of gendered norms and their facility with the concept itself. Through a discussion of diverse pieces of evidence from the socio-historical context, including numerous relatively explicit statements about gender, I have described ideas about gender that would have been intelligible in that context even if the authors were not aware or conscious of them. In this respect, this study shows how the court tales of Daniel (re)produce configurations of gender from the socio-historical context even though that cultural work never rises to the foreground in the stories. Regardless of authorial intention or consciousness, I hope that scholars will no longer be able to read these stories without seeing how the characters produce masculinity in routine interactions.

The arguments in this study create space to consider several additional topics, four of which I will note specifically. First, this project shows the potential of reading any biblical text in light of cultural configurations of gender even when gender may not be an explicit topic. Such work has been pursued in biblical studies, but I have provided a thorough discussion of methodological issues associated with this mode of analysis and a systematic evaluation of the available evidence for claims scholars have made about masculinity in the Hebrew Bible and its ancient Near Eastern context. A study of masculinity in other court tales in the Hebrew Bible, Esther and the Joseph novella in particular, would extend this work. While feminist biblical scholarship has considered many issues in Esther, the topic of masculinity remains significantly underdeveloped. For instance, while Haman brags about his many sons (Esth 5:11), each of them is killed (9:7–14). Attentiveness to the importance of producing sons to perpetuate the father's name for a culturally predominant masculinity heightens the negative depiction of Haman's downfall. In the Joseph novella, displays of knowledge are especially powerful (Gen 40–41). This study provides a foundation to consider each story on their own and how they relate to each other with respect to ideas about gender.

Second, I did not discuss the apocalyptic sections of Daniel. Unlike the exceedingly knowledgeable interpreter in the court tales, the apocalyptic sections of Daniel present the protagonist as one who needs assistance interpreting his own dreams (7:15–16) or what he reads in Jeremiah (9:22). Daniel even fails to understand the significance of one of his dreams after Gabriel explains it to him (8:27).

Daniel is also afraid or alarmed as a result of what he sees (7:15, 28; 8:17, 27). At one point, Daniel even reports: "Strength did not remain in me. My vigor was turned against me toward destruction. I retained no strength" (10:8). Even as knowledge and writing remain powerful matters in the apocalyptic section of Daniel (12:1), the differently masculine Daniel of the court tales departs in some ways from this construction of gender as the book unfolds. This study provides a foundation for studying masculinity in the apocalyptic sections of Daniel and the combined product that became the book of Daniel.

Third, in considering the phenomena of scribal masculinity in the Hebrew Bible and its ancient Near Eastern context, I restricted the scope to include only those recurring dynamics that could illumine the court tales of Daniel. This work provides a point of departure for a comprehensive study of scribal masculinity in the ancient Near East that can assess whether there were differences between the ways scribes in various cultural groups in the ancient Near East negotiated predominant configurations of masculinity.

Fourth, this study has incorporated recent scholarship on masculinity that has not yet entered biblical studies. In this respect, one significant contribution of this project is the way it sketches the parameters of a culturally predominant masculinity and the ways in which a scribal masculinity could be produced in negotiation with it. This argument contributes to a fuller understanding of the multiple masculinities in the Hebrew Bible and how they are (re)produced in a variety of hierarchical relationships.

9.3 Revisiting the issues

9.3.1 A question of method: how to study gender in biblical literature?

A major task for gender studies in the Hebrew Bible is assessing how texts portray characters with respect to cultural norms of gender.[1] In Chapter 2, I discussed an approach to address the issue of how to study gender in biblical literature even when a text does not bring gender to the foreground. Working with the idea that configurations of gender change across time and cultures demands a historical approach that begins by locating the text in a socio-historical context and subsequently analyzing sources from that setting to cultivate an awareness of configurations of gender in that context. Attention should be given to sources from the cultural group that produced the text as well as other proximate cultural groups. For organizing those sources, I proposed two types of evidence: relatively explicit statements about gender and implicit depictions.

Several factors influenced my decision to begin with the court tales of Daniel and subsequently consider the historical context. First, scholarship on masculinity in the Hebrew Bible and the ancient Near East inevitably influenced my analysis of the court tales of Daniel. Beginning with a reading of the court tales of Daniel in light of categories scholars have utilized in discussing masculinity in the ancient Near East enabled me to articulate those ideas from the outset. Making these concepts explicit at the start made it easier to evaluate them in terms of the socio-historical context in which the stories emerged. Second, the sequence I adopted allowed me to assess the evidence for previous claims about gender in the ancient world in a thorough and systematic fashion. Issues of methodology have been neglected in previous scholarship, a point that became especially apparent in light of the minimal evidence supporting suggestions that persuasive speech was part of an ancient Israelite masculinity. At this stage in the development of gender studies in the Hebrew Bible and its cultural contexts, reviewing the evidence and arguments made about the data remains important. As scholarship grows on gender in the Hebrew Bible and its ancient Near Eastern context, this sort of work may become less necessary as scholarly awareness of ancient configurations of gender develops. Third, beginning with the texts showed what was at stake and what could be gained by a thorough consideration of the socio-historical context from the outset. The order of analyzing the text and sources from the socio-historical context may vary. But attentiveness to both is crucial. While my historical approach to gender in the court tales of Daniel may differ from some feminist or queer approaches that are primarily interested in the implications of biblical texts for modern readers, they are not incompatible.[2] Despite the difficulties, tentativeness, and contingency of all historical inquiry, including this one, the understanding of gender I adopted demands a historical approach.

The categories of evidence I proposed provide a heuristic way of sorting and approaching it. A relatively explicit statement about gender, which directly associates an action or characteristic with being (like) or becoming male or female, provides the most compelling evidence, though its significance is not always straightforward. For instance, the Philistines' rallying cry in 1 Sam 4:9 ("become men and engage in war") clearly equates masculinity with physical strength and war. Yet Jeremiah's resistance to Yahweh's call ("I do not know how to speak because I am only a boy") proved challenging to assess (1:6). A valuable project that would facilitate gender studies in the Hebrew Bible would be to compile all relatively explicit statements about gender in the Hebrew Bible itself as well as in texts from the ancient Near East. These statements should be organized by topic, time periods, and genres of literature. Likewise, additional studies of the construction of gender in legal material from both the Hebrew Bible and the ancient Near East will develop scholarly knowledge about gendered norms and values in ways that may provide conceptual categories for analyzing other genres (e.g., narratives).[3] For implicit statements, which provide the most abundant data, I suggested three criteria: repetition, general consistency, and ideology. Though I did not work extensively with these criteria in this study due to the short length of the court tales of Daniel, it would be worthwhile to work with and refine them in relation to a longer text with more numerous female characters (e.g., Genesis).

An important issue to clarify when studying gender in biblical literature is how a scholar understands the key term "gender." While Judith Butler has provided a productive way of studying gender for biblical scholars, I also turned to sociological studies of gender. Lacking direct access to the authors of biblical literature, biblical scholars cannot adopt sociological methods, such as participant observation or interviews. Yet sociological scholarship provides clarity on key conceptual distinctions and dynamics that may or may not be relevant in any particular instance. Moreover, responding to calls for closer work between scholars of gender inside and outside biblical studies requires conversing in scholarly concepts in the areas where such ideas were formulated and continue to be refined.[4] Clearly, biblical scholars must take care to avoid making the evidence fit concepts developed elsewhere and sociological studies of gender in the modern world cannot fill gaps in knowledge about the ancient world. But I have shown that some important concepts and distinctions from critical studies of masculinity in the modern world illumine the court tales of Daniel, including the possibility for multiple masculinities to be produced in hierarchical relationships and that deviating from a situationally predominant masculinity might not impede the (re)production of gendered inequality. For biblical scholars, shifting to study masculinit*ies* risks finding a new masculinity in each male character, reducing masculinity to everything that a male character does. To further unlink the study of men and masculinity, additional work is needed on masculinity among female characters in the Hebrew Bible as well as its ancient Near Eastern context.[5] In reading the court tales of Daniel informed by sociological scholarship on gender, I have shown that it is a generative perspective on gender for biblical scholars to adopt.

9.3.2 *What happens when a narrative character deviates from culturally predominant norms of gender?*

Working from the perspective that cultural configurations of gender are not naturally or essentially related to particular bodies, one expects to find instances of characters in texts deviating from gendered norms. This study provides a few instances to assess what happens when a character deviates from culturally predominant gendered norms.

The representation of Daniel and his colleagues presents an instance where characters clearly deviate from predominant gendered norms. Their masculinity is produced through a negotiation that accepts an equation of a predominant masculinity and (re)produces it through a different configuration of practices. Their deviations clearly show that gendered norms do not naturally or essentially flow from particular bodies. But their masculinity does not subvert gendered inequality in the cultural context because it accepts equations of a predominant masculinity without challenging those basic ideas.

The negative depictions of the physical appearance of various kings contain another example wherein a deviation from gendered norm might not undermine that norm. Less-than-positive descriptions of a king's physical appearance occur at narrative junctures when his power is undermined, he is forced into a subordinate position, or when displaying fear. The text uses a king's poor physical appearance in these cases as a rhetorical strategy of negatively characterizing him.

Accordingly, his deviation from the expectation that he should look the best as the culturally dominant male does not challenge the equation of good looks with power or prestige. While the narrative may expose that configuration of gender as a product of cultural conventions, for the rhetorical strategy to be effective, it requires and (re)produces the idea that most powerful male should look the best.

While God deviates from a thread of a culturally predominant masculinity when he fails to protect his people by placing them into the hand of a foreign king, he repeatedly intervenes in the remainder of the court tales to protect his own. This example introduces a dynamic wherein a character initially deviates from and later repeatedly conforms to a particular gendered norm. The repetitiveness of God's subsequent success in protecting his own suggests that the court tales have no interest in questioning the idea that God ought to and can protect his people. God's initial deviation exposes that gendered norm as the product of cultural processes, but the stories do not challenge that thread of a culturally predominant masculinity. Rather the stories (re)produce that thread in repeatedly showing God's ability to protect his own.

In light of these examples from the court tales of Daniel, I offer a few general parameters for assessing the implications of a character deviating from predominant configurations of gender within the cultural context. First, when deviations (re)produce an aspect of a predominant configuration of gender through different practices, they are not likely to challenge gendered inequality. Second, when a text depicts an individual departing from a gendered norm as a narrative strategy of negatively characterizing that person, the deviation may not necessarily undermine that norm. Finally, when assessing individual deviations from gendered norms at a point in the narrative, the larger context should also be considered. These parameters are not exhaustive and are only intended to be suggestive. Considering additional examples will lead to additional ways of assessing what occurs when textual characters depart from configurations of gender.

9.3.3 *Political implications of a study of masculinity in biblical literature*

My argument that the court tales of Daniel (re)produce gendered inequality in their cultural context raises an issue I identified in Chapter 2: whose interests are served by producing knowledge about masculinity in the Hebrew Bible?[6] I cannot offer an assessment of all studies of masculinity in the Hebrew Bible, each of which should be evaluated on its own terms.[7] But I will offer my thoughts about the social interests served in this study and expect that others will identify additional interests served through it.

I begin with the unavoidable and obvious answer: this study serves my interests. I am a white heterosexual male who has attended institutions of higher learning in the United States. This project represents the culmination of numerous years of study in an attempt to display knowledge sufficient to obtain an academic degree with social status that will enable me to become a credentialed biblical scholar and hopefully attain gainful employment in the field. I have sought to benefit from critical approaches to gender, including feminism and queer theory. Yet through this study, I intend to contribute to these approaches and the political movements that are integral to them in ways that may begin to challenge aspects of my own location as an interpreter. In this respect, I submit that this study serves more than my own interests, even with the potential to work against some of them by raising consciousness about several important points.

With few exceptions, biblical scholars have not noticed masculinity in these stories even as they have been concerned about social identity.[8] In this study, I have shown how the court tales of Daniel engage and (re)produce culturally particular configurations of masculinity. This part of my argument raises awareness about the extent to which these stories are androcentric, as feminist scholars have been at pains to critique in other portions of biblical literature,[9] both in the obvious ways that they focus on male characters and the less-noticed ways that they (re)produce cultural norms of masculinity. Deryn Guest cogently describes the political implications of an argument like this one: "If we hope for social and political transformation, the removal of invisibility is absolutely key."[10] Moreover, I have shown that doing gender in the court tales of Daniel occurs in everyday activities even though this work never becomes explicit. This part of my argument aligns with the key sociological idea that gender is produced in routine interactions even when individuals may not be conscious of or intend this work to occur.[11] By showing this dynamic in these ancient stories, I intend to raise consciousness about it for my readers in the hope that they will become aware of how gender happens in the course of their own everyday interactions.

Second, even as I have shown the androcentric biases of these stories, I have also argued that there is no single construction of masculinity in the Hebrew Bible. There are, rather, multiple masculinities in the Hebrew Bible, and the court tales of Daniel present a compelling example of a masculinity that was less common in the cultural context. Moreover, this study has shown that the masculinities in this collection of ancient texts were produced in relation to changing and diverse socio-historical contexts, underscoring the point that configurations of gender have not and need not always be the same. This aspect of my study impedes appeals to a construct of "biblical manhood" as part of an attempt to define modern ideas about gender. Rather than finding solid ground for such political goals in the modern world, this study suggests that those interested in such an effort will find a shifting and changing "ground."

Third, my argument draws attention to a dynamic where doing gender differently may be instrumental in (re)producing gendered inequality rather than dismantling it. I do not mean to suggest that this dynamic is unique to the court tales of Daniel.[12] A key concept from sociological research on masculinity proves insightful here: a complicit masculinity, which simultaneously deviates and benefits from a predominant configuration of masculinity.[13] Many individuals today are complacent knowing that they do not participate in predominant configurations of masculinity in the modern world. Yet they may also miss or underestimate the extent to which their own departures and their own practices may simultaneously (re)produce gendered inequality. Individuals and communities must consider the implications of this point in light of unique and diverse contexts. This argument functions to encourage reflection and awareness about this issue in considering a concrete example of it in the court tales of Daniel.

Finally, I will suggest an area related to the dynamics described above that deserves considerable reflection, both generally and in the specific example involving knowledge: biblical scholars and biblical studies, a field male scholars continue to dominate. The Society of Biblical Literature (SBL) reports that in 2004 there were 6,636 members.[14] Approximately 78 percent of those members identified as male and 22 percent as female. Prior to 2004, SBL did not keep such records about its members. The situation remains very similar over a decade later in 2015: of the 8,058 total members, approximately 76 percent reported as male and 24 percent as female. A similar portrait of biblical scholars emerges when considering presidential leadership for the SBL. Since the 1980s, the decade in which a woman became president of the SBL for the first time (Elizabeth Schüssler Fiorenza in 1987), only nine of the thirty-seven presidents have been women, amounting to approximately 24 percent.[15] Although the situation since 2010 has changed significantly, with four of six presidents being female, if including the 110 years prior to the first female president of the SBL, that percentage dwindles significantly. A recent and very thorough collection of essays on methods of interpreting the Hebrew Bible produces a similar image of biblical scholars.[16] This volume contains twenty-eight contributions, twenty-one written by men (75 percent) and seven by women (25 percent). Considering various major commentary series produces a similar image of biblical scholars. For instance, the Hermeneia commentary series currently covers twelve books from the Hebrew Bible in a total of seventeen volumes. All of the authors are male.[17] The Anchor Bible Commentary series contains fifty-three volumes covering each book of the Hebrew Bible.[18] Only one of these volumes was written by a woman, the volume on Zephaniah by Adele Berlin. Two volumes, covering Haggai and Zechariah, were co-written by Carol Meyers and Eric Meyers. Similarly, the Old Testament Library Series, which includes commentaries and other major works on the Hebrew Bible, has 64 volumes, 6 of which were written by women.[19] Finally, I know of only one introductory textbook on the literature and study of the Hebrew Bible authored by a woman.[20]

Any number of other factors need to be considered in assessing the extent to which biblical studies remains a field dominated by men, such as publications in journals, number of faculty members at various institutions, either with or without tenure, as well as students admitted into PhD programs. Feminist biblical scholars have clearly critiqued the predominance of men in biblical scholarship. In suggesting these small points of data, I add another voice to those feminist critiques of a persistent issue. Moreover, adducing such fragments of evidence that attest to the dominance of men in biblical studies does not even begin to address more difficult and important questions about the gendering of biblical scholarship. For instance, what are the predominant discursive modes of presenting knowledge, either in professional conferences or publications? How do those configurations of practice fit in relation to gendered norms and stereotypes in modern contexts? What are the valued types of knowledge and approaches to producing it in biblical scholarship? Are the answers to such questions implicitly gendered? Similarly, what are desirable qualities in a biblical scholar, and to what extent are those characteristics implicitly or explicitly gendered? Even as I have no intention of answering such difficult questions in this context, this book raises awareness about them through considering the production of gender in an ancient text. Whether answers to these problems will be found in the same text or in the broader collection of ancient texts within which it is now located remains something for future work to assess. The political contributions of this study are: (1) to raise consciousness of persistent dynamics that contribute to the (re)production of gendered inequality; (2) to draw attention to the diversity of masculinities in biblical literature; and (3) to show the androcentric biases and assumptions in a particular section of the Hebrew Bible.

9.3.4 Disciplinary fit of a study of masculinity in biblical literature

Considering the political implications of this project provides a point of departure for revisiting another issue I articulated in Chapter 2: how does a study of masculinity fit in relation to existing approaches to the topic of gender in biblical literature? To put the issue more pointedly, how do the political implications of this study promote or work against agendas in other approaches? To frame this issue, I revisit a concept Guest introduces: rather than assessing a project as "feminist" or "queer" based on the social location of the interpreter, one can approach this question in terms of what the article or book accomplishes or does.[21] Or to play on a common convention of referring to a piece of scholarship as a "work" that forces this issue: what work does this work do? Through these conceptual moves, Guest creates room for "queer straight feminists" and "profeminist gender traitors."[22] Though not without potential for criticisms based upon my described social location, I submit that this study aligns and allies with feminist and queer biblical scholarship as part of a developing area of gender studies.

While feminist biblical scholarship has become increasingly diverse in some respects,[23] a critique of the androcentrism of biblical literature and its interpreters is a point of commonality.[24] Through calling attention to the obvious point that the court tales of Daniel focus on male characters and the less-noticed ways that the stories (re)produce configurations of masculinity in their cultural context, this study aligns with a major emphasis and goal of feminist biblical scholarship. Likewise, this project raises awareness about a subtle dynamic that (re)produces gendered inequality in the context of routine interactions regardless of whether people are conscious about it or intend it to occur. This project participates in the goal of dismantling gendered inequality in the modern world by seeking to raise consciousness. These aspects of this study align with emphases and political concerns of feminist biblical scholarship.

The relationship of this project with queer biblical scholarship may initially appear less compelling in comparison with its connections to feminist biblical scholarship. Though there are diverse approaches to queer biblical scholarship, Ken Stone suggests this unifying concern: "a critical interrogation and active contestation of the many ways in which the Bible is and has been read to support heteronormative and normalizing configurations of sexual practices and sexual identities."[25] Studying masculinity in the court tales of Daniel left little to comment on concerning sexuality, except in so far as Daniel and his colleagues do not appear married or to have produced (male) children. But many biblical scholars adopting a queer approach are primarily concerned with gender without connecting the analysis to sexuality.[26] A queer aspect of these projects emerges through troubling an exclusively and narrowly binary configuration of gender required by heteronormative constructions of sexuality. Indeed, Judith Butler's important book *Gender Trouble*, a highly influential work for queer theory, emerged as a feminist project on gender.[27] From this vantage point, troubling gendered categories simultaneously disrupts a heteronormative framework, though the connection has not always been explicit or central to queer biblical scholarship. This project aligns with queer biblical scholarship by showing the diversity of constructions of masculinities in biblical literature. By showing that masculinity in biblical literature is not one but rather plural, this argument contributes to the disruption of an exclusively binary configuration of gender required by a heteronormative ideology.

In drawing from and seeking to align and ally with feminist and queer biblical scholarship, this work participates in a burgeoning area of "gender studies" in the field. This location renders studies of masculinity in biblical literature, including this one, intellectually and politically accountable to the critical approaches upon which they rely. Intellectual accountability is needed to show the ways in which the topic depends entirely on the contributions of feminist and queer scholarship. Political accountability ensures that studying this topic cannot remain a "neutral" project of intellectual curiosity. In future work, studying masculinity in biblical literature may become more than a topic of study, perhaps its own critical approach aligned with others in gender studies. For that development to occur, such scholarship will need a defined political agenda and goals that can distinguish and align it in relation to the others. The political agenda of critiquing the oppression of women and promoting gendered equality in feminist biblical scholarship is clear. Likewise, queer biblical scholarship has a clear political goal of dismantling oppression and inequality based upon categories of sexuality. For studies of masculinity in the Hebrew Bible to become more than a topic, a defined political agenda will be necessary. Though the agenda of consciousness raising in this project moves in that direction, doing something about that raised consciousness is a crucial next step.

Notes

1. Deryn Guest, *Beyond Feminist Biblical Studies*, The Bible in the Modern World 47 (Sheffield: Sheffield Phoenix, 2012), 20; Beatrice Lawrence, "Gender Analysis: Gender and Method in Biblical Studies," in *Method Matters: Essays on the Interpretation of the Hebrew Bible in Honor of David L. Petersen*, eds. Joel M. LeMon and Kent Harold Richards, RBS 56 (Atlanta: Society of Biblical Literature, 2009), 335; Ken Stone, "Gender Criticism: The Un-Manning of Abimelech," in *Judges & Method: New Approaches in Biblical Studies*, ed. Gale A. Yee, 2nd ed. (Minneapolis: Fortress, 2007), 192.
2. For two feminist opinions about the place of historical approaches in considering the implications of biblical texts for modern readers, see Pamela Thimmes, "What Makes a Feminist Reading Feminist? Another Perspective," in *Escaping Eden: New Feminist Perspectives on the Bible*, eds. Harold C. Washington, Susan Lochrie Graham, and Pamela Thimmes (New York: New York University Press, 1999), 132–40; Phyllis A. Bird, "What Makes a Feminist Reading Feminist? A Qualified Answer," in Washington, Graham, and Thimmes, *Escaping Eden*, 124–31. For an example of queer biblical criticism narrowly focused on the implications of biblical texts for modern readers, see Timothy R. Koch, "Cruising as Methodology: Homoeroticism and the Scriptures," in *Queer Commentary and the Hebrew Bible*, ed. Ken Stone, JSOTSSup 334 (Sheffield: Sheffield Academic, 2001), 169–80.
3. See Cheryl B. Anderson, *Women, Ideology, and Violence: Critical Theory and the Construction of Gender in the Book of the Covenant and the Deuteronomic Law* (New York: T&T Clark, 2004); Mark K. George, "Masculinity and Its Regimentation in Deuteronomy," in *Men and Masculinity in the Hebrew Bible and Beyond*, ed. Ovidiu Creangă, The Bible in the Modern World 33 (Sheffield: Sheffield Phoenix, 2010), 64–82.
4. Pamela J. Milne, "Toward Feminist Companionship: The Future of Feminist Biblical Studies and Feminism," in *A Feminist Companion to Reading the Bible: Approaches, Methods and Strategies*, eds. Athalya Brenner and Carole Fontaine (Sheffield: Sheffield Academic, 1997), 39–60; Martti Nissinen, "Biblical Masculinities: Musings on Theory and Agenda," in *Biblical Masculinities Foregrounded*, eds. Ovidiu Creangă and Peter-Ben Smit, Hebrew Bible Monographs 62 (Sheffield: Sheffield Phoenix, 2014), 271–85.
5. For this suggestion, see also Guest, *Beyond Feminist Biblical Studies*.
6. Framing the question in this way draws from J. Cheryl Exum, "Feminist Criticism: Whose Interests Are Being Served?" in Yee, *Judges & Method*, 65–89.
7. For an assessment of some previous work in these terms, see Guest, *Beyond Feminist Biblical Studies*, 135–42.
8. A notable exception is approximately two pages in T. M. Lemos, "'They Have Become Women': Judean Diaspora and Postcolonial Theories of Gender and Migration," in *Social Theory and the Study of Israelite Religion: Essays in Retrospect and Prospect*, ed. Saul M. Olyan (Atlanta: Society of Biblical Literature, 2012), 102–4. Additionally, see Carol A. Newsom, "Daniel," in *Women's Bible Commentary, Revised and Updated*, eds. Carol A. Newsom, Sharon H. Ringe, and Jacqueline E. Lapsley, 3rd ed. (Louisville: Westminster John Knox, 2012), 293–98. Newsom concentrates her comments on the feminist potential of Daniel's critique of imperial power rather than analyzing the book in terms of cultural configurations of masculinity. For some recent examples that do not address social identity in terms of gender, see Anathea Portier-Young, "Languages of Identity and Obligation: Daniel as a Bilingual Book," *VT* 60 (2010): 98–118; Matthew S. Rindge, "Jewish Identity Under Foreign Rule: Daniel 2 as a Reconfiguration of Genesis 41," *JBL* 129 (2010): 85–104.
9. See, for instance, Kathleen M. O'Connor, "The Feminist Movement Meets the Old Testament: One Woman's Perspective," in *Engaging the Bible in a Gendered World:*

An Introduction to Feminist Biblical Interpretation in Honor of Katharine Doob Sakenfeld, eds. Linda Day and Carolyn Pressler (Louisville: Westminster John Knox, 2006), 12.

10 Guest, *Beyond Feminist Biblical Studies*, 128.
11 See Cecilia L. Ridgeway, *Framed by Gender: How Gender Inequality Persists in the Modern World* (New York: Oxford University Press, 2011).
12 For some sociological case studies showing how deviations from predominant gendered norms (re)produce gendered inequality, see Catherine Connell, "Doing, Undoing, or Redoing Gender? Learning from the Workplace Experiences of Transpeople," *Gender & Society* 24 (2010): 31–55; Jesse Wozniak, and Christopher Uggen, "Real Men Use Nonlethals: Appeals to Masculinity in Marketing Police Weaponry," *Feminist Criminology* 4 (2009): 275–93; J. Edward Sumerau, "'That's What a Man Is Supposed to Do': Compensatory Manhood Acts in an LGBT Christian Church," *Gender & Society* 26 (2012): 461–87.
13 This idea is especially clear in R. W. Connell, *Masculinities*, 2nd ed. (Berkeley: University of California Press, 2005), 79–80. For further discussion, see Chapter 3 in this study.
14 Numbers as reported through the SBL "Facts and Figures," Online: www.sbl-site.org/SBLDashboard.aspx.
15 "Past Presidents of SBL," Online: www.sbl-site.org/assets/pdfs/pastpresidents.pdf.
16 Joel M. LeMon, and Kent Harold Richards, eds., *Method Matters: Essays on the Interpretation of the Hebrew Bible in Honor of David L. Petersen*, RBS 56 (Atlanta: Society of Biblical Literature, 2009).
17 A list of volumes and authors can be found online at http://store.augsburgfortress.org/store/productfamily/92/Hermeneia-series. The all-male author list of the Hebrew Bible portion of the commentary series remains when including Enoch and Fourth Ezra.
18 A list can be found online at http://yalepress.yale.edu/SeriesPage.asp?Series=144.
19 A list can be found online at www.wjkbooks.com/Products/CategoryCenter/BSE:OTL/Old-Testament-Library.aspx?categoryId=BSE%3aOTL&categoryId=BSE%3aOTL&categoryId=BSE%3aOTL&categoryId=BSE%3aOTL&categoryId=BSE%3aOTL&categoryId=BSE%3aOTL&categoryId=BSE%3aOTL.
20 Corinne L. Carvalho, *Encountering Ancient Voices: A Guide to Reading the Old Testament*, 2nd ed. (Winona, MN: Saint Mary's Press, 2010).
21 Guest, *Beyond Feminist Biblical Studies*, 152–62, esp. 162.
22 Ibid., 152 and 157.
23 For an assessment of how feminist biblical scholarship is rather homogenous with respect to its liberal feminist emphases, see Esther Fuchs, "Biblical Feminisms: Knowledge, Theory and Politics in the Study of Women in the Hebrew Bible," *BibInt* 16 (2008): 205–26.
24 See note 9 above.
25 Ken Stone, "Queer Commentary and Biblical Interpretation: An Introduction," in Stone, *Queer Commentary and the Hebrew Bible*, 33.
26 See, for instance, Ken Stone, "Lovers and Raisin Cakes: Food, Sex and Divine Insecurity in Hosea," in Stone, *Queer Commentary and the Hebrew Bible*, 116–39; Deryn Guest, "From Gender Reversal to Genderfuck: Reading Jael Through a Lesbian Lens," in *Bible Trouble: Queer Reading at the Boundaries of Biblical Scholarship*, eds. Teresa J. Hornsby and Ken Stone, SemeiaSt 67 (Atlanta: Society of Biblical Literature, 2011), 9–44.
27 Butler is not unique in observing the interconnections between categories of gender and sexuality or the way that a normative heterosexual framework requires only two genders. See also, for example, Gayle Rubin, "The Traffic in Women: Notes on the 'Political Economy' of Sex," in *Toward an Anthropology of Women*, ed. Rayna R. Reiter (New York: Monthly Review Press, 1975), 157–210.

BIBLIOGRAPHY

Ackerman, Susan. "Why Is Miriam Also Among the Prophets? (And Is Zipporah Among the Priests)." *JBL* 121 (2002): 47–80.
Ahituv, Shmuel. *Echoes from the Past: Hebrew and Cognate Inscriptions from the Biblical Period*. Jerusalem: Carta, 2008.
Alter, Robert. *The Art of Biblical Narrative*. New York: Basic Books, 1981.
Anderson, Cheryl B. *Women, Ideology, and Violence: Critical Theory and the Construction of Gender in the Book of the Covenant and the Deuteronomic Law*. New York: T&T Clark, 2004.
Bahrani, Zainab. *Rituals of War: The Body and Violence in Mesopotamia*. New York: Zone Books, 2008.
Bar-Efrat, Shimeon. *Narrative Art in the Bible*. Sheffield: Almond Press, 1989.
Barber, Kristen. "The Well-Coiffed Man: Class, Race, and Heterosexual Masculinity in the Hair Salon." *Gender & Society* 22 (2008): 455–76.
Barnett, Richard David. *Sculptures from the North Palace of Ashurbanipal at Nineveh (668–627 B.C.)*. London: British Museum, 1976.
———. *Sculptures from the Southwest Palace of Sennacherib at Nineveh*. London: British Museum, 1998.
———. *The Sculptures of Aššur-Nasir-Apli II, 883–859 B.C., Tiglath-Pileser III, 745–727 B.C. [and] Esarhaddon, 681–669 B.C., from the Central and South-West Palaces at Nimrud*. London: British Museum, 1962.
Bartholomaeus, Clare. "'I'm Not Allowed Wrestling Stuff': Hegemonic Masculinity and Primary School Boys." *Journal of Sociology* 48 (2012): 227–47.
Beasley, Christine. "Rethinking Hegemonic Masculinity in a Globalizing World." *Men and Masculinities* 11 (2008): 86–103.
Beauliu, Paul-Alain. "The Babylonian Background of the Motif of the Fiery Furnace in Daniel 3." *JBL* 128 (2009): 273–98.
Bellis, Alice Ogden. *Helpmates, Harlots, and Heroes*. 2nd ed. Louisville: Westminster John Knox, 2007.
Bergmann, Claudia D. "'We Have Seen the Enemy, and He Is Only a She': The Portrayal of Warriors as Women." Pages 129–42 in *Writing and Reading War: Rhetoric, Gender, and Ethics in Biblical and Modern Contexts*. Edited by Brad E. Kelle and Frank Ritchel Ames. SymS 42. Atlanta: Society of Biblical Literature, 2008.
Biggs, Robert D. "The Babylonian Sexual Potency Texts." Pages 71–78 in Parpola and Whiting, *Sex and Gender in the Ancient Near East*.

BIBLIOGRAPHY

———. *Šà.zi.ga: Ancient Mesopotamian Potency Incantations*. TCS 2. Locust Valley, NY: J. J. Augustin, 1967.

Bird, Phyllis A. "What Makes a Feminist Reading Feminist? A Qualified Answer." Pages 124–31 in Washington, Graham, and Thimmes, *Escaping Eden*.

Bly, Robert. *Iron John: A Book About Men*. Reading, MA: Addison-Wesley, 1990.

Boer, Roland. *The Earthy Nature of the Bible: Fleshly Readings of Sex, Masculinity, and Carnality*. New York: Palgrave Macmillan, 2012.

———. "Of Fine Wine, Incense and Spices: The Unstable Masculine Hegemony of the Book of Chronicles." Pages 20–33 in Creangă, *Men and Masculinity in the Hebrew Bible and Beyond*.

———. "Too Many Dicks at the Writing Desk, or How to Organise a Prophetic Sausage Fest." *Theology and Sexuality* 16 (2010): 95–108.

Bolger, Diane, ed. *Gender Through Time in the Ancient Near East*. Lanham, MD: AltaMira Press, 2008.

Boling, Robert. *Judges: Introduction, Translation, and Commentary*. AB. Garden City, NY: Doubleday, 1975.

Bonfiglio, Ryan P. "Archer Imagery in Zechariah 9:11–17 in Light of Achaemenid Iconography." *JBL* 131 (2012): 507–27.

Brayford, Susan. "Feminist Criticism: Sarah Laughs Last." Pages 311–32 in LeMon and Richards, *Method Matters*.

Brenner, Athalya, ed. *A Feminist Companion to Prophets and Daniel*. Sheffield: Sheffield Academic, 2001.

———. *A Feminist Companion to Esther, Judith, and Susanna*. Sheffield: Sheffield Academic, 1995.

———. "Self-Response to 'Who's Afraid of Feminist Criticism?'" Pages 245–46 in Brenner, *A Feminist Companion to Prophets and Daniel*.

———. "Who's Afraid of Feminist Criticism? Who's Afraid of Biblical Humour? The Case of the Obtuse Foreign Ruler in the Hebrew Bible." Pages 228–45 in Brenner, *A Feminist Companion to Prophets and Daniel*.

Brenner, Athalya, and Fokkelien van Dijk-Hemmes. *On Gendering Texts: Female and Male Voices in the Hebrew Bible*. New York: Brill, 1993.

Briant, Pierre. *From Cyrus to Alexander: A History of the Persian Empire*. Translated by Peter T. Daniels. Winona Lake, IN: Eisenbrauns, 2002.

Bridges, Tristan, and C. J. Pascoe. "Hybrid Masculinities: New Directions in the Sociology of Men and Masculinities." *Sociology Compass* 8 (2014): 246–58.

Browne, Irene, and Joya Misra. "The Intersection of Gender and Race in the Labor Market." *Annual Review of Sociology* 29 (2003): 487–513.

Bryan, Betsy. "Evidence for Female Literacy from Theban Tombs of the New Kingdom." *Bulletin of the Egyptological Seminar* 6 (1985): 17–32.

Bucholtz, Mary. "The Feminist Foundations of Language, Gender, and Sexuality Research." Pages 23–47 in Ehrlich, Meyerhoff, and Holmes, *The Handbook of Language, Gender, and Sexuality*.

Buss, Martin J. *The Prophetic Word of Hosea*. Berlin: Verlag Alfred Töpelmann, 1969.

Butler, Judith. *Gender Trouble: Feminism and the Subversion of Identity*. 2nd ed. New York: Routledge, 2010.

Buysse, Jo Ann M., and Melissa Sheridan Embser-Herbert. "Constructions of Gender in Sport: An Analysis of Intercollegitate Media Guide Cover Photographs." *Gender & Society* 18 (2004): 66–81.

BIBLIOGRAPHY

Caminos, Richard A. *Late-Egyptian Miscellanies*. London: Oxford University Press, 1954.

Camp, Claudia V. *Ben Sira and the Men Who Handle Books: Gender and the Rise of Canon-Consciousness*. Hebrew Bible Monographs 50. Sheffield: Sheffield Phoenix, 2013.

———. "The Female Sage in Ancient Israel and in the Biblical Wisdom Literature." Pages 185–204 in Gammie and Perdue, *The Sage in Israel*.

Carr, David M. *Writing on the Tablet of the Heart: Origins of Scripture and Literature*. Oxford: Oxford University Press, 2005.

Carrigan, Tim, Bob Connell, and John Lee. "Toward a New Sociology of Masculinity." *Theory and Society* 14 (1985): 551–604.

Carvalho, Corinne L. *Encountering Ancient Voices: A Guide to Reading the Old Testament*. 2nd ed. Winona, MN: Saint Mary's Press, 2010.

Chafetz, Janet Saltzman, ed. *Handbook of the Sociology of Gender*. New York: Kluwer Academic/Plenum Publishers, 1999.

Chapman, Cynthia R. *The Gendered Language of Warfare in the Israelite-Assyrian Encounter*. HSM 62. Winona Lake, IN: Eisenbrauns, 2004.

———. "Sculpted Warriors: Sexuality and the Sacred in the Definition of Warfare in the Assyrian Palace Reliefs and in Ezekiel 23:14–17." Pages 1–17 in *The Aesthetics of Violence in the Prophets*. Edited by Chris Franke and Julia M O'Brien. LHBOTS 517. New York: T&T Clark, 2010.

Charpin, Dominique. *Reading and Writing in Babylon*. Translated by Jean Marie Tood. Cambridge, MA: Harvard University Press, 2010.

Cifarelli, Megan. "Gesture and Alterity in the Art of Aššurnaṣirpal II of Assyria." *Art Bulletin* 80 (1998): 210–28.

Clines, David J. A. "Being a Man in the Book of the Covenant." Pages 3–9 in *Reading the Law: Studies in Honor of Gordon J. Wenham*. Edited by J. G. McConville and Karl Möller. LHBOTS 461. London: T&T Clark, 2007.

———. "Dancing and Shining at Sinai: Playing the Man in Exodus 32–34." Pages 54–63 in Creangă, *Men and Masculinity in the Hebrew Bible and Beyond*.

———. "David the Man: The Construction of Masculinity in the Hebrew Bible." Pages 212–43 in *Interested Parties: The Ideology of Writers and Readers of the Hebrew Bible*. 2nd ed. Sheffield: Sheffield Academic, 2009.

———. "Final Reflections of Biblical Masculinity." Pages 234–39 in Creangă, *Men and Masculinity in the Hebrew Bible and Beyond*.

———. "He-Prophets: Masculinity as a Problem for the Hebrew Prophets and Their Interpreters." Pages 311–28 in *Sense and Sensitivity: Essays on Reading the Bible in Memory of Robert Carrol*. Edited by Alastair G. Hunter and Philip R. Davies. JSOTSup 348. Sheffield: Sheffield Academic, 2002.

———. "Loin-Girding and Other Male Activities in the Book of Job." (n.d.). http://academia.edu/2469762/Loingirding_and_Other_Male_Activities_in_the_Book_of_Job.

———. "Why Is There a Song of Songs, and What Does It Do to You If You Read It?" Pages 94–121 in *Interested Parties: The Ideology of Writers and Readers of the Hebrew Bible*. 2nd ed. Sheffield: Sheffield Academic, 2009.

Cohen, Ada. *Art in the Era of Alexander the Great: Paradigms of Manhood and Their Cultural Traditions*. Cambridge: Cambridge University Press, 2010.

Coles, Tony. "Negotiating the Field of Masculinity: The Production and Reproduction of Multiple Dominant Masculinities." *Men and Masculinities* 12 (2009): 30–44.

Collins, John J. *Daniel: A Commentary on the Book of Daniel*. Hermeneia. Minneapolis: Fortress, 1993.

BIBLIOGRAPHY

Collins, Patricia Hill. *Black Feminist Thought: Knowledge, Consciousness, and the Politics of Empowerment*. 2nd ed. New York: Routledge, 2009.
Collins, Paul. "Trees and Gender in Assyrian Art." *Iraq* 68 (2006): 99–107.
Collins, Paul, Lisa Baylis, and Sandra Marshall. *Assyrian Palace Sculptures*. Austin: University of Texas Press, 2009.
Collins, Rebecca L. "Content Analysis of Gender Roles in Media: Where Are We Now and Where Should We Go?" *Sex Roles* 64 (2011): 290–98.
Connell, Catherine. "Doing, Undoing, or Redoing Gender?: Learning from the Workplace Experiences of Transpeople." *Gender & Society* 24 (2010): 31–55.
Connell, R. W. *Gender and Power*. Sydney: Allen and Unwin, 1987.
―――. *Masculinities*. 2nd ed. Berkeley: University of California Press, 2005.
Connell, R. W., and James W. Messerschmidt. "Hegemonic Masculinity: Rethinking the Concept." *Gender & Society* 19 (2005): 829–59.
Conybeare, F. C., J. Rendel Harris, and Agnes Smith Lewis. *The Story of Aḥiḳar from the Aramaic, Syriac, Arabic, Armenian, Ethiopic, Old Turkish, Greek and Slavonic Versions*. Cambridge: Cambridge University Press, 1913.
Cottingham, Marci D. "Recruiting Men, Constructing Manhood: How Health Care Organizations Mobilize Masculinities as Nursing Recruitment Strategy." *Gender & Society* 28 (2014): 133–56.
Cowley, A. E. *Aramaic Papyri of the Fifth Century*. Oxford: Clarendon, 1923.
Craven, Toni. "Daniel and Its Additions." Pages 191–94 in *The Women's Bible Commentary*. Edited by Carol A. Newsom and Sharon H. Ringe. Louisville: Westminster John Knox, 1992.
Creangă, Ovidiu. "Introduction." Pages 3–14 in Creangă and Smit, *Biblical Masculinities Foregrounded*.
―――, ed. *Men and Masculinity in the Hebrew Bible and Beyond*. The Bible in the Modern World 33. Sheffield: Sheffield Phoenix, 2010.
―――. "Variations on the Theme of Masculinity: Joshua's Gender In/stability in the Conquest Narrative." Pages 83–109 in Creangă, *Men and Masculinity in the Hebrew Bible and Beyond*.
Creangă, Ovidiu, and Peter-Ben Smit, eds. *Biblical Masculinities Foregrounded*. Hebrew Bible Monographs 62. Sheffield: Sheffield Phoenix, 2014.
Cunningham, Sheryl, David Domke, Kevin Coe, Anna Fahey, and Nancy van Leuven. "Accruing Masculinity Capital: Dominant and Hegemonic Masculinities in the 2004 Political Conventions." *Men and Masculinities* 16 (2013): 499–516.
Davies, Philip R. "Reading Daniel Sociologically." Pages 345–61 in *The Book of Daniel in the Light of New Findings*. Edited by A. S. van der Woude. Leuven: University Press, 1993.
Day, Linda. "Wisdom and the Feminine in the Hebrew Bible." Pages 114–27 in Day and Pressler, *Engaging the Bible in a Gendered World*.
Day, Linda, and Carolyn Pressler, ed. *Engaging the Bible in a Gendered World: An Introduction to Feminist Biblical Interpretation in Honor of Katherine Doob Sakenfeld*. Louisville: Westminster John Knox, 2006.
Denny, Kathleen E. "Gender in Context, Content, and Approach: Comparing Gender Messages in Girl Scout and Boy Scout Handbooks." *Gender & Society* 25 (2011): 27–47.
Deutsch, Francine M. "Undoing Gender." *Gender & Society* 21 (2007): 106–27.
DiPalma, Brian Charles. "De/Constructing Masculinity in Exodus 1–4." Pages 36–53 in Creangă, *Men and Masculinity in the Hebrew Bible and Beyond*.

Duncanson, Claire. "Forces for Good? Narratives of Military Masculinity in Peacekeeping Operations." *International Feminist Journal of Politics* 11 (2009): 63–80.

Ebeling, Jennie R. *Women's Lives in Biblical Times*. New York: T&T Clark, 2010.

Eck, Beth A. "Compromising Positions: Unmarried Men, Heterosexuality, and Two-Phase Masculinity." *Men and Masculinities* 17 (2014): 147–72.

Ehrlich, Susan, and Miriam Meyerhoff. "Introduction: Language, Gender, and Sexuality." Pages 1–20 in Ehrlich, Meyerhoff, and Holmes, *The Handbook of Language, Gender, and Sexuality*.

Ehrlich, Susan, Miriam Meyerhoff, and Janet Holmes, eds. *The Handbook of Language, Gender, and Sexuality*. Malden, MA: Wiley-Blackwell, 2014.

Eilberg-Schwartz, Howard. *God's Phallus and Other Problems for Men and Monotheism*. Boston: Beacon, 1994.

Exum, J. Cheryl. "Feminist Criticism: Whose Interests Are Being Served?" Pages 65–89 in Yee, *Judges & Method*.

Ezzell, Matthew B. "'I'm in Control': Compensatory Manhood in a Therapeutic Community." *Gender & Society* 26 (2012): 190–215.

Fewell, Danna Nolan. *Circle of Sovereignty: Plotting Politics in the Book of Daniel*. Nashville: Abingdon, 1991.

———. "Reading the Bible Ideologically: Feminist Criticism." Pages 268–82 in *To Each Its Own Meaning: An Introduction to Biblical Criticisms and Their Application*. Edited by Steven L. McKenzie and Stephen R. Haynes. Louisville: Westminster John Knox, 1999.

Fincke, Jeanette C. "The Babylonian Texts of Nineveh: Report on the British Museum's 'Ashurbanipal Library Project.'" *AfO* 50 (2003): 111–49.

Fitzmyer, Joseph A. *The Aramaic Inscriptions of Sefire*. Rome: Pontifical Biblical Institute, 1967.

Fontaine, Carole R. "'Be Men, O Philistines' (1 Samuel 4:9): Iconographic Representations and Reflections on Female Gender as Disability in the Ancient World." Pages 61–72 in *This Abled Body: Rethinking Disabilities in Biblical Studies*. Edited by Hector Avalos, Sarah J. Melcher, and Jeremy Schipper. SemeiaSt 55. Atlanta: Society of Biblical Literature, 2007.

Foucault, Michel. *Discipline and Punish: The Birth of the Prison*. Translated by Alan Sheridan. New York: Vintage Books, 1995.

———. *History of Madness*. Edited by Jean Khalfa. Translated by Jonathan Paul Murphy and Jean Khalfa. New York: Routledge, 2006.

———. *The History of Sexuality: An Introduction*. Translated by Robert Hurley. New York: Vintage Books, 1990.

Frymer-Kensky, Tikva. *Reading the Women of the Bible*. New York: Schocken, 2002.

Fuchs, Esther. "Biblical Feminisms: Knowledge, Theory and Politics in the Study of Women in the Hebrew Bible." *BibInt* 16 (2008): 205–26.

———. "The History of Women in Ancient Israel: Theory, Method, and the Book of Ruth." Pages 211–31 in *Her Master's Tools? Feminist and Postcolonial Engagements of Historical-Critical Discourse*. Edited by Caroline Vander Stichele and Todd Penner. GPBS 8. Atlanta: Society of Biblical Literature, 2005.

———. "Men in Biblical Feminist Scholarship." *JFSR* 19 (2003): 93–114.

———. *Sexual Politics in the Biblical Narrative: Reading the Hebrew Bible as a Woman*. JSOTSup 310. Sheffield: Sheffield Academic, 2000.

———. "Status and Role of Female Heroines in the Biblical Narrative." Pages 77–84 in *Women in the Hebrew Bible: A Reader*. Edited by Alice Bach. New York: Routledge, 1999.

Gammie, John G., and Leo G. Perdue, *The Sage in Israel and the Ancient Near East*. Winona Lake, IN: Eisenbrauns, 1990.

Garr, W. Randall. *Dialect Geography of Syria-Palestine, 1000–586 B.C.E*. Philadelphia: University of Pennsylvania Press, 1985.

Garrison, Mark B. "Achaemenid Iconography as Evidenced by Glyptic Art: Subject Matter, Social Function, Audience and Diffusion." Pages 115–63 in *Images as Media: Sources for the Cultural History of the Near East and the Eastern Mediterranean (1st Millenium BCE)*. Edited by Christoph Uehlinger. OBO 175. Fribourg: University Press, 2000.

———. "Archers at Persepolis: The Emergence of Royal Ideology at the Heart of Empire." Pages 337–60 in *The World of Achaemenid Persia: History, Art and Society in Iran and the Ancient Near East*. Edited by John Curtis and St John Simpson. New York: I. B. Tauris, 2010.

———. "The Heroic Encounter in the Visual Arts of Ancient Iraq and Iran C. 1000–500 B.C." Pages 151–74 in *The Master of Animals in Old World Iconography*. Edited by D. B. Counts and B. Arnold. Budapest: Archaeolingua, 2010.

———. "Royal Achaemenid Iconography." Pages 566–95 in *The Oxford Handbook of Ancient Iran*. Edited by D. T. Potts. Oxford: Oxford University Press, 2013.

Garrison, Mark B., and Margaret Cool Root. *Seals on the Persepolis Fortification Tablets, Volume I: Images of Heroic Encounter*. OIP 117. Chicago: Oriental Institute of the University of Chicago Press, 2001.

George, Mark K. "Masculinity and Its Regimentation in Deuteronomy." Pages 64–82 in Creangă, *Men and Masculinity in the Hebrew Bible and Beyond*.

Gilders, William K. "Anthropological Approaches: Ritual in Leviticus 8, Real or Rhetorical?" Pages 233–50 in LeMon and Richards, *Method Matters*.

———. *Blood Ritual in the Hebrew Bible: Meaning and Power*. Baltimore: Johns Hopkins University Press, 2004.

Glancy, Jennifer A. "The Accused: Susanna and Her Readers." Pages 288–302 in Brenner, *A Feminist Companion to Esther, Judith, and Susanna*.

Goffman, Erving. *Gendered Advertisements*. New York: Harper and Row, 1974.

Goldingay, John. *Daniel*. WBC. Dallas: Word Books, 1989.

———. "Hosea 1–3, Genesis 1–4, and Masculist Interpretation." *HBT* 17 (1995): 37–44.

Goss, Robert E., and Mona West, eds. *Take Back the Word: A Queer Reading of the Bible*. Cleveland, OH: Pilgrim Press, 2000.

Green, Adam Isaiah. "Queer Theory and Sociology: Locating the Subject and Self in Sexuality Studies." *Sociological Theory* 25 (2007): 26–45.

Grelot, Pierre. *Documents Araméens D'Égypte*. Paris: Les Éditions du Cerf, 1972.

Grene, David, trans. *The History: Herodotus*. Chicago: University of Chicago Press, 1987.

Guest, Deryn. *Beyond Feminist Biblical Studies*. The Bible in the Modern World 47. Sheffield: Sheffield Phoenix, 2012.

———. "From Gender Reversal to Genderfuck: Reading Jael Through a Lesbian Lens." Pages 9–44 in Hornsby and Stone, *Bible Trouble*.

———. "Looking Lesbian at the Bathing Bathsheba." *BibInt* 16 (2008): 227–62.

Guest, Deryn, Robert E. Goss, Mona West, and Thomas Bohache, eds. *The Queer Bible Commentary*. London: SCM, 2006.

Gunn, David, and Danna Nolan Fewell. *Narrative in the Hebrew Bible*. New York: Oxford University Press, 1993.

Hackett, Jo Ann. "Hebrew (Biblical and Epigraphic)." Pages 139–56 in *Beyond Babel: A Handbook for Biblical Hebrew and Related Languages*. Edited by John Kaltner and Steven L. McKenzie. RBS 42. Atlanta: Society of Biblical Literature, 2002.

Haddox, Susan E. "(E)Masculinity in Hosea's Political Rhetoric." Pages 174–200 in *Israel's Prophets and Israel's Past: Essays on the Relationship of Prophetic Texts and Israelite History in Honor of John H. Hayes*. Edited by Brad E. Kelle and Megan Bishop Moore. LHBOTS 446. New York: T&T Clark, 2006.

———. "Favoured Sons and Subordinate Masculinities." Pages 2–19 in Creangă, *Men and Masculinity in the Hebrew Bible and Beyond*.

———. *Metaphor and Masculinity in Hosea*. StBibLit 141. New York: Peter Lang, 2011.

Harris, Rivkah. "The Female 'Sage' in Mesopotamian Literature (With an Appendix on Egypt)." Pages 3–18 in Gammie and Perdue, *The Sage in Israel*.

Hartman, Louis F. *The Book of Daniel*. AB. Garden City, NY: Doubleday, 1978.

Hays, Christopher B. "Chirps from the Dust: The Affliction of Nebuchadnezzar in Daniel 4:30 and Its Ancient Near Eastern Context." *JBL* 126 (2007): 305–25.

Hearn, Jeff. "A Multi-Faceted Power Analysis of Men's Violence to Known Women: From Hegemonic Masculinity to the Hegemony of Men." *The Sociological Review* 60 (2012): 589–610.

Hearn, Jeff, Marie Nordberg, Kjerstin Andersson, Dag Balkmar, Lucas Gottzén, Roger Klinth, Keith Pringle, and Linn Sandberg. "Hegemonic Masculinity and Beyond: 40 Years of Research in Sweden." *Men and Masculinities* 15 (2012): 1–25.

Hennen, Peter. *Faeries, Bears, and Leathermen: Men in Community Queering the Masculine*. Chicago: University of Chicago Press, 2008.

Hirose, Akihiko, and Kay Kei-ho Pih. "Men Who Strike and Men Who Submit: Hegemonic and Marginalized Masculinites in Mixed Martial Arts." *Men and Masculinities* 13 (2010): 190–209.

Hoffner, Harry A. "Symbols for Masculinity and Femininity: Their Use in Ancient Near Eastern Sympathetic Magic Rituals." *JBL* 85 (1966): 326–34.

Hoftijzer, J., and K. Jongeling. *Dictionary of the North-West Semitic Inscriptions*. Leiden: Brill, 1995.

Holm, Tawny L. *Of Courtiers and Kings: The Biblical Daniel Narratives and Ancient Story-Collections*. EANEC 1. Winona Lake, IN: Eisenbrauns, 2013.

Holmes, Mary. *What Is Gender? Sociological Approaches*. Los Angeles: Sage, 2007.

Hornsby, Teresa J., and Ken Stone, eds. *Bible Trouble: Queer Reading at the Boundaries of Biblical Scholarship*. SemeiaSt 67. Atlanta: Society of Biblical Literature, 2011.

Huehnegard, John. *A Grammar of Akkadian*. Winona Lake, IN: Eisenbrauns, 2000.

Humphreys, W. Lee. "Life-Style for Diaspora: A Study of the Tales of Esther and Daniel." *JBL* 92 (1973): 211–23.

Jacobs, Sandra. "Divine Virility in Priestly Representation: Its Memory and Consummation in Rabbinic Midrash." Pages 146–70 in Creangă, *Men and Masculinity in the Hebrew Bible and Beyond*.

Kang, Miliann. *The Managed Hand: Race, Gender, and the Body in Beauty and Service Work*. Berkeley: University of California Press, 2010.

Kelle, Brad E. *Hosea 2: Metaphor and Rhetoric in Historical Perspective*. AcBib 20. Atlanta: Society of Biblical Literature, 2005.

Kelso, Julie. *O Mother, Where Art Thou? An Irigarayan Reading of the Book of Chronicles*. London: Equinox, 2007.

Kennelly, Ivy, Sabine N. Merz, and Judith Lorber. "What Is Gender." *American Sociological Review* 66 (2001): 598–605.

Kent, Roland G. *Old Persian: Grammar, Texts, Lexicon*. New Haven: American Oriental Society, 1950.

Koch, Timothy R. "Cruising as Methodology: Homoeroticism and the Scriptures." Pages 169–80 in Stone, *Queer Commentary and the Hebrew Bible*.

Krafchick, Jennifer L., Toni Schindler Zimmerman, Shelley A. Haddock, and James H. Banning. "Best-Selling Books Advising Parents about Gender: A Feminist Analysis." *Family Relations* 54 (2005): 84–100.

Kuhrt, Amélie. *The Persian Empire: A Corpus of Sources from the Achaemenid Period*. New York: Routledge, 2007.

Lan, Pei-Chia. *Global Cinderellas: Migrant Domestics and Newly Rich Employers in Taiwan*. Durham: Duke University Press, 2006.

Lapsley, Jacqueline E. *Whispering the Word: Hearing Women's Stories in the Old Testament*. Louisville: Westminster John Knox, 2005.

Lawrence, Beatrice. "Gender Analysis: Gender and Method in Biblical Studies." Pages 333–48 in LeMon and Richards, *Method Matters*.

Lee, Eunny P. "Ruth the Moabite: Identity, Kinship, and Otherness." Pages 89–101 in Day and Pressler, *Engaging the Bible in a Gendered World*.

LeMon, Joel M. "Yahweh's Hand and the Iconography of the Blow in Psalm 81:14–16." *JBL* 132 (2013): 865–82.

LeMon, Joel M., and Kent Harold Richards, eds. *Method Matters: Essays on the Interpretation of the Hebrew Bible in Honor of David L. Petersen*. RBS 56. Atlanta: Society of Biblical Literature, 2009.

Lemos, T. M. "'They Have Become Women': Judean Diaspora and Postcolonial Theories of Gender and Migration." Pages 81–109 in *Social Theory and the Study of Israelite Religion: Essays in Retrospect and Prospect*. Edited by Saul M. Olyan. Atlanta: Society of Biblical Literature, 2012.

Levine, Amy-Jill. "'Hemmed in on Every Side': Jews and Women in the Book of Susanna." Pages 303–23 in Brenner, *A Feminist Companion to Esther, Judith, and Susanna*.

Lichtheim, Miriam. *Ancient Egyptian Literature: A Book of Readings*. Vol. 2. Berkeley: University of California Press, 1976.

Lindenberger, James M. "Ahikar: A New Translation and Introduction." Pages 479–507 in *The Old Testament Pseudepigrapha*. Edited by James H. Charlesworth. Vol. 2. Garden City, NY: Doubleday, 1985.

———. *The Aramaic Proverbs of Ahiqar*. Baltimore: Johns Hopkins University Press, 1983.

Lipka, Hilary. "Masculinities in Proverbs: An Alternative to the Hegemonic Ideal." Pages 86–103 in Creangă and Smit, *Biblical Masculinities Foregrounded*.

Lorber, Judith. *Paradoxes of Gender*. New Haven: Yale University Press, 1994.

Löwisch, Ingeborg. "Gender and Ambiguity in the Genesis Genealogies: Tracing Absence and Subversion through the Lens of Derrida's Archive Fever." Pages 60–73 in *Embroidered Garments: Priests and Gender in Biblical Israel*. Edited by Deborah W. Rooke. Sheffield: Sheffield Phoenix, 2009.

Lucal, Betsy. "What It Means to Be Gendered Me: Life on the Boundaries of a Dichotomous Gender System." *Gender & Society* 13 (1999): 781–97.

Macwilliam, Stuart. "Ideologies of Male Beauty and the Hebrew Bible." *BibInt* 17 (2009): 265–87.

———. *Queer Theory and the Prophetic Marriage Metaphor in the Hebrew Bible*. Sheffield: Equinox, 2011.

Marcus, Michelle. "Geography as Visual Ideology: Landscape, Knowledge, and Power in Neo-Assyrian Art." Pages 193–208 in *Neo-Assyrian Geography*. Edited by Mario Liverani. Rome: Universita di Roma, 1995.

Marcus, Ralph, trans. *Josephus*. 9 vols. LCL. Cambridge, MA: Harvard University Press, 1963.

McCall, Leslie. "The Complexity of Intersectionality." *Signs* 30 (2005): 1771–1800.

Merill Willis, Amy C. "Heavenly Bodies: God and the Body in the Visions of Daniel." Pages 13–37 in *Bodies, Embodiment, and Theology of the Hebrew Bible*. Edited by S. Tamar Kamionkowski and Wonil Kim. LHBOTS 465. New York: T&T Clark, 2010.

Messerschmidt, James W. "And Now, The Rest of the Story: A Commentary on Christine Beasley's 'Rethinking Hegemonic Masculinity in a Globalizing World.'" *Men and Masculinities* 11 (2008): 104–8.

———. "Engendering Gendered Knowledge: Assessing the Academic Appropriation of Hegemonic Masculinity." *Men and Masculinities* 15 (2012): 56–76.

———. "Goodbye to the Sex-Gender Distinction, Hello to Embodied Gender: On Masculinities, Bodies, and Violence." Pages 71–88 in *Sex, Gender, and Sexuality: The New Basics: An Anthology*. Edited by Abby L. Ferber, Kimberly Holcomb, and Tre Wentling. New York: Oxford University Press, 2009.

———. *Hegemonic Masculinities and Camouflaged Politics: Unmasking the Bush Dynasty and Its War Against Iraq*. Boulder, CO: Paradigm Publishers, 2010.

Messner, Michael A. "Barbie Girls versus Sea Monsters: Children Constructing Gender." *Gender & Society* 14 (2000): 765–84.

———. "When Bodies Are Weapons: Masculinity and Violence in Sport." *International Review for the Sociology of Sport* 25 (1990): 203–20.

Meyers, Carol L. *Discovering Eve: Ancient Israelite Women in Context*. Oxford: Oxford University Press, 1988.

———. *Rediscovering Eve: Ancient Israelite Women in Context*. Oxford: Oxford University Press, 2012.

Mills, Sara, and Louise Mullany. *Language, Gender and Feminism: Theory, Methodology and Practice*. New York: Routledge, 2011.

Milne, Pamela J. "Toward Feminist Companionship: The Future of Feminist Biblical Studies and Feminism." Pages 39–60 in *A Feminist Companion to Reading the Bible: Approaches, Methods and Strategies*. Edited by Athalya Brenner and Carole Fontaine. Sheffield: Sheffield Academic, 1997.

Minchin, Elizabeth. *Homeric Voices: Discourse, Memory, Gender*. Oxford: Oxford University Press, 2007.

Mitchell, Christine. "1 and 2 Chronicles." Pages 184–91 in Newsom, Ringe, and Lapsley, *Women's Bible Commentary*.

Moore, Stephen D. "Final Reflections on Biblical Masculinity." Pages 240–55 in Creangă, *Men and Masculinity in the Hebrew Bible and Beyond*.

———. "'O Man, Who Art Thou . . . ?' Masculinity Studies and New Testament Studies." in *New Testament Masculinities*. Edited by Stephen D. Moore and Janice Capel Anderson. Semeia St 45. Atlanta: Society of Biblical Literature, 2003.

Moore, Stephen D., and Janice Capel Anderson. "Taking It Like a Man: Masculinity in 4 Maccabees." *JBL* 117 (1998): 249–73.

Muraoka, Takamitsu, and Bezalel Porten. *A Grammar of Egyptian Aramaic*. Leiden: Brill, 1998.

Nelson, Richard. "The Double Redaction of the Deuteronomistic History: The Case Is Still Compelling." *JSOT* 29 (2005): 319–37.

Newsom, Carol A. "Daniel." Pages 293–98 in Newsom, Ringe, and Lapsley, *Women's Bible Commentary*.

———. *Daniel: A Commentary*. OTL. Louisville: Westminster John Knox, 2014.

———. "Women as Biblical Interpreters Before the Twentieth Century." Pages 11–23 in Newsom, Ringe, and Lapsley, *Women's Bible Commentary*.

Newsom, Carol A., Sharon H. Ringe, and Jacqueline E. Lapsley, eds. *Women's Bible Commentary, Revised and Updated*. 3rd ed. Louisville: Westminster John Knox, 2012.

Niditch, Susan. *Judges: A Commentary*. OTL. Louisville: Westminster John Knox, 2008.

Nimchuk, Cindy L. "The 'Archers' of Darius: Coinage or Tokens of Royal Esteem?" *Ars Orientalis* 32 (2002): 55–79.

Nissinen, Martti. "Biblical Masculinities: Musings on Theory and Agenda." Pages 271–85 in Creangă and Smit, *Biblical Masculinities Foregrounded*.

———. *Homoeroticism in the Biblical World: A Historical Perspective*. Translated by Kirsi Stjerna. Minneapolis: Augsburg Fortress, 1998.

O'Connor, Kathleen M. "The Feminist Movement Meets the Old Testament: One Woman's Perspective." Pages 3–26 in Day and Pressler, *Engaging the Bible in a Gendered World*.

Olson, Dennis T. "Untying the Knot? Masculinity, Violence, and the Creation-Fall Story of Genesis 2–4." Pages 73–86 in Day and Pressler, *Engaging the Bible in a Gendered World*.

Olyan, Saul M. *Rites and Rank: Hierarchy in Biblical Representations of Cult*. Princeton: Princeton University Press, 2000.

Parpola, Simo, and Kazuko Watanabe, eds. *Neo-Assyrian Treaties and Loyalty Oaths*. SAA 2. Helsinki: Helsinki University Press, 1998.

Parpola, S., and R. M. Whiting, eds. *Sex and Gender in the Ancient Near East: Proceedings of the 47th Rencontre Assyriologique Internationale, Helsinki, July 2–6, 2001*. Helsinki: Neo-Assyrian Text Corpus Project, 2002.

Pascoe, C. J. *Dude, You're a Fag: Masculinity and Sexuality in High School*. Berkeley: University of California Press, 2007.

Paul, Shalom M. *Amos: A Commentary on the Book of Amos*. Hermeneia. Minneapolis: Fortress, 1991.

———. "The Shared Legacy of Sexual Metaphors and Euphemisms in Mesopotamian and Biblical Literature." Pages 489–98 in Parpola and Whiting, *Sex and Gender in the Ancient Near East*.

———. *Studies in the Book of the Covenant in the Light of Cuneiform and Biblical Law*. Leiden: Brill, 1970.

Pearce, Laurie E. "The Scribes and Schools of Ancient Mesopotamia." Pages 2265–78 in Sasson, et. al., *Civilizations of the Ancient Near East*.

Piacentini, Patrizia. "Scribes." *OEAE* 3 (n.d): 187–192.

Polaski, Donald C. "Mene, Mene, Tekel, Parsin: Writing and Resistance in Daniel 5 and 6." *JBL* 123 (2004): 649–69.

Porada, Edith. *The Art of Ancient Iran: Pre-Islamic Cultures*. New York: Crown Publishers, Inc., 1965.

Portier-Young, Anathea. *Apocalypse Against Empire: Theologies of Resistance in Early Judaism*. Grand Rapids: Eerdmans, 2011.

———. "Languages of Identity and Obligation: Daniel as a Bilingual Book." *VT* 60 (2010): 98–118.

Pritchard, James B., ed. *Ancient Near Eastern Texts Relating to the Old Testament*. Princeton: Princeton University Press, 1969.

Reade, Julian E. "The Neo-Assyrian Court and Army: Evidence from Sculptures." *Iraq* 34 (1972): 87–112.

Rendsburg, Gary A. "A Comprehensive Guide to Israelian Hebrew: Grammar and Lexicon." *Orient* 38 (2003): 5–35.

Ridgeway, Cecilia L. *Framed by Gender: How Gender Inequality Persists in the Modern World*. New York: Oxford University Press, 2011.

Rindge, Matthew S. "Jewish Identity under Foreign Rule: Daniel 2 as a Reconfiguration of Genesis 41." *JBL* 129 (2010): 85–104.

Risman, Barbara J. "From Doing to Undoing: Gender as We Know It." *Gender & Society* 23 (2009): 81–84.

———. "Gender as a Social Structure: Theory Wrestling with Activism." *Gender & Society* 18 (2004): 429–50.

Robins, Gay. "Some Principles of Compositional Dominance and Gender Hierarchy in Egyptian Art." *Journal of the American Research Center in Egypt* 31 (1994): 33–40.

Rohr, Richard. *Soul Brothers: Men of the Bible Speak to Men Today*. New York: Orbis Books, 2004.

Rollston, Christopher A. *Writing and Literacy in the World of Ancient Israel: Epigraphic Evidence from the Iron Age*. ABS 11. Atlanta: Society of Biblical Literature, 2010.

Rooke, Deborah W., ed. *A Question of Sex?: Gender and Difference in the Hebrew Bible and Beyond*. Hebrew Bible Monographs 14. Sheffield: Sheffield Phoenix, 2007.

Root, Margaret Cool. "From the Heart: Powerful Persianisms in the Art of the Western Empire." Pages 1–29 in *Asia Minor and Egypt: Old Cultures in a New Empire. Proceedings of the Groningen 1988 Achaemenid History Workshop*. Edited by Heleen Sancisi-Weerdenburg and Amélie Khurt. Achaemenid History 6. Leiden: Nederlands Instituut voor het Nabije Oosten, 1991.

———. *King and Kingship in Achaemenid Art: Essays on the Creation of an Iconography of Empire*. Acta Iranica 19. Leiden: Brill, 1979.

Roth, Martha T. *Law Collections from Mesopotamia and Asia Minor*. 2nd ed. WAW 6. Atlanta: Scholars Press, 1997.

Rubin, Gayle. "The Traffic in Women: Notes on the 'Political Economy' of Sex." Pages 157–210 in *Toward an Anthropology of Women*. Edited by Rayna R. Reiter. New York: Monthly Review Press, 1975.

Rudy, Rena M., Lucy Popova, and Daniel G. Linz. "The Context of Current Content Analysis of Gender Roles: An Introduction to a Special Issue." *Sex Roles* 62 (2010): 705–20.

Rufus, Quintus Curtius. *History of Alexander*. Translated by John C. Rolfe. 2 vols. Loeb Classical Library. Cambridge, MA: Harvard University Press, 1946.

Sachau, E. *Aramäische Papyrus Und Ostraka Aus Einer Jüdischen Militär-Kolonie Zu Elephantine*. Vols 1–2. Leipzig: Hinrichs, 1911.

Sampson, Emily. "Daniel, Belshazzar, and Julia: The Rediscovery of the Translation of Julia E. Smith (1792–1886)." Pages 262–82 in Brenner, *A Feminist Companion to Prophets and Daniel*.

Sasson, Jack, John Baines, Gary Beckman, and Karen S. Rubinson, eds. *Civilizations of the Ancient Near East*. Vol. IV. New York: Charles Scribner's Sons, 1995.

Sawyer, Deborah F. "Gender Criticism: A New Discipline in Biblical Studies or Feminism in Disguise?" Pages 2–17 in Rooke, *A Question of Sex?*

Schectman, Sarah. *Women in the Pentateuch: A Feminist and Source-Critical Analysis*. Hebrew Bible Monographs 23. Sheffield: Sheffield Phoenix, 2009.

Schilt, Kristen. *Just One of the Guys? Transgender Men and the Persistence of Gender Inequality*. Chicago: University of Chicago Press, 2010.

Schippers, Mimi. "Recovering the Feminine Other: Masculinity, Femininity, and Gender Hegemony." *Theory and Society* 36 (2007): 85–102.

Schmidt, E. F. *Persepolis I*. OIP 68. Chicago: University of Chicago Press, 1953.

Scholz, Susanne, ed. *Feminist Interpretation of the Hebrew Bible in Retrospect*. Recent Research in Biblical Studies 5. Sheffield: Sheffield Phoenix, 2013.

———. *Introducing the Women's Hebrew Bible*. New York: T&T Clark, 2007.

Seow, Choon Leong. *Daniel*. WC. Louisville: Westminster John Knox, 2003.

Shows, Carla, and Naomi Gerstel. "Fathering, Class, and Gender: A Comparison of Physicians and Emergency Medical Technicians." *Gender & Society* 23 (2009): 161–87.

Siculus, Diodorus. *The Library of History*. Translated by C. Bradford Welles. 12 vols. LCL. Cambridge, MA: Harvard University Press, 1963.

Smith-Christopher, Daniel. *A Biblical Theology of Exile*. OBT. Minneapolis: Fortress, 2002.

Soggin, J. Alberto. *Judges: A Commentary*. Translated by John Bowden. OTL. Philadelphia: The Westminster Press, 1981.

Speer, Susan A., and Elizabeth Stokoe. "An Introduction to Conversation and Gender." Pages 1–28 in *Conversation and Gender*. Edited by Susan A. Speer and Elizabeth Stokoe. Cambridge: Cambridge University Press, 2011.

Stanton, Elizabeth Cady. *The Woman's Bible*. Mineola, NY: Dover, 2002.

Steinberg, Naomi. "Feminist Criticism." Pages 163–92 in *Methods for Exodus*. Edited by Thomas B. Dozeman. New York: Cambridge University Press, 2010.

Stone, Ken. "Gender Criticism: The Un-Manning of Abimelech." Pages 183–201 in Yee, *Judges & Method*.

———. "Lovers and Raisin Cakes: Food, Sex and Divine Insecurity in Hosea." Pages 116–39 in Stone, *Queer Commentary and the Hebrew Bible*.

———. "Queer Commentary and Biblical Interpretation: An Introduction." Pages 11–34 in Stone, *Queer Commentary and the Hebrew Bible*.

———, ed. *Queer Commentary and the Hebrew Bible*. JSOTSSup 334. Sheffield: Sheffield Academic, 2001.

———. "Queer Reading Between Bible and Film: Paris Is Burning and the 'Legendary Houses' of David and Saul." Pages 75–98 in Hornsby and Stone, *Bible Trouble*.

Strawn, Brent A. "Jeremiah's In/Effective Plea: Another Look at נער in Jeremiah I 6." *VT* 45 (2005): 366–77.

———. "'A World Under Control': Isaiah 60 and the Apadana Reliefs from Persepolis." Pages 85–116 in *Approaching Yehud: New Approaches to the Study of the Persian Period*. Edited by Jon L. Berquist. SemeiaSt 50. Atlanta: Society of Biblical Literature, 2007.

Stronach, David. "Early Achaemenid Coinage: Perspectives from the Homeland." *IrAnt* 24 (1989): 255–83.

Sumerau, J. Edward. "'That's What a Man Is Supposed to Do': Compensatory Manhood Acts in an LGBT Christian Church." *Gender & Society* 26 (2012): 461–87.

Sunderland, Jane, and Lia Litossetliti. "Current Research Methodologies in Gender and Language Study: Key Issues." Pages 1–18 in *Gender and Language Research Methodologies*. Edited by Kate Harrington, Lia Litosetliti, Helen Sauntson, and Jane Sunderland. New York: Palgrave Macmillan, 2008.

Talbot, Kirsten, and Michael Qualye. "The Perils of Being a Nice Guy: Contextual Variation in Five Young Women's Constructions of Acceptable Hegemonic and Alternative Masculinities." *Men and Masculinities* 13 (2010): 255–78.

Taylor, Frank. "Content Analysis and Gender Stereotypes in Children's Books." *Teaching Sociology* 31 (2003): 300–311.

Thimmes, Pamela. "What Makes a Feminist Reading Feminist? Another Perspective." Pages 132–40 in Washington, Graham, and Thimmes, *Escaping Eden*.

Toorn, Karel van der. *Scribal Culture and the Making of the Hebrew Bible*. Cambridge: Harvard University Press, 2007.

Trible, Phyllis. "Depatriarchalizing in Biblical Interpretation." *JAAR* 41 (1973): 30–48.

———. *God and the Rhetoric of Sexuality*. OBT. Minneapolis: Fortress, 1978.

———. *Texts of Terror: Literary-Feminist Readings of Biblical Narratives*. Philadelphia: Fortress, 1984.

Udry, J. Richard. "Biological Limits of Gender Construction." *American Sociological Review* 65 (2000): 443–57.

Valeta, David M. "The Book of Daniel in Recent Research (Part One)." *CurBR* 6 (2008): 330–54.

———. *Lions and Ovens and Visions: A Satirical Reading of Daniel 1–6*. Hebrew Bible Monographs 12. Sheffield: Sheffield Phoenix, 2008.

van Deventer, H. J. M. "Another Wise Queen (Mother) – Women's Wisdom in Daniel 5.10–12?" Pages 247–61 in Brenner, *A Feminist Companion to Prophets and Daniel*.

Vigneau, André. *Encyclopédie Photographique de L'art, Le Musée Du Louvre*. Vol. 1. Paris: Editions TEL, 1935.

Vogt, S. J., ed. *A Lexicon of Biblical Aramaic Clarified by Ancient Documents*. Translated by J. A. Fitzmyer. 2nd ed. Roma: Gregorian & Biblical Press, 2011.

Walls, Neal H. *Desire, Discord, and Death: Approaches to Ancient Near Eastern Myth*. Boston: American Schools of Oriental Research, 2001.

Waltke, Bruce K., and M. O'Connor. *An Introduction to Biblical Hebrew Syntax*. Winona Lake, IN: Eisenbrauns, 1990.

Washington, Harold C. "'Lest He Die in the Battle and Another Man Take Her': Violence and the Construction of Gender in the Laws of Deuteronomy 22." Pages 185–213 in *Gender and Law in the Hebrew Bible and the Ancient Near East*. Edited by Victor H. Matthews, Bernard M. Levinson, and Tikva Frymer-Kensky. New York: T&T Clark, 2004.

———. "Violence and the Construction of Gender in the Hebrew Bible: A New Historicist Approach." *BibInt* 5 (1997): 324–63.

Washington, Harold C., Susan Lochrie Graham, and Pamela Thimmes, eds. *Escaping Eden: New Feminist Perspectives on the Bible*. New York: New York University Press, 1999.

Weigl, Michael. *Die Aramäischen Achikar-Sprüche Aus Elephantine Und Die Alttestamentliche Weisheitsliteratur*. BZAW 399. Berlin: Walter de Gruyter, 2010.

Wente, Edward F. "The Scribes of Ancient Egypt." Pages 2211–21 in Sasson, et. al., *Civilizations of the Ancient Near East*.

Wernberg-Møller, Preben. *The Manual of Discipline*. STDJ 1. Grand Rapids: W.B. Eerdmans, 1957.
West, Candace, and Sarah Fenstermaker. "Doing Difference." *Gender & Society* 9 (1995): 8–37.
West, Candace, and Don H. Zimmerman. "Accounting for Doing Gender." *Gender & Society* 23 (2009): 112–22.
———. "Doing Gender." *Gender & Society* 1 (1987): 125–51.
West, Mona. "Daniel." Pages 427–31 in Guest, et. al., *The Queer Bible Commentary*.
———. "Reading the Bible as Queer Americans: Social Location and the Hebrew Scriptures." *Theology and Sexuality* 10 (1999): 28–42.
Williams, Christine L. "The Glass Escalator: Hidden Advantages for Men in the 'Female' Professions." *Social Problems* 39 (1992): 253–67.
Wingfield, Adia. "Racializing the Glass Escalator: Reconsidering Men's Experiences with Women's Work." *Gender & Society* 23 (2009): 5–26.
Winter, Irene J. "The Body of the Able Ruler: Toward an Understanding of the Statues of Gudea." Pages 151–66 in *On Art in the Ancient Near East: Volume II From the Third Millenium B.C.E.* Edited by Irene J. Winter. Leiden: Brill, 2010.
———. "Sex, Rhetoric, and the Public Monument: The Alluring Body of Naram-Sîn of Agade." Pages 11–26 in *Sexuality in Ancient Art: Near East, Egypt, Greece, and Italy*. Edited by Natalie Boymel Kampen. Cambridge: Cambridge University Press, 1996.
Wozniak, Jesse, and Christopher Uggen. "Real Men Use Nonlethals: Appeals to Masculinity in Marketing Police Weaponry." *Feminist Criminology* 4 (2009): 275–93.
Wright, Jacob L. "Commensal Politics in Ancient Western Asia: The Background to Nehemiah's Feasting (Part I)." *ZAW* 122 (2010): 212–33.
———. "Commensal Politics in Ancient Western Asia: The Background to Nehemiah's Feasting (Continued, Part II)." *ZAW* 122 (2010): 333–52.
———. "Making a Name for Oneself: Martial Valor, Heroic Death, and Procreation in the Hebrew Bible." *JSOT* 36 (2011): 131–62.
Wright, Jacob L., and Michael J. Chan. "King and Eunuch: Isaiah 56:1–8 in Light of Honorific Burial Practices." *JBL* 131 (2012): 99–119.
Xenophon. *Cyropaedia*. Translated by Walter Miller. 2 vols. LCL. Cambridge, MA: Harvard University Press, 1914.
Yee, Gale A., ed. *Judges & Method: New Approaches in Biblical Studies*. 2nd ed. Minneapolis: Fortress, 2007.
———. *Poor Banished Children of Eve: Woman as Evil in the Hebrew Bible*. Minneapolis: Fortress, 2003.
Ziegler, Christiane. *Les Statues Égyptiennes de l'Ancien Empire*. Paris: Réunion des Musées Nationaux, 1997.

INDEX

Abednego 1, 40–2, 46, 52–3n36, 54n46, 55n48, 96, 110–11, 121, 122, 124; *see also* Daniel
Abigail 112n5, 116
Abimelech 68
Abishag 112n5
Abraham (patriarch) 68, 80n69, 127n20; and Sodom and Gomorrah 127n20
Absalom 16, 56n63, 103–4, 112n5
Achaemenid art 65
Achaemenid Empire 65
Achaemenids 62
Akkadian (language) 53–4n44, 67, 75n5
Alexander (the Great) 106
Amos: book of 128n30; the prophet 128n30
Anchor Bible Commentary series 138
androcentrism 5, 130; of biblical literature 2–4, 137, 139
Antiochus IV 5n2
anxiety 43, 47, 55n57; gendered 42–4; masculine 80n73; about name 91
Aramaic (language) 2, 51n29, 52n35, 54n44, 56n64, 89, 99n50, 110, 129n41
Arioch 38–9, 51n22, 51n29, 53n40, 124
Armenian (language) 100n60
Ashurbanipal 51n24, 88, 98–9n37
Assyrians 1, 98–9n37; *see also* Neo-Assyrian
Azariah *see* Abednego

Baal 73
Babylon 1, 34–5, 37–9, 46, 56n62, 60, 80n69, 80n73, 83, 124
Babylonian kingdom 57n74
Bathsheba 116
Beasley, Christine 24, 31n43

beauty 101, 112n5; female 101, 103, 112n5, 112n6; male 5, 101–6, 108–11, 112n5, 112n6, 131; and masculinity 34, 101, 103; physical 33–5, 70, 105; and power 103–5, 108–11, 113n20, 131, 136; and social position 105–6, 108, 110, 136
Belshazzar 44–6, 47, 49, 56n64, 57n75, 58, 74, 96, 110, 120, 124–5, 131; as problem son 44–6, 47, 49, 58, 74, 131; *see also* writing on the wall
Belteshazzar 56n62
Ben Sira 69, 90–2, 96–7n4, 99n51, 100n57
biblical criticism *see* biblical scholarship
biblical scholarship 25, 29n20, 138–9; feminist approach 2–4, 5, 6–7n6, 7n7, 7n11, 7n12, 7–8n13, 13–15, 18n14, 18n22, 19n24, 27n1, 132, 134, 139–40, 141n2, 142n23; gendering of 139; as male-dominated field 138–9; masculist approach 13–14; queer approach 3, 5, 8n21, 8–9n26, 13–15, 18n22, 19n31, 134, 139–40, 141n2
Butler, Judith 3, 4, 8n24, 10n36, 19n25, 21, 22, 134, 140, 142n27

Chaldeans 35, 52–3n36, 83, 124
Chapman, Cynthia 17n8, 17n10, 60, 71–2, 80n73, 81n92
Chronicles (books of) 56n63, 69
Clines, David J. A. 3–4, 9n28, 9n29, 13, 15–16, 17n5, 18n20, 28–9n19, 40, 53n43, 92, 101–3, 112–13n10, 115–17, 126n9, 126n14, 127n20, 127n22
Connell, R. W. (Raewyn) 21–4, 29n20, 29n28, 29–30n29, 30n31, 30n41, 31n43, 95, 100n73

INDEX

court tales of Daniel 1–5, 5n1, 5–6n2, 6n3, 11, 14, 16, 21, 26–7, 33–6, 38–9, 41, 42, 44, 46–9, 49n3, 50n9, 51–2n31, 52n35, 52–3n36, 55n59, 57n76, 58–9, 61, 64, 66, 71, 73, 74, 83–4, 87, 90, 95–6, 103, 108, 115, 117, 119–25, 127n23, 129n40, 131–9; absence of women in 96, 139; androcentrism of 5, 130, 137, 139; beauty in 101, 103, 108–11; discourse in 115–25; masculinity in 14, 16, 21, 33–49, 74, 96, 97n8, 101, 109, 111, 115, 123, 125, 130, 132–3, 140; origin of 75n5; predominant masculinity and 58–75; scribal masculinity in 83–96
Cyrus 47, 57n74, 104–6

Daniel 1, 4, 5, 27, 33–6, 38–49, 50n11, 51n14, 51n19, 51n22, 51n27, 51n29, 51–2n31, 52n35, 52–3n36, 53n39, 53n40, 56n62, 56n64, 57n78, 58, 74, 82n102, 83–4, 95–6, 100n74, 115, 121–5, 130–3, 135, 140; appearance/beauty of 103, 108–11; and his colleagues 1, 4, 5, 27, 33–6, 38, 40–1, 46, 47, 48–9, 50n11, 51n19, 53n40, 58, 74, 82n102, 83–4, 95–6, 100n74, 103, 109, 111, 124, 130–1, 135, 140; diet of 35, 74, 109–10, 115, 123–4; dream interpretation 36–40, 42–5, 48, 49, 53n40, 55n59, 96, 120, 122, 123; interpretation/reading of writing on the wall 96; and lion pit 1, 46, 48, 74, 111; loyalty to God 47; loyalty to king 47, 57n78; masculinity of 109, 122, 130, 135; and name 44, 48, 96; and powerful knowledge 38–9, 43, 45, 48, 96
Daniel (book of) 1–4, 5–6n2, 7n13, 33–6, 38–40, 42–6, 49n3, 50n11, 51n27, 51n29, 51–2n31, 52n35, 52–3n36, 53n40, 54n46, 55n54, 56n61, 56n62, 56n64, 57n75, 74, 75n5, 90, 96, 100n74, 109–11, 120–5, 129n38, 129n40, 131, 133, 141n8; apocalyptic section of 132–3
Darius I 50n7, 53n38, 57n75, 61, 62, 64, 70, 77n18, 106, 107, 121–3, 131
Darius the Mede 45, 46–7, 57n74
David, King 1, 16, 17n5, 56n63, 60, 67, 101–3, 115–16, 127n20; beauty of 101–3, 112n8; persuasiveness of 116

Deborah (judge) 68, 116
Deuteronomistic History (DtrH) 60, 69, 76n13, 116, 119
Deuteronomy 60, 68, 76n13, 79n65, 82n97
Dinah 82n97
Diodorus 106
discourse 25–6, 39, 115, 117–22, 125, 125n1, 127n23; advice as 124–5; confessions as 122–3, 125, 131–2; critique as 125; decrees as 120–2, 125, 129n40, 131; dream interpretation as 120, 125; to do gender 5, 39, 115, 118–20, 125, 131; and masculinity 121, 122, 127–8n25; persuasive speech as 115, 117, 127n23; titles as 123–4, 125; *see also* "doing gender"
"doing gender" 21–3, 26, 28n12, 28n13, 39, 91, 95, 115, 118–19, 132, 137; through discourse 118–22, 125, 131
doing masculinity 25, 26, 37, 89, 93, 116, 121
dominance: male 24, 26, 27, 30–1n41, 35, 61, 72, 74; masculine 33, 58

eastern diaspora 59
Eglon 44
Egypt, ancient 50n11, 52n35, 53n39, 55n48, 75n5, 84–7, 89; 20th dynasty 86; iconography 78n47, 98n23; king of 100n60; New Kingdom era 84, 97n5
Egyptians 60
Eliab 102
Elijah (prophet) 116
Elisha (prophet) 116
English (language) 65, 105, 113n20, 123, 129n40; and gendered bias 65, 112n5
Esther 132; book of 132
ethnicity 1, 34, 38, 124
eunuchs 35–6, 55n51, 98n34, 99n48
Exodus (book of) 20n44, 68, 72, 112–13n10, 113n20, 115, 116, 119, 127n20
Ezekiel (book of) 4, 93, 100n66, 127n22

femininity 31n42, 31n43, 42, 55n54, 78n51, 81n78; doing 116; military defeat as 60–1, 126n14; and provisioning 81n78
feminism 3, 5, 7n7, 7n12, 13, 15, 137
fiery furnace 1, 41, 46, 55n48, 74, 111, 121
Foucault, Michel 29n28

158

INDEX

Fuchs, Esther 4, 18n20, 79n51, 79n65, 81n78

Gabriel (angel) 132
Garrison, Mark B. 62, 65
gender 8n17, 10n36, 12–13, 15, 16, 18n22, 19n31, 21–3, 26, 28n8, 33, 34, 36, 38, 39, 40, 48, 50n9, 54n45, 57n80, 59–60, 64–6, 68, 70, 72, 76n9, 85, 86, 87, 91, 92, 100n74, 101, 110, 115–18, 123, 125, 127n18, 127–8n25, 131–2, 134–5, 137, 140; binary construction of 3, 5, 8n24, 16, 140; categories of 15, 142n27; construction of 8n24, 16, 48, 65, 133, 134; criticism 18n16, 18n17; culturally specific ideas/configurations of 12–13, 21, 31n55, 121, 131–7; hierarchy 30n41, 72; identity 22, 141n8; production of 26, 139; relations 23; vs. sex 2; sociological approaches to 13, 21, 55n49, 132; *see also* "doing gender"; gender studies; norms
gendered equality 140
gendered inequality 2, 5, 26, 95, 96, 127–8n25, 131, 135–40, 142n12
gender studies 1, 4, 5, 11, 14, 16, 119, 130, 133–4, 139–40
Genesis (book of) 2, 25, 73, 79n65, 80n68, 80n69, 82n97, 82n103, 115, 117, 127n20, 132, 134
Gibeonites 82n97
Gideon 59–60
God 4, 5, 13, 25, 33–5, 38–49, 53n39, 55n57, 55n59, 56n61, 58–9, 68, 73, 74, 91, 92–3, 96, 100n74, 109, 111, 112–13n10, 115–16, 121–2, 124, 127n18, 127n20, 131–2, 136; as dominant male 35, 47, 49, 74, 132; masculinity of 47, 74; sovereignty of 47, 56n61; *see also* Yahweh
Goldingay, John 13–14, 18n22
Goliath 102–3
Greece, ancient 63
Greek (language) 2, 56n64, 66, 75n5, 78n50, 90, 104, 106–7
Guest, Deryn 4, 14, 15–16, 17n4, 19n25, 20n38, 137, 139

Haggai (book of) 138
Haman 132
Hananiah *see* Shadrach
Hebrew (language) 2, 54n44, 56n64, 101, 110, 113n20, 119, 123, 129n41

Hebrew Bible 1, 5, 5n1, 9n28, 11, 13–14, 19n31, 22, 34, 36, 41, 42, 44, 50n9, 56n63, 59, 67–9, 80n69, 92–3, 95–6, 100n65, 116, 117, 138–9; androcentrism of 3–4, 5; beauty in 101–4, 108, 112n5, 112n6; court tales in 5n1; female prophets in 126n12; femininity in 78n50; gender in 72, 92–3, 101, 132; gender studies in 1, 4, 5, 11, 16, 130, 133–4; masculinity in 9n28, 13–15, 16, 22–3, 33, 35, 37, 39, 41, 58–60, 79n61, 101–2, 115, 125, 127n22, 130, 132–3, 136–7, 140; motherhood in 78n50; patriarchy in 78n50; persuasive speech in 118; prophetic literature in 17n8; prophetic speech in 127n22; rituals of blood manipulation in 54n45; texts written by women in 119, 128–9n35; women in 126n12, 135
Hebrews 60
Hellenistic period, early 1, 6n2, 33, 59, 75n5, 106–7, 127n23
Hephaestion 106
Hermeneia commentary series 138
Herodotus 58, 59, 66, 69
heteronormative framework 15, 140
Hezekiah (prophet) 51n19, 69
Hittite culture 63
Hoffner, Harry A. 58, 59, 64, 67
Hosea (book of) 18n22, 73
Huldah 116

identity 54n45; gender 22; gendered 12, 39, 118; sexual 140; sexualized 118; social 1, 39, 65, 123, 137, 141n8; socially constructed 47
intersectionality 23, 29n22
Isaac (patriarch) 80n69
Isaiah: book of 51n19, 55n51, 80n69, 127n22; prophet 55n51, 60, 116
Israel: ancient 4, 14, 36, 50n6, 63, 68, 73, 81n78, 93, 97n5, 101, 115, 116, 119, 126n14, 128n30, 128–9n35, 134; nation of 25
Israelites 101

Jacob/Israel (patriarch) 80n69
Jael 16, 68, 76n12
Jefferson's Bible 2
Jehoiakim, King 1, 34, 36, 55n59
Jeremiah: book of 17n3, 60, 116–17, 132; prophet 60, 116–17, 134

159

INDEX

Jerome (saint) 53n39
Jerusalem 16, 53n40, 93
Jesse 102
Jether 59–60
Jews 44
Joab 60
Job: book of 17n3, 92–3, 127n18; prophet 92–3, 127n18
Joseph (patriarch) 80n69, 103–4, 109, 112n5, 132
Josephus 51n19, 51n20, 100n74
Joshua: book of 115–16; prophet 115–16
Judah 1, 34, 38, 51n19, 51n27, 58, 108, 124; Yehud 44
Judahites 38, 51n19
Judaism 44
Judeans 1, 4, 40, 46, 124
Judges (book of) 16, 17n3, 59–60, 68, 76n12, 116, 117, 119

Kelso, Julie 56n63, 69, 80n70
king: as shepherd-provider 80n73; as title 123–4; as warrior-protector 80n73
Kings (books of) 1, 17n3, 59, 60, 100n65, 110, 112n5, 116, 117
knowledge 33–40, 42–6, 48–9, 74, 93, 109, 125, 130–2; gendering of 125; as masculine 35–6, 50n9, 120, 125; power of 34, 39–40, 43–5, 48, 50n9, 51–2n31, 84, 92–3, 96, 109, 127n18, 130, 132

lion's den/pit 1, 46, 48, 74, 111

Macwilliam, Stuart 103–4
Manasseh 69
masculinities 4, 5, 13, 17n4, 22–7, 29n19, 30n29, 30–1n41, 31–2n55, 34, 37, 38, 68, 94, 95, 100n70, 122, 133, 135, 137, 139–40; in biblical literature 140; hegemonic 30–1n41, 31–2n55, 100n70; hierarchy of 68, 122, 133, 135; non-hegemonic 23, 31–2n55; traditional 13
masculinity 1–5, 8n21, 9n28, 11, 13–15, 17n5, 18n16, 18n17, 20n44, 21–7, 30n31, 31n43, 31n43, 33, 36, 40, 46, 48, 51n14, 55n54, 55n55, 59–60, 65, 68, 76n13, 78n50, 83, 85, 91, 93–5, 100n68, 103, 118, 125, 127n17, 133; adult 117; complicit 24, 137; concept of 22; configurations of 1, 4, 5, 33, 36, 42–4, 48, 49, 55n54, 64, 74, 96, 111, 120, 123, 125, 128n25, 130–1, 133, 137, 139, 141n8; culturally dominant 24, 123; culturally predominant 5, 43, 49, 58, 59, 65–6, 69–71, 74, 79n61, 82n102, 83–7, 90–1, 94–6, 120–3, 130–3, 136; definition 23; dominant 24–5, 31n43; dominate/dominating 31n43; hegemonic 21, 23–5, 27, 27n6, 29n20, 30n31, 30–1n41, 31n42; invisibility of 65; of knowledge 36–9; and martial prowess 4, 34, 59, 64, 66, 67–71, 74, 76n16, 79n61, 86–7, 94, 113n27; as military victory 60–1; Near Eastern 59, 67; non-predominant 26; norms of 34, 37, 39, 49, 116, 131, 137; predominant 24–6, 37, 42, 46, 48–9, 60–2, 64–7, 73–4, 83–91, 94–6, 97n8, 100n68, 135–7; and producing sons/children 5, 34, 49, 58–9, 64, 67–71, 74, 79n61, 80n73, 84, 91, 120, 130, 132; and protection 33, 43, 46, 58, 65, 70–1, 73–4, 80n73, 81n92, 82n97, 120, 122, 130; and provision 33, 43, 58, 62, 71–4, 80n73, 81n90, 82n97, 82n98, 120, 130; royal 71, 117; and strength 86, 90, 92, 116, 134; studies 14–15, 18n20, 19n26, 21, 23–4, 27n6, 100n68, 135, 139–40; subordinate 24–5; and/of violence 13–14, 18n22, 36–9, 41, 43, 47–8, 49, 59, 64–7, 90, 94, 113n16, 117, 120–2, 130; and war 60, 65, 68, 103, 113n16, 117, 120, 130, 134; *see also* beauty; doing masculinity; persuasive speech; power; scribal masculinity
masculinizing ritual 64
Meshach 1, 40–2, 46, 52–3n36, 54n46, 55n48, 96, 110–11, 121, 122, 124; *see also* Daniel
Mesopotamia 55n48, 72, 75n5, 97n5, 113n27
Mesopotamian culture 37
Messerschmidt, James 21, 23–4, 29n20, 30n29, 30n31, 30–1n41, 31n42, 31n43
Middle Assyrian laws 72
Midianite kings 59–60
Mishael *see* Meshach
Moses 103, 112–13n10, 113n20, 115–16, 127n20; and golden calf 127n20

Nahum: book of 17n3; prophet 1, 60
name: immortality of 90–1, 96, 100n74; perpetuation of father's/passing on of

INDEX

5, 40, 44, 46, 58, 67, 69–70, 74, 79n65, 80n68, 84, 95, 120, 130–2; *see also* name-making
name-making 67–8, 79n61, 131; through martial prowess 67–71; and procreation 67–8, 74, 79n65, 80n69, 80n73, 83–5, 87, 91, 95; and scribal masculinity 84–5, 87; and war 67–8, 71, 87; and wisdom 90–1
Nathan (prophet) 116
Near East, ancient 1, 5, 33–7, 42–4, 50n6, 50n11, 57n69, 59, 64, 67, 72–3, 75n5, 78n30, 80n73, 83–4, 89–96, 96–7n4, 100n74, 101–2, 104, 107–8, 112n7, 130, 132–5
Nebuchadnezzar, King 1, 34–49, 51n22, 52–3n36, 53n40, 54n46, 55n48, 55n57, 55n59, 56n61, 56n64, 57n75, 58, 74, 83, 109–10, 121–2, 124, 125, 129n40, 131; court of 101; dreams of 36–40, 42–5, 48, 53n40, 54n46, 55n57, 55n59, 120; statue of 40, 42, 54n46, 131
Neo-Assyrian 17n8, 17n10, 55n54, 60–1, 71, 80n73, 87, 89, 98n34; art 55n54, 61, 87–9; curses of feminization 60, 80n73, 81n92; Empire 80n73; eunuchs 98n34; feasting 82n98; iconography 81n92, 87, 98–9n37; kings 55n55, 71, 81n92, 82n98, 89; sources 72, 81n92
Neo-Babylonian period 87
Newsom, Carol A. 2, 35, 42, 45, 50n11, 51n14, 51–2n31, 53n39, 55n54, 56n61, 56n62, 56n64, 57n75, 100n60, 109, 110, 114n34, 141n8
New Testament 9n28; masculinity in 9n28
Nineveh 60, 98–9n37, 99n41, 99n42
norms: cultural 4, 17n5, 22, 34, 37, 39, 49, 60, 109, 131–3, 137; deviations from 13, 15–16, 26, 31n55, 116, 135–6, 142n12; gendered 1, 4, 6n5, 11–13, 15–16, 21, 26, 59, 60, 86, 92, 96, 109, 116, 126n14, 130, 132–6, 139, 142n12; of masculinity 34, 37, 39, 49, 116, 131, 137; subversion of 15–16, 26, 109

Old Testament Library Series 138

Papyrus Anastasi 50n11, 98n21
Papyrus Lansing 86–7, 89
Pascoe, C. J. 25–6, 118–19

patriarchs 25, 82n97, 82n103, 115; *see also names of individual patriarchs*
patriarchy 23, 78n50, 79n65, 95
Pentateuch 119
Persepolis 65
Persian (language) 65, 75n5
Persian empire 62, 66, 78n38
Persian iconography 55n60, 62, 64, 73, 77n23, 107; archer/bow imagery 62, 64–5, 73, 78n30; combat encounter/motif 65–6, 71, 73, 78n38; control encounter/balancing motif 65–6, 81n81
Persian period 53n38, 55n60, 61, 62, 64, 66, 69, 71, 73–4, 87, 101, 104, 106–7, 127n23; late 1, 6n2, 33, 59
Persians 47, 57n74, 62, 65–6, 70, 73, 104; and beauty 104, 106–7; and feasting 73–4; masculinity of 70
persuasive speech 33–5, 37, 39, 115–18, 125, 125n1, 126n9, 127n18, 127n20, 127n23, 127n24, 134; gendering of 116, 118; and masculinity 115, 117, 125, 126n9, 127n23; power of 115, 118
Pharaoh 20n44, 44, 109, 115
Philistines 11, 12, 22, 60, 134
power 5, 23–5, 31n43, 34–5, 40–9, 53n39, 53n40, 54n45, 55n48, 65–6, 73, 84–7, 90–6, 103–11, 115, 118, 120–2, 126n9, 130, 132, 135–6; God's 42–3, 46, 125, 131; imperial 1, 6n3, 141n8; intellectual 51–2n31; through/of knowledge/wisdom 34, 36–40, 43–5, 48, 50n9, 51–2n31, 84, 92, 94, 130, 133; male 13; and male beauty 33–6, 103–4, 108–11, 130, 131; through martial prowess 87, 94; as masculine/and masculinity 65–7, 90, 92, 94, 95, 126n9; military 62, 65; of persuasive speech 115; position(s) of 5, 24, 31n43, 37, 106, 107, 110, 113n22, 120, 131; reproductive 64; in the scribal profession 85–7, 93; social 106, 107, 113n22; through violence 34, 68, 84, 130; of/through words 91–2, 100n65, 126n9
prophets 100n74, 116, 126n12, 127n22; *see also names of individual prophets*
Proverbs (book of) 94, 100n70
Psalms: 45 102–3; 80 112–13n10; 104 112–13n10; 127 79n61

161

INDEX

Qohelet 94–5
queen, the 1, 44–5, 56n64, 96, 106, 123–5, 129n42
queer theory 5, 137, 140

Rachel (matriarch) 112n5
Rahab 116
Rebekah (matriarch) 112n5
Rehoboam 56n63, 69
Revelation (book of) 2
Root, Margaret Cool 53n38, 62, 65, 106–7
royal lineage 69
Ruth: book of 52n34, 79n65; matriarch 79n65

Sabbath 55n51
Samuel: books of 16, 17n3, 17n5, 22, 60, 67, 101–2, 112n8, 116, 117, 127n20, 134; prophet 102, 116
Sarah (matriarch) 82n97, 112n5
"Satire on the Trades, The" 85–6, 97–8n19
Saul, King 60, 67, 102, 112n8, 127n20
scribalism 50n11, 92–3, 95; *see also* scribal masculinity
scribal masculinity 5, 35, 50n11, 83–96, 96–7n4, 120, 130–1, 133; and name-making 84–5, 87, 91, 100n74; socio-economic status of 86, 90, 92–5, 100n66, 131; *see also* power
Semitic languages 123, 129n41
Sennacherib, King 89–90, 98–9n37, 99n41, 99n42
sex 22; -category 22, 23, 26, 33; discourse 25; vs. gender 2
sexuality 15, 19n31, 25, 64, 140, 142n27; categories of 142n27; hetero- 118; heteronormative constructions of 140; homo- 128n25
Shadrach 1, 40–2, 46, 52–3n36, 54n46, 55n48, 96, 110–11, 121, 122, 124; *see also* Daniel
Shimei 60
Sirach (book of) 90–1, 99n51, 99n54
Sisera 16; *see also* Jael
Sisyngambris 106; *see also* Alexander (the Great)
social constructionist approach 4, 27n3
Society of Biblical Literature (SBL) 3; as male-dominated organization 138, 142n114

Solomon, King 1, 56n63, 60, 69, 116
Song of Songs (book) 18n20, 53–4n44, 112n6
Stanton, Elizabeth Cady 2, 6n6, 7n11, 7n12, 14; *Woman's Bible, The* 2
strength, as masculine 35, 86, 116
subordination, ritual of 40–2, 47, 49, 54n45, 54n46, 55n48, 74, 110, 121, 124, 131
Susa 50n7
Susanna 2, 8n13, 56n64

Tamar 79n65, 112n5
Trible, Phyllis 6–7n6

Ugarit culture 63

violence 76n13, 80n73; gendering of 60, 76n12; and masculinity 13–14, 18n22, 36–9, 41, 43, 47–8, 49, 59, 64–6, 90, 94, 113n16, 117, 120–2, 130; and power 34, 66, 84, 130

war/warfare 1, 33, 76n13, 78n47, 79n65, 80n73, 87–9; as culturally masculine 66, 76n14, 103; gendering of 66, 76n12, 76n14; heroic death in 67; and masculinity 60, 66, 68, 103, 113n16, 117, 120, 130, 134; and name-making 67–8, 71, 87
weakness, as feminine 35
West, Candace 18n13, 22–3, 28n8, 28n12, 54n45
women, subordination of 23, 31n42
"Words of Ahikar" 89–90, 91, 100n60, 129n41
Wright, Jacob L. 57n69, 67–8, 73
writing on the wall 1, 110, 120, 125

Xenophon 104–6
Xerxes 61, 70

Yahweh 34–6, 38, 44, 55n51, 55n59, 60, 68, 73, 80n69, 93, 102, 104, 116–17, 128n30, 134

Zechariah (book of) 138
Zephaniah (book of) 138
Zimmerman, Don 18n13, 22–3, 28n8, 28n12, 54n45